THE ALLIANCE FOR YOUNG ARTISTS & WRITERS PRESENTS

THE BEST TEEN

WRITING OF 2011

EDITED BY
ALEXANDRA FRANKLIN

2010 SCHOLASTIC
AWARDS PORTFOLIO
GOLD MEDAL RECIPIENT

FOREWORD BY
MYLA GOLDBERG
1989 Scholastic Award Winner

Cover Image: **Cody Castro,** *Isolation,* Photography, Age 18, NY

For information or permission, contact:
Alliance for Young Artists & Writers
557 Broadway
New York, NY 10012
www.artandwriting.org

Copy editor: Adrienne Onofri

Copyright © 2011 Alliance for Young Artists & Writers
Printed in the United States of America
Anthology printing, September 2011
ISBN-978-545-42996-2
ISBN-0-545-42996-X

The Best Teen Writing of 2011 is dedicated to the National Writing Project. The Alliance and the NWP launched a partnership in 2008 with the shared vision that talented young writers should receive recognition and publication opportunities. Since then, the NWP has been instrumental in expanding the reach of the Scholastic Writing Awards through its robust national network of innovative and extraordinarily dedicated teachers. The mission of the NWP is to focus the knowledge, expertise and leadership of America's educators on sustained efforts to improve writing and learning for all students. The Alliance staff would like to particularly thank the NWP national staff, including Sharon Washington, executive director; Elyse Eidman-Aadahl, director of national programs and site development; and Tanya Baker, director of national programs, for their collaborative and brilliant spirit as some of the Alliance's most valued "thinking partners."

About The Best Teen Writing of 2011

The works featured in *The Best Teen Writing of 2011* are selected from this year's Scholastic Art & Writing Awards, a national program presented by the Alliance for Young Artists & Writers, which recognizes talented teenagers in the visual and literary arts. The Awards were founded in 1923 to celebrate the accomplishments of creative students and to extend to them opportunities for recognition, exhibition, publication and scholarships.

In 2011, more than 185,000 artworks and manuscripts were submitted in 29 categories to regional affiliates across the country. Professionals reviewed the works for excellence in three core criteria: technical skill, originality and the emergence of a personal vision or voice.

More than 1,425 students received National Awards and joined the ranks of such luminaries as Richard Avedon, Truman Capote, Bernard Malamud, Carolyn Forché, Sylvia Plath, Joyce Carol Oates, Robert Redford and Andy Warhol, who all won Scholastic Awards when they were teenagers.

This year, 456 teens were recognized as the best young writers in the country. The works selected for this publication represent the diversity of the National Award winners, including age and grade, gender, genre, geography and subject matter. They also present a spectrum of the insight and creative intellect that inform many award-winning pieces.

A complete listing of National Award winners and examples of winning works of art and writing can be found on our website at www.artandwriting.org. There, you will also find information about how to enter the 2012 Scholastic Art & Writing Awards, a list of our scholarship partners, and ways that you can partner with the Alliance to support young artists and writers in your community.

2011 National Writing Jurors

We are grateful to this year's panel of jurors for their commitment to finding compelling young voices.

DRAMATIC SCRIPT
Regie Cabico
Ari Handel
Joanna Settle

HUMOR
Kathryn Erskine
Stephen Sherrill
Steve Young

JOURNALISM AND PERSUASIVE WRITING
Susan Cain
Thom Duffy
Greg Merkle
Kevin Olivas

PERSONAL ESSAY/ MEMOIR
Matt de la Pena
Sharifa Rhodes Pitts
Gary Soto
Jim Stahl
Ned Vizzini
Vicky Wilson

POETRY
Nikki Giovanni
Aracelis Girmay
David Hernandez
Alice Quinn
Zach Savich
Vijay Seshadri

SCIENCE FICTION/ FANTASY
Courtney Eldridge
Gerald Richards
Julia Whicker

SHORT SHORT STORY
Susan Barnett
Marjorie Celona
Rene Saldana

SHORT STORY
Charisse Carney Nunes
Adele Griffin
Cristina Henriquez
Laura McNeal
Courtney Sheinmel
Catharine Stimpson

GENERAL WRITING PORTFOLIO
Jesse Browner
Davy Rothbart
Darcey Steinke

NONFICTION WRITING PORTFOLIO
Melissa Fay Greene
John Hockenberry
Lauren Keane
Margy Rochlin

AMERICAN VOICES
Tanya Baker
Angie Frazier
Lis Harris
Joseph Legaspi
Lauren Myracle
Deji Olukotun
Jon Skovron
Francisco Stork
Chuck Wentzel

CREATIVITY & CITIZENSHIP
Sarah Darer Littman
Trent Reedy
Olugbemisola Rhuday-Perkovich

NEW YORK LIFE AWARD
Laura Davis
Patricia McCormick

CONTENTS

GOLD, SILVER AND AMERICAN VOICES MEDALS

POETRY

Personal Essay/Memoir

Science Fiction/Fantasy

Dramatic Script

Journalism

Persuasive Writing

Humor

Short Short Story

Short Story

Editor's Introduction

I wanted this job a lot. I was pretty brassy about it, too; I can admit that. I had just graduated from high school in Jackson, Mississippi. I was in New York, I was a Portfolio Gold Medalist, and I had this idea that everything I ever wanted was falling into my lap. I spent most of the awards week begging Alex Tapnio to let me be the editor of the next year's *Best Teen Writing* anthology. I sent emails. I was, basically, very annoying.

Exactly one year later, I was in Manhattan again, at dinner with the Alliance staff after the awards ceremony at Carnegie Hall. I had a brand-new name tag with my name above the word STAFF (I took pictures of this and sent it to my parents, who were suitably impressed). "You know what I remember most about you?" Alex said, referring to our encounter in 2010. "You were totally gunning for that editor's job. I mean, you really wanted it."

I really did. I wanted to be involved. I wanted to be the one who got to wade through the manuscripts, meeting the new writers, soaking up the new voices.

I started going through the pool of award-winning writing in March, and I didn't surface for months. My three roommates got used to waking up in the morning to find me already sitting at our kitchen table, fixated on a piece of short fiction or a collection of poetry, my coffee cold and untouched at my elbow. I couldn't tear myself away. I wanted to read everything twice. The vastness of the job revealed itself later, when I had to start narrowing down the manuscripts from the original stack. I had spent hours every day with these exquisite pieces of writing, falling in love over and over. I couldn't imagine selecting only a few pieces. I suggested a multivolume set; the Alliance politely rejected my suggestion. At least I tried.

The writing in this collection represents a few of the strongest voices from 2011's writing award winners. It's a complicated spectrum of stories—shockingly funny, devastating, wry, tragic—but, regardless of genre or tone, each individual voice is stunning. These writers handle words with an expert touch that is rare for their age. They are very, very good at their craft, and this is only the beginning. I am immensely honored to have been among the first to read the new literary voices of this generation.

Particularly in a career like writing, you never get anywhere alone. I'd like to first thank the Alliance for Young Artists & Writers for the years of opportunities, encouragement and affirmation. Thanks to Lisa Feder-Feitel for being such a warm and motherly source of comfort, to Katie Babick and Michael Vinereanu for more than I can list here, to Kerri Schlottman for keeping me on track, and to Alex, Danniel, Nick, John Sigmund, John Kollmer, Nora, Dominic, Kat, and Virginia for making me feel at home and helping me in countless ways every day. Special gratitude goes to Dr. Paul Smith, for being wise, encouraging and in love with words; and to my family, who has come to accept that maybe this writing thing isn't just a phase. Specifically, thank you to my mother, who helped put together my first book when I was four. (We've come a long way since then, haven't we?) I also owe a lot to Dan, for his infinite patience when I hit the workahol a little too hard, and to Claire, whose chai lattes got me through plenty of days of nonstop reading.

And finally—most significantly—thank you to all of the young writers whose work was under consideration for this anthology. I know your names and your stories, and I have no doubt that I will encounter them again. Let this be the beginning and not the end. Find out what drives you to write, what gets under your skin, what makes writing feel like a compulsion and not a hobby, and chase that inspiration. But even if you decide that you are not, ultimately, a writer, I truly believe that you will each do great things. I can only echo what Rilke writes in *Letters to a Young Poet*: "Your life will still find its own paths from there, and that they may be good, rich, and wide is what I wish for you, more than I can say."

—Alexandra Franklin

FOREWORD

If you're reading this, chances are that while others are playing outside, or hanging out with their friends, you or somebody you know can often be found holed up somewhere writing. I'm now going to go out on a limb and say chances are that not everyone has always "gotten" this whole writing thing, and that there have been times when you or this somebody you know has entertained fantasies that you were a mutant, or an alien, or left on a random doorstep. Or maybe there have just been times when you've felt lonely or terminally weird. To which I'd like to say, Congratulations! As far as I can tell, this is how being a writer begins. At least, that's how it began for me.

I was one of those kids who loved playing imaginary games. Whether I was alone or with a friend, I was pretty much always making stuff up. In second grade, I learned how to write down the made-up stuff, which was when I started telling people that I wanted to be a writer. As I got older, I started going to summer camps where I could take writing classes—you know, for fun—and when I thought about the grown-up version of my life, I pictured a book on a bookstore shelf with my name on it. To my mind, there was no more powerful object. By making up a story, I transported myself to a world of my own invention; by writing it down, I took other people there with me. I couldn't imagine why anyone would want to do anything else.

By the time I'd heard about the Scholastic Writing Awards, my desire to be a writer had solidified from a childhood fantasy into something that was beginning to worry my parents. I had no backup plan, no alternate path to pursue, and no role models. Neither of my parents wrote, or were particularly artsy. In between fantasizing that I was a mutant, or an alien, or left on a random doorstep, I stuck some poems in an envelope and sent them to New York City. I'd pretty much forgotten about the contest when a return letter arrived—but to this day I remember where I was standing when I opened the envelope and learned that I was one of the Scholastic Awards' first-place winners. For the first time in my life, it seemed like someone other than me was saying that this whole being-a-writer thing might be possible.

What I did after that is different from what other aspiring writers have done, and probably different from what you did (or will do), because despite what might be nice to believe, there's no one right way to do it. Here's the important part: I read and wrote all the time. For me, that included going to college, but not going to graduate school. Instead, I found a cheap place to live so that I could write a lot and not have to work very much. I found an agent after finishing my first novel, and then spent a year and a half being rejected by every publisher in the United States. I wrote a second novel while working at a part-time job that barely covered my rent and instant ramen but that gave me four days a week to write, my assumption being that I would again get universally rejected. I figured if I kept at it long enough, I'd eventually write a novel that someone, somewhere, would have to like. Maybe I'd be forty or fifty years old when this happened, but I didn't care: I had found a way to be a grown-up and still make stuff up, and that seemed worth any amount of instant ramen. Happily, I didn't have to wait until I was middle-aged. My second novel, *Bee Season,* did get published and all of the sudden the thing I'd been dreaming about since I was seven years old—of a book with my name on it on a bookstore shelf—was no longer just another product of my imagination.

It's hard to be a writer, and not everyone who deserves success finds it, but if you're interested, here's some advice: Learn to love revision. Of the quarter million words available to you in the English language, make sure you're using just the right ones. And then, get ready for the utter joy that will transmogrify you when you've captured a moment or a person or an emotion exactly the way you want to capture it, pinning it there on the page for everyone else to see. In the meantime, check out these pages. I have a feeling you'll be seeing some of these names again.

—Myla Goldberg

PORTFOLIO GOLD MEDALS

Graduating high school seniors may submit a portfolio of three to eight works for review by authors, educators and literary professionals. Winners of the General Writing Portfolio and Nonfiction Portfolio Gold Medals each receive a $10,000 scholarship.

Victoria Ford, 17
Governor's School for the Arts and Humanities
Greenville, SC
Teacher: Scott Gould

*Victoria Ford is from Greenville, South Carolina, and will attend the
University of Pennsylvania. She admires poet Larry Levis and memoirist
Abigail Thomas. Her family is the inspiration for much of her work, and
she feels that writing is a healing process.*

LIKE AN EVENT HORIZON
Personal Essay/Memoir

Except I wouldn't have quite used those words the summer my
older brother Theo left Hickory Ridge. Maybe because I didn't know
enough about science or the sky to mark that night as something
close to a phenomenon, some boundary in space time. But a summer
like that: after a windstorm in June uprooted a magnolia tree and it
soaked in the neighborhood pool for over a month, hurting the feelings of
a few, chubby Hispanic children who lived in my building so much
so that they would experience small bouts of rage, tossing fallen walnuts,
balls of laundry lint, broken toys and their own tennis shoes across
the pool's fence, screaming sheepishly to their mothers *Fix it, Fix it.*
Mama, we're hot and sticky and the bathtub at home is no more fun.
And there was Midnight, my neighbor's black German shepherd,
howling until sunrise on some mornings. Maybe he was starving?
Maybe he was hurting from the chain that kept him incarcerated in
the supply closet? And there was the yellow caution tape wrapped
around our stairwell after the middle-aged couple in the flat upstairs
ended the week with another fistfight—over a lost key or a missed
call or whatever it took to turn people against the ones they loved. There
was all of that, everything that made each of us in Apartment 75 a little
more lonesome in the Carolina heat, a little more miserable.

It's been a year since Theo left and the air conditioner in almost
every apartment this week is broken. It's hot. Actually, it's more than
one hundred degrees outside but if you're in here with me, watching

my younger brother Johnjohn water a pile of leaves in the living room, you're wishing you were in his hands, because the beads of sweat forming above your lip make your body thirst more than anything has before. I feel as though everything is beginning to take on more weight. The kitchen wallpaper unbuttons itself from the corners, rolling slowly toward the center, and the leaves on my mother's banana plant on the windowsill sag to the floor like the neck of a swan.

My mother woke early this morning, tearing through the house and knocking over picture frames in the narrow spine of our hallway. She remembers—of course she remembers. Just last year on this day, she claimed Theo "divorced from the family forever." I figured she felt the same angst, maybe even heartache, I had when he told me his secret: how he planned to hitch a ride back to Memphis because he couldn't stand the thought of being around her after she got out of prison. I didn't blame him. We hadn't always felt this way. Before we moved to Hickory Ridge, my mother was serving a sentence of eleven months and twenty-nine days at a penal farm in Memphis. I remember the last visit we made to see her before my brothers and I moved to South Carolina. An officer patted her down in the prison's gym right in front of us. His hands moved from her denim work shirt to her jeans and rolled down to the soles of her bleached sneakers. She didn't flinch. She stood there and spread her arms apart as if she waited to be raised onto a cross.

I could tell by the look in Theo's eyes, the way his pupils twitched, that he couldn't take it. A part of him wanted to hurt the officer. But our mother passed through the inspection quickly, and when she sat with us, I placed my hand on Theo's shaking knee. When we finally started talking, all our mother could think about was getting out. She wanted us to tell her if she looked ready to come back into the real world. Did she look good enough to be seen by her old friends? Was she fat? I didn't know what to say. Of course you're not, or you look fine as you want to be. The idea of my mother getting out was frightening, for me at least. I wasn't ready for the drinking to start up again, the screaming, the sudden outbursts of rage she experienced if the house wasn't clean, or if we were too quiet, or if she just felt the urge to get her hands on something, to twist or hit. Theo was the one to speak up. He held one of her hands and looked at her for a moment. I wonder if we saw the same woman. The woman who made us heart-shaped pancakes on Valentine's Day? The woman who once chased us with a baseball bat around the house when we were ten or eleven? The woman sitting in front of us then, who had been reduced to burning colored pencils for eyeliner? Maybe he didn't see any of those women. He just told her that she was beautiful and, honestly, shouldn't give a damn what people thought. And we didn't cry, just laughed at how silly we felt. All of us in that prison.

Kevin Hong, 17
Walnut Hill School
Natick, MA
Teacher: Allan Reeder

Kevin Hong resides in Needham, Massachusetts. His influences include Joseph Brodsky, Rainer Maria Rilke and Jorge Luis Borges. He will attend Harvard College, where he plans to continue writing.

THE SPECTRUM
Short Story

Shen, the house painter, could see the family inside, in the lighted kitchen, engulfed in the vapors from the huge pot of soup. They seemed very full and happy. The boy, seven or eight years old, occasionally leaned back in his chair to throw out a belch whose volume Shen could gauge from the laughter of his parents on either side, and they would ladle more soup into his bowl, and smack their lips at the meat that slid off the bone (he could see steam slip from the bone as well). The room looked hot. It rose in Shen's eyes like a loaf of bread, so when the wife stepped outside and called up to the roof to invite him and his crew in for some turkey soup—so cold today, she said—it was all Shen could do to swallow his saliva and say, "No, thank you. We have food in the van." The wife went in. He pointed his pressure hose at the skylight to blot out his view of the kitchen.

The Harpers' house seemed always to be full of light. The curtains were open during the day, when Mrs. Harper did housework, and sun flooded the windows, washed over shadows like a tide, sunk into the hardwood floors. In the morning, Shen liked to work on the front of the house, the east side, where the sun warmed his back. From that side, he could see the family room and the dining room on the first floor, and Mr. Harper's study and the master bedroom on the second. There was a small balcony just above the front door from which he could see the foyer, the grand staircase leading to the second floor, and a large chandelier. The light hung twelve feet from the floor on a long, gold chain. It looked like a giant crystal bowl and twinkled throughout the day.

The living room and the kitchen were on the west side. The sunroom, white with white tiles, abutted the kitchen to the south. Its roof was lower than that of the rest of the house. Sunlight congregated there late morning and into the afternoon, through its glass doors and windows, and through the two skylights on the roof. Shen was standing atop the sunroom now. It was here, by the skylights, that he could observe the Harpers' dinner in the kitchen. He was washing the south wall of the second floor and attic. The pressure hose roared against it, and mist formed a rainbow in the air. Amid the noise, Shen peered down and imagined their conversation, the clatter of dishes and silverware.

At dusk, he descended from the roof. He called out to Bo and Sunny, who shut off the water and began loading the van. Shadows broke over the backyard as the last of the sun touched the west side of the house, which glistened like the surface of a lake. The light in the kitchen grew only brighter. It looked as if the Harpers were swimming in it. Shen walked to the driveway and started the van. Jazz was playing on the radio, and he lit a cigarette while he waited for Bo and Sunny to finish packing up. They were arguing about the Rockets game when they clambered in. They were both young. Bo, a squat, red-faced man, insisted that this was their lucky year. Sunny, dark-skinned and rough, insulted each of the starters, Bo and then Bo's mother.

"Your arguments have no substance," Bo said. "That's why you're so crude. It's a shield you use to hide your vacuousness."

"Vacuum my ass," Sunny said. "Slob. Go stuff your face with a watermelon."

Shen said nothing. He put the van in gear and pulled out of the driveway.

***

Shen had looked at Mr. Harper with surprise at their first meeting, when the man, tall and barrel-chested and with the ruddy beard of a poet, said, "We'll be keeping the same color, the peach." He hadn't even glanced at the color scheme. Shen looked up from it, and Mr. Harper was staring at him, as if daring him to make a snide remark. But the house painter knew little English, and instead had shaken the husband's hand. They smiled at each other. Shen tried to make his eyes say "Women" with a sly, knowing twinkle, and Mr. Harper responded with a shrug, as if he had long ago yielded control over his own aesthetic to his wife. Shen had never married, but he had been in love, once.

In any case, Shen discovered that he liked the peach paint. It wasn't too bright, and it contrasted nicely with the evergreen and maple flanking the house. At sunset, from the driveway, the house seemed to glow with the kind of energy that old temples give off, that resonates long after the mosaics have chipped and the walls have cracked.

After the day of power washing, Shen and his crew began to scrape. They laid blue canvas and bedspreads over the bushes and small trees surrounding the house, and then, in the late morning, climbed their ladders armed with putty knives and heat guns. From up high, the house felt like a huge boat surrounded by water, and up on the scaffolds they were like sailors in the crow's nests. Mr. Harper had gone off to work, and the boy was at school. With the gun, Shen loosened old paint from the wall and then slid his knife into the pockets of air and peeled. When he stepped down from his ladder for a smoke, he glimpsed Mrs. Harper in the living room. He was on the east side, but through the opening in the wall of the family room he could make out her figure, poised over a low table covered with a mound of clothes.

She could have been a dancer, judging by her motions. She was tall and slender, with long legs and a graceful neck. She wore her hair in a ponytail that whipped from shoulder to shoulder as she worked. It was dark brown, but when sunlight caught it, refracted through its wisps, her hair turned red, nearly the color of the Japanese maple in the front yard. Shen walked by the living room windows during the crew's lunch break. It was hard to see inside the house because of the way the sun, just past its zenith, glanced off the glass, but he could discern Mrs. Harper's silhouette, now bending, now lifting the hamper, now propping it on her hip. Each form melted into the next. He watched her glide from the living room toward the stairs as if the floor were covered with ice.

The Harpers' cat also roamed the house. He was orange with yellow stripes, and he liked to prowl up and down the stairs. Once in a while, on his patrol, he would stop at the top and look at the chandelier. His head would tilt to one side, hinged on some vertebra between mild curiosity and keen interest, and his tail would swing in a slow arc, as if he were calculating the velocity of some invisible pendulum, some unseen momentum of the chandelier.

All of the flaking paint had been scraped away by lunch. In the afternoon, the crew used electric sanders to feather the clapboards. Shen ignored the incessant grinding; he focused instead on the flurries of dust that rose into the sun's scope and then floated to the ground or were dispersed by a breeze. Some of it swirled around his arms and head and shined, shot through with light. He felt as if he were inside a snow globe. He sanded with his right hand, and with his left he could feel tremors running through the wall, could imagine the sound shaking the rooms inside.

He was on the balcony in the early afternoon when Mrs. Harper was sweeping the foyer. She moved backward toward the stairs, her steps light and delicate, and bowed down with broom and dustpan as if coaxing some intangible force toward her. When she reached the stairs, she turned and started up, straightening her back. Then, suddenly—it must have been a rush of blood, Shen thought—she swayed to the side and caught herself on the railing. She rested the broom and dustpan beside her and rubbed her eyes. Shen saw her insert a pinky into her left ear, as if it were waterlogged or had an itch. She stayed there for half a minute, slouched, breathing slowly. Then, continuing up the stairs, she looked to her left and saw Shen.

He had stopped working. The balcony creaked as he started and shifted his weight, realizing where he was, what he was doing. His electric sander was still on, whining, running against air. Mrs. Harper looked annoyed, or maybe just surprised; her brow was furrowed and her mouth was slightly open, her nostrils flared. She must have felt uneasy, at least. Bits of sun had spun themselves into her hair.

Shen broke first; he gave a little smile and then moved out of the window's frame and began sanding again. His right hand was numb from the machine's vibrations. After a minute, he couldn't help but glance back inside. Mrs. Harper was going back down the stairs, broom and dustpan in hand again, sweeping each step. When she reached the bottom, she crossed the foyer and entered the kitchen, probably for a glass of water. A moment later, the cat appeared on the stairs, and Shen followed it down as well.

The cat, he'd noticed, moved slowly and kept low, as if searching for a purpose. Maybe he thought he would happen upon one, catch it scurrying toward a mouse hole or a crack in the wall. After lunch, Shen had caught sight of the cat swiping at the galaxies that Mrs. Harper beat from the family room curtains. He turned around and around as dust eddied in the air. Shen was about to name the cat Curly, for his dexterous tail, or Li Po—the cat was certainly a thinker, a poet, and probably a drunk—when the creature, in the midst of a universe of particles, suddenly pounced at Mrs. Harper, hackles up. He opened his mouth and showed her his teeth. Mrs. Harper stepped toward him brandishing her duster, and he—Li Po, Shen finally decided—ducked through her legs and dashed up the stairs.

Late that day Shen saw Mrs. Harper again, in the master bedroom. He was on his ladder at the southeast corner of the house. She had drawn the curtains, but they were thin, and he could make her out, sprawled face-up on the king bed. He turned off the electric sander so she would not be disturbed, and the stirring of leaves in the trees filled him.

Li Po trotted in and leaped to Mrs. Harper's side; he nuzzled her as if to make amends, and she stroked his neck and behind his ears. She reached behind her head to undo her ponytail, and her hair spilled onto the pillow. Li Po nestled on her belly. They looked very peaceful together and lay there until the school bus squealed. Then Mrs. Harper started, sat straight up. The cat toppled from her body and slinked away. Shen turned from the window to see the yellow bus at the end of the driveway and the Harpers' little boy emerging from it, his book bag jouncing. The boy stopped at the mailbox to retrieve the day's mail and then ran toward the house, his arms laden. Shen looked back into the bedroom, but the woman was gone.

Below, the front door opened, and Mrs. Harper met her son outside. The boy dropped the mail onto the ground as she knelt and kissed his cheek. When he pressed his face into his mother's chest and reached his arms up around her neck, her hair fell about his head like a private forest. She was murmuring something into his ear, and he was giggling. Then Mrs. Harper stood, and the boy scampered about, picking up the envelopes and magazines that had scattered on the ground. He said something about a Mrs. Patterson—Mrs. Patterson had read them a story about a hippo, and they were learning how to write lowercase letters in cursive. Shen did not understand.

The boy collected the last piece of mail and went inside the house, and his mother followed. She looked up just before she closed the door, looked up and to the left at Shen on his perch. Shen pretended to be inspecting the window frames. Then the door shut. He suddenly felt dizzy. He stepped down from the ladder and ambled to the driveway for a smoke.

After the sanding, they washed the house again. The paint that remained on the walls was dull, de-glossed. The house looked old and mottled, as if it had risen from the earth. But the family inside, at dinner that evening, looked as cheerful as ever. From the roof of the sunroom, Shen saw Mrs. Harper lean her head against her husband's shoulder as he served vegetables, saw his arm around her. Their son's face was as round and as bright as a porcelain doll's. Mr. Harper tousled his hair, and then they fell to eating. As shadows consumed the backyard, the kitchen's light stayed strong. It bloomed into the dark. Shen shut off his hose and called out to Bo and Sunny. They began loading the van.

***

They waited a day for the house to dry and then began to apply the primer. Sunny and Bo started at opposite ends of the west wall and worked toward the middle, while Shen worked alone on the east side. The stuff smelled strongly, as if demanding his attention. There were three days of painting—one for the primer and two for the finish. He worked patiently, slowly, as he covered the clapboards; there was no rush, and he did not want to get tired.

He began at the upper-left corner of the wall. He painted from left to right until the entire level was done, and then moved down a few rungs on his ladder. Again and again he climbed down the ladder, repositioned it and climbed back up. When he finally did feel weary, he turned around and lay back on the ladder's rungs. He breathed deeply and closed his eyes, or squinted into the sun. These moments, he felt almost completely detached from the earth. Only a few metal bars held him up from the ground thirty feet below.

During lunch, the crew sat around a crockpot of rice and a foil container full of pork cuts. Bo produced an embroidered handkerchief from his pocket and wiped sweat from his face.

"Have you met someone?" Sunny asked.

Bo grinned."No kidding," Sunny said.

Bo wrinkled his nose. "But this paint," he said. "What a caustic stench! I think I'm going stupid."

"Too late," Sunny said, and laughed.

"Seriously," Bo said, "my eyes feel swollen. I feel like there's a probe poking around in my nose. I think I'm developing a condition."

Shen smiled to himself; Bo and Sunny were young and inexperienced. He didn't mind the paint so much. He had never really minded uncomfortable sensations; he had learned to shut them out. He remembered a time long ago, in elementary school, when all the students went out during recess with buckets of feces to fertilize the garden in the square. Pairs of students walked through the furrows, one ahead of the other, sharing the load of a bucket that swung from the middle of a pole resting on their shoulders. The furrows were like balance beams; they were careful not to fall over. Sometimes they sang, and the melodies floated from their mouths and over their heads like wisps of smoke. Shen remembered this as he watched Sunny and Bo go back and forth. He wanted to tell the two of them what he was thinking, but he left it alone.

"You get used to it" was all he said. Then he stood up and returned to work.

But he found himself dozing off in the afternoon. The paint, or maybe the sun, dulled his senses to the point where he swayed on the ladder, half-asleep. His ears felt stuffed; he suddenly wanted to drop everything, his paintbrush, his heavy bucket. He wouldn't have cared if the paint splashed against the canvas on the ground, splattered on the lawn and the walkway and the front steps. He got down from the scaffold and, rubbing his temples, shuffled down the driveway. He leaned against the van and tried to take in some fresh air, but it was no use. He lit a cigarette. His head kept buzzing. Then he saw the school bus lurching down the street. It pulled up in front of him and belched its exhaust.

Shen straightened, dropped his cigarette and smashed it under his heel. The door of the bus opened and the Harpers' little boy hopped out. He was wearing a blue jacket with a big hood drawn over his head. His brown hair framed his eyes and pale cheeks. He looked up at Shen and squinted, until Shen stepped forward and his shadow fell upon the boy like a cloak. He must have looked like a giant silhouette against the sun. He remembered the first time he had seen a deer—how, at his slightest movement, the creature caught wind and ran away. He felt slow and awkward in front of the boy.

"What's your name?" he asked. His voice was raspy.

"Joel," the boy said. He blinked, and looked down at Shen's feet and up again. His eyes were light gray, almost translucent. He was missing one of his front teeth. "What's yours?"

"Shen."

Joel Harper put out his right hand. Shen took it gingerly in his. He felt like a child in the boy's eyes.

"That's a funny name," Joel said. "Where did you get it?"

"From my parents," Shen said. "From China."

"China!" Joel said. "What's China like?"

Shen opened his mouth to speak, and then faltered. "What's it like?" he said.

Joel nodded.

He did not know how to answer the question. What did the boy want to know? Would he understand if Shen tried to explain customs, cultures and histories that were entirely foreign to him? Had the boy any perception of distance and time? What did he know of hills like giant hands, terraced fields, sun spreading on land and lake like a copper mirror?

"Very big," Shen said. The rest of it he held under his tongue.

"How far away?" Joel said.

Shen thought again. "Very far."

His arm felt rusty in its socket, but he lifted it and gestured toward the west. He made a throwing motion, as if he had a spear in his hand and he could follow its arc. Joel followed it with him.

"I'm going to travel around the world someday," the boy said. "I'm going to be an explorer." He took a step toward the mailbox.

"Good," Shen said, "very good." His English was loud and abrupt.

His heart was caught in his throat.

"But I wouldn't want to go fast," Joel said. "I wouldn't want to go around the world in eighty days. I want to see everything! I'd want to go around the world in"—he scratched his head, and his hood slipped off—"ten hundred years."

Sunlight set off his hair, which took on the same red hue as his mother's. He opened the mailbox and peered inside, and then, with both hands, brought out a large envelope and several magazines and letters. The envelope was almost as big as his torso. Shen thought he could have scooped him up with one arm and lifted him onto his shoulders. Joel smiled and stepped past him on the driveway.

"Nice meeting you," the boy said, glancing back. "Bye."

"Yes, good," Shen said, as Joel walked away. "Goodbye."

The boy clutched the mail to his chest as he trundled up to the house. On cue, the front door opened, and Mrs. Harper stepped outside. Joel ran into her outstretched arms. Shen saw her look down the driveway at him and thought he saw a frown. Then they were inside, the door shut. Shen blinked at the sun, stretched his arms and walked slowly back. He climbed his ladder and resumed work. The primer stung his nostrils, but he welcomed it. He moved his brush in a long, simple phrase.

***

At dusk, he sat by one of the skylights on the roof of the sunroom. Sunny and Bo were finishing the north side of the house. Sunny was making fun of one of Bo's few and fleeting conquests, and Bo's protests fluttered through the air. The house smelled of vitriol, but the roof received occasional breezes that filled the trees. Shen breathed deeply and looked at the clouds smoldering from the setting sun.

He lay back, and his mind's magician flung his cards out in the sky. Shen surveyed them as a feudal lord surveys his many acres. Closer, Joel's face, scrunched, looking into the sun. Beyond that, the boy stooping to pick up a piece of mail from the ground. Then Shen recalled his collection of cigarette cartons, which, in his youth, were tradable items—Golden Gate, Triple Happiness, Lucky Red. His father, barefoot on the cement of the kitchen floor, running in place to keep warm. His brother gnawing on a stale rice cake. Chi Li, the ladies' man, burning the sky on his motorcycle, the only motorcycle in town, colorful streamers flowing from the handlebars. The exhaust, a shooting star.

He saw a woman sitting up in bed, combing her long, black hair, both straps of her nightgown loose about her arms. One slender leg slipped out from under the sheets and dangled over the side of the bed; her foot arched toward the ground, perfectly pointed, as if poised to enter a body of water. Shen turned and looked down through the skylight into the Harpers' kitchen.

They were seated around the table as usual. Mr. Harper was carving a roasted chicken. Mrs. Harper was ladling soup. Joel blew on the soup in his bowl and watched the steam that rose and wove itself into latticework. What did the boy see? A bridge, maybe, or a pair of trapeze artists in a circus act, a tower—and then Shen noticed that the boy was looking at him. He froze, afraid that Joel had spotted him, but realized in a moment that the boy could see nothing beyond the skylight; it was too dark outside. Nevertheless, Shen climbed down from the roof, careful not to make any noise, and smoked a cigarette in the driveway. He waited in the van for Bo and Sunny to finish painting. When they were done, they loaded the van. In the rearview mirror, as Shen steered away, the sun's last light gilded the house.

***

The work continued on schedule. The crew began applying the first finish. Shen noted as he climbed his ladder that the leaves were changing. The trees that bordered South Street branched out toward each other, forming a natural arbor or columned passageway that was tinged with red and yellow.

On their break, mid-morning, Bo recited poetry. They smoked in a circle by the van, and Bo waved his cigarette in the air, creating skinny rivers, curling shapes. He never really inhaled on the cigarette; he just liked to hold it. He was especially fond of the ancient poet Du Fu:

"The trees shed leaves that rustle, rustle down,
And endlessly, the river surges, surges on.

A guest of autumn's sorrow, of ten thousand miles,
Of a hundred years of ills, I climb the terrace alone."

Sunny laughed at him. "A poet now, eh?" he said. "No wonder the ladies are so hot for you."

"Don't make fun of poetry just because you can't understand it," Bo said.

"Du Fu, tofu," Sunny said. "Get over yourself. I can live without that sentimental crap, thank you very much."

"What do you think, boss?" Bo said.

Shen took a long drag and let the smoke out slowly. It rolled up his face like a thin veil. He didn't really understand the ancient poets, but Bo looked very earnest. Cigarette ash crumbled onto Bo's left boot.

"I guess it's nice," Shen said, and smiled. He stubbed his cigarette as Bo raised his fist in triumph. Sunny snorted and headed back to work.

It was Saturday, and the Harpers were all home. Mr. Harper had spent much of the morning surrounded by his books. As he painted the east wall, Shen had seen him in his study, which was papered with a colorful array of sticky notes that he arranged and rearranged in columns. They were lesson plans, maybe, or story lines. Mr. Harper was a teacher, Shen knew. He had said so when they met. He taught English at the university. The walls of his study were lined with hundreds of books. Shen wondered how old it smelled, how the scent of dog-eared paper filled the room.

Downstairs, Joel was putting together a puzzle in the family room while Mrs. Harper lay on the couch, flipping through the pages of a magazine. Joel looked frail and pretty, unlike his father, but Shen noted with amusement the similarity of their actions. He could watch Mr. Harper organize his notes in different orders, and then work down the ladder to see his son finding a piece that fit, the head of a giraffe, or a zebra's tail. Li Po, the cat, meandered up and down the stairs, dividing his time between the two rooms. Mr. Harper let him rest in his lap without breaking concentration; Joel, when Li Po jumped onto the coffee table and stepped on the puzzle, gathered him up in his arms and buried his face in the fur.

In the afternoon, Shen moved to the roof of the sunroom to paint the south wall. Sunny was below, painting the wall of the first floor. The day was at its crest, and Shen felt as tall as the trees, whistled as they did when the wind bustled by. Looking up at the tips of the branches, he felt more than human, or maybe less, like pure air.

The feeling reminded Shen of a place he had visited in his youth, a mountain spring. The water there was pure, and the trees all around were flushed with sun. Gold dappled the ground. A very old man had set up a business there selling prayer flags and blessings, five yuan each, to those who came to drink the water of the spring. For an extra five, one could drink from his gnarled hands. Shen told this to Sunny, who, taking a break, had climbed to the top of his ladder and propped his arms on the roof to listen. He laughed when Shen told him about the hands, and Shen did too. He felt good; he painted as he talked, freely and smoothly, using the entire length of his arm. Then he heard a sound from inside the house. It was almost imperceptible—a dull clatter, like the far-off clapping of wooden chimes.

Shen put his hand up; Sunny had heard it too. The young man climbed up to the roof and crawled to one of the skylights. He peered in and let out a grunt.

"It's the boy," he said. "He's broken a plate."

Shen laid down his brush and joined Sunny by the skylight. Noodles and shards of ceramic were strewn across the kitchen tiles. The nucleus of the mess was at Joel's feet, which were splattered with red sauce. Mr. Harper was there, full-blooded. Mrs. Harper was on one knee, her arms wrapped around her son, her cheek pressed against his. The man was yelling, but his voice was muffled through the window. He jabbed his index finger at Joel and at the floor. Joel's mother shouted back and held the boy tighter. The man kicked a fragment of the plate and left the kitchen.

Sunny chuckled. "Brings back memories, huh?" he said.

Shen didn't answer. He watched Mrs. Harper dry the boy's tears—which had given his face some color, a hint of pink—and the two of them cleaned up. Joel would not let go of his mother's hand; he held on to it as he bent to pick up shards of the plate. His mother swept the noodles with a broom. Li Po walked among the mess. He sniffed daintily at a meatball and then turned his head with disgust.

"What a baby," Sunny said. "Times sure have changed. A prime example of the decadence of society, as Bo would put it." He crawled back to his ladder, stepped down and resumed painting the south wall.

Shen remained watching Joel and his mother as they disposed of the mess. Then Joel left the kitchen for the family room, while Mrs. Harper turned to the sink. She bowed her head, filled a pot halfway with water and restarted the stove. Shen held his breath as she leaned over the marble countertop, her hair spread out across her shoulders, and then let it out slowly, steadily. The sounds of cars passing on the road and the wind rolling into the trees came back to him. They carried him back to his work.

***

The crew finished on Sunday evening. Sunny and Bo began rolling up the canvas and sheets around the house. Shen breathed better, now that the trees and bushes were once again thrown open to the air. They were shadowy in the dim light, like gargoyles on silent guard. Mr. Harper came outside to inspect the work; he started at the driveway, walked around the house and then returned, nodding to himself. The house, shining with new energy, cut into the sky.

Shen watched Mr. Harper from a few paces away. The man stood tall in the driveway in a T-shirt and shorts. He seemed oblivious to the evening chill. Shen felt angry after what he had witnessed the previous day. It occurred to him, for a moment, that he could speak his mind. Or he could show the man how he felt with merely a word or two, a dismissal, a cold shoulder. He wouldn't, though. Strangely, watching, he admired Mr. Harper, not only for the way he put his hands in his pockets, brows knit in concentration, and let the spirit of the house fill him—he was its patron and its owner, even if he disagreed with its color—but also for the way he seemed to understand matters without knowing anything about them, in the way he cast his eye over the detail of the window frames, could see past the finish to the primer and the sanding, to the power wash of the first day, even though it was dim out, even though he really couldn't see much.

"It looks great," Mr. Harper said. "Really fine." He put his hands together—hands like slabs of meat—and rubbed them. He looked at Shen and smiled through his dense beard. His eyes twinkled, and the painter remembered the joke that they had shared together at the start, and wondered if Mr. Harper remembered. Feeling ashamed, Shen merely nodded and looked away.

Then, from the driveway, they heard the storm door swing open. Joel's shout rang out like a shrill violin.

"Bunker's on the chandelier!"

Shen's first reaction was confusion. He did not know what a bunker was. He saw that Mr. Harper was equally as surprised and bewildered; his mouth opened but emitted no sound as he stumbled toward the house. Joel held the door. Mr. Harper ran inside and stopped in the foyer. Shen could see him looking up, hands outstretched, swaying as if he were under a fly ball. Then he realized, and suddenly felt as if he had known it all along, as if the fact had always been with him and had resurfaced at its calling: Bunker was Li Po. Bunker was the cat. The cat had jumped onto the chandelier.

Bo had been carrying a stepladder to the van when Joel shouted. Now Shen took the ladder from him and shouldered it. He went as quickly as he could to the door; seeing him, Joel opened it, saying nothing, only staring, distressed, and Shen angled the ladder through. Mrs. Harper was at the top of the staircase, leaning over the banister toward the chandelier, which was jerking to and fro. Crystals were being knocked loose from it by the four legs that had fallen between the fixture's rings and were each scrabbling for a foothold. Several crystals had already exploded on the ground; Mr. Harper was trying to catch the others before they shattered.

Shen unfolded the ladder and climbed up. He averted his eyes from the light that was intensified by the glass prisms. The three members of the house were shouting over each other—"Watch your feet, Joel!" "Hannah, come down!" "That's glass on the floor!" "Bunker, stop kicking!"—but as Shen reached the top of the ladder, they drew together at the bottom of the stairs and squinted up at the painter. Shen's head was above the light now, and he could see into the bowl of concentric rings, the cat squirming there, and through the rings, he could see the floor lit with stars.

"Watch out!" Joel said. "He doesn't like strangers!"

Bunker yowled as Shen reached into the chandelier and lifted him. The cat twisted and kicked against Shen's chest. Shen could feel the cat's muscles churning, his spine's incredible torque. In his right arm, the body felt almost liquid, like marbles rolling over and over each other. He held the cat tightly against him as he stepped down the ladder. As soon as both of his feet were on the foyer floor, the cat sprang off into the kitchen. Joel hollered and ran after him. The painter straightened and adjusted his coat, which had been perforated by the cat's claws, and then he felt his heart pounding, felt blood pump in every part of his body. He saw Mrs. Harper slip her arm through her husband's. She gave Shen a funny look. He was startled to be so close to her. She was probably remembering the balcony window. And maybe, from inside, she had seen Joel talking with him. Her hair was crimson in the light and her skin was pale.

"Thank you," Mr. Harper said. "I mean, sorry, and thank you."

"No, no," Shen said. He scratched his head and felt paint chips. It was very bright in the foyer. The chandelier was still swinging; the crystals' spectral fragments met the glass that had spread across the floor. The Harpers remained staring at him, as if they expected him to do something, to make a joke or take a bow.

"Yes," Mrs. Harper said, looking down, "yes—thanks." She scuffed a slippered foot against the floor and cleared away a constellation of glass.

Joel came back with Bunker in his arms and elbowed his way in between his parents. He was grinning.

"He's from China!" Joel called out, his voice full of awe.

Mr. Harper laughed. "Oh, is that right? How do you know?"

"He told me!" Joel said. "His name is Shen, and he's from China."

Shen saw Mrs. Harper frown.

"Looks like you've made a new friend," Mr. Harper said.

"How big is China, Dad?"

"How big?" Mr. Harper said. "How big? Let's see. You know my library?"

"Yes."

"There are many books in that library, right?"

"Right!"

"Well," he said, kneeling down, "if you took every single book in that library, and you counted every single word—no, every single letter in every single book—you wouldn't reach half the number of people that live in China."

Joel's mouth fell open. The Harpers looked to Shen for verification. Shen nodded dumbly. The room was moving with colors. The shadows of the Harpers, the railing, the flower vase by the stairs lunged to and fro.

"Well, say goodbye to Shen now," Mr. Harper said to Joel. "He's very tired. He's had a long day."

"Bye," Joel said, as Mrs. Harper stepped behind the boy and put her hands on his shoulders.

Shen pressed down on the bottom step of the ladder to fold it up. He shouldered it as Mr. Harper held the door open.

"Thanks again," the man said, and they shook hands. Then Shen walked out. It was dark outside after the brightness of the foyer. Shadows were thin and long on the front yard. He heard the door shut behind him. Bo and Sunny were waiting in the driveway. He gave them the ladder to secure to the top of the van, and he climbed into the driver's seat.

He switched the engine on, and then the heat. Jazz was playing on the radio, the same station as always. Shen did not know the names of the songs or the players, but he could pick up on colors in the sounds that splashed through the van. The saxophone and the cymbals were an orange—acrid but still sweet—that shocked the stretched canvas of air. Bo and Sunny climbed in. Shen pulled down on the gearshift and the van responded like a bull, yoked. He turned right out of the driveway, and the house crossed the length of the rearview mirror. Light burgeoned, soft and gold, from the skylights on the roof of the sunroom where he had worked and rested and watched.

For a mile or so, in his mind he picked his way through the house as if he were exploring an ancient ruin. He saw the boy's muddy shoes just inside the door, a bed of sunlight by the balcony window, the cat's sides rising and falling as he breathed into a weightless sleep. A wonderland of dust, Mrs. Harper's hair spilling down like a cataract, blankets thrown clear of a bad dream. He smelled clean clothes, breathed in a vase of purple flowers. Each sign of life—a curtain moving, a door ajar—seemed to open some reservoir of memory, still full, huge and silent except for drops of water, condensed on the ceiling, that fell into the pool, echoing.

He wondered what had gone through Mrs. Harper's head when she had seen him staring through the balcony window. Why she had stumbled so on the stairs, almost swooned. And what had Joel thought of him as he stood in the driveway in his heavy boots, eclipsing the sun? How had Mr. Harper judged him after inspecting the work, and after Shen had rescued the cat from the chandelier?

It was no wonder to him how the cat had gotten there. Shen could see him at his regular perch at the top of the stairs. He could see him stretch out like an accordion and vault onto the banister and then, with another fearsome leap, reach for the bowl of light. It was less a reach than it was a return, as if the cat had been attached to an invisible, elastic cord, had pulled back as far as he could and then rebounded. Shen saw the crystals again, tripped like a minefield, betraying for a moment all their brilliance. He blinked and the colors were still in his eyes.

"So, what was that anyway, boss?" Sunny called out from the back over the music.

"Nothing," Shen said. "Their cat was stuck."

Sunny and Bo laughed. "I'm going to miss them," Sunny said. "Especially that little crybaby. Some entertainment during the long hours."

"Oh, like you never shed a tear when you were a child," Bo said.

"I never said I didn't. Difference is, my father beat them out of me."

"Maybe that's why you've got such a cold exterior," Bo said. "You've got issues. The thing about the past is, it'll keep growing and growing, and one day it's all you'll have left."

"Shut up," Sunny said. "It's you who keeps growing. Lose some weight, why don't you? The beers can't keep up. Speaking of which…"

Shen stayed quiet as the two men talked. He drove slowly; the van's headlights illuminated only the immediate road. He rolled down his window to feel the air and heard the trees that arched overhead. He felt as if he were going through a long, winding tunnel. The car was a spirit level, very small and even and centered. Night dragged like a woolen train. Shen reminded himself to send the Harpers' bill and stepped down from the remains of the roof. Pressing the pedal, he felt the engine stir underfoot.

Amanda Unger, 17
Bayonne High School
Bayonne, NJ
Teacher: Charlann Meluso

Amanda Unger is from Bayonne, New Jersey. In her writing, she tries to give readers a different perspective on situations that would ordinarily be deemed negative; she is inspired by the work of Chuck Palahniuk and Ray Bradbury. She will double major in creative writing and graphic design at New Jersey City University.

WISHBONES
Short Story

Liam first notices it in Elijah's ankles.

In his Achilles tendons, really. Known in the medical world as the calcaneal tendons. But Liam is nowhere near a doctor, and therefore he only thinks of them as the taut tendons at the back of Elijah's ankles. Attaching his heels to his ankles to his calves. All his muscles that Liam notices are becoming so very small and his joints are bony, but Elijah assumes it's not obvious because he's already so very thin. And he's justified in that, because Liam didn't notice for a long time.

But Liam did notice, eventually. He noticed those ankles.

Normally, guys have thinner legs than girls do. Liam knows this; he's seen enough smooth, bare women and their long and short legs to know that their legs are proportioned differently. One of the last girls he'd met, with her lazy bedroom eyes, she'd said she was jealous of guys because their legs were always slender and gorgeous without effort. And that she had a swimmer friend who waxed his legs smooth, and she was always so jealous of them. Needless to say, Liam hadn't called her for a second time around, but it had got him thinking, looking. And men have lankier ones with long calves and tight muscles. Naturally with prominent tendons and tight soleus muscles and everything else.

But Elijah's tendons are practically wishbones, his skin tight around them. Practically raw red.

Liam's not sure when he first noticed them. But he'd been looking ever since. He supposes it must have been one morning or evening or something when Elijah didn't have boots or socks or pants on. It's like when you're dreaming—you never remember the beginning of one, you always end up in the middle of it. And for Liam, it's like a confusing, frightening, recurring dream. Looking around in the middle of the dream, he remembers Elijah lying on his stomach on the bed, fingers roaming over the keyboard on the laptop. His legs bent at the knees to expose his ankles to the still air. Swinging them back and forth like a schoolgirl. Looking around in the middle of the dream, he remembers Elijah in swim trunks at the beach and his tendons are beaten by the saltwater and the sand in the air and they're practically raw red like they've got sunburn but they don't.

Looking around in the middle of the dream, he remembers Elijah standing on the scale in the bathroom, staring down at numbers, and he can tell by the tension in his shoulders that he's not happy with them. His ankles are so thin and the Achilles tendons protrude obstructively. And Liam just stands in the doorway staring at him and his skinny legsarmswaist that he'd never thought much of until now.

Liam doesn't say anything. About the scale, about his ankles. About Elijah pushing his food around his plate with nonchalance instead of eating it. He doesn't. It's just not the time, not his place. He will let this go on for as long as it must. Liam used to think Elijah would eat when he wasn't around. Elijah comes out with them at night and says he's not hungry, or he doesn't feel well. The excuses all start to add up, and Liam begins to keep track of them. Nerves before a show. Jet lag from the flight. Too tired to bother worrying about his stomach fucking growling.

Elijah's fingers are as slender as the cigarettes he smokes. His hipbones jut at the waist of his pants, and he tugs them down an extra inch so he can look in the mirror and feel proud of himself. Look at those hipbones. And he'd run cigarette fingers over them. They glide like smoke. Look how shapely you're becoming. It's a twisted kind of vanity, an attraction to his deprived insides. If only he could be chiseled like a Greek statue, perfect proportions and achingly desirable angles. His skin's already porcelain, already marble and wonderful, and he just needs to have a carved anatomy. Just a little bit more bone. Just another size down. That's all he keeps telling himself before he pulls on a shirt and it's tight because it's a size smaller than it should be. Because he wants to feel his ribs poking out like ivory piano keys he'll never learn to play. The keys his brother can play and he watches him and envies him and runs cigarettes over his ribs and it's almost there. It's almost like playing the piano.

Liam is losing the ability to even recognize his brother. They're subtle, the changes in him, but they're there. And Liam notices the way it swallows a bit more of him every time Elijah lets his stomach swallow itself. His cheekbones seem higher, a sick kind of sexy each time Elijah smiles at the camera. It makes him look taller, not that he even needs it with his ridiculous natural height, and he towers over Liam. It almost makes Liam feel overweight in comparison. And Liam can see all the joints in Elijah's hands as he grips the microphone and sings his lungsheartstomach out into it and the fans fucking scream when Elijah's skeletal hips show below the hem of his shirt, stretching his arms up to the stars.

For a split second, Elijah feels absolutely beautiful.

And his calcaneal tendons are cut open, blistering tenderly as the backs of his boots chafe against them. He runs around on stage like it's all okay, but his socks are blood-stained at the end of the night when he undresses in the hotel room. He hisses out chewed serpentine swears when he dabs them with alcohol and bandages them. And he cries when they start bleeding ugly all over again and again but it's worth it. It's all worth it.

An agent says Elijah looks mighty thin lately, and Elijah giggles like a girl and says he's really not. But she compares a recent picture of him to an older one and, yes, his bones are more pronounced and his eyes more sunken and Elijah shrugs a shoulder. Stress from being on tour, he says, he's homesick and tired. Says he always gets like this being on the bus all the time. Liam looks pointedly away from the camera, watching the concave hollows of Elijah's cheeks and the jugular in his neck and he knows that Elijah never used to be like this. Even stressed, even homesick. Even tired of being on the bus.

He watches Elijah absently scratch at his ankle and he knows.

Elijah lets his bony frame fall down on the couch next to Liam one evening, and he's in sweats to cover up how goddamn thin he is. As if Liam can't tell. And he cuddles up to Liam, mumbling that he's cold and Liam feels warm against him and Liam knows it's because he has virtually no body fat. He's always cold. But he plays the role of the good big brother and wraps his arm around Elijah and keeps him warm. Keeps him happy—or tries to, at least. Because he doesn't talk as openly to Liam as he used to, not anymore. He bundles it up and spits it out with his weight. This is just one thing that won't be shared between twins.

Sometimes he wonders if George and Frank notice. Or anyone on the cast with them. Does anyone realize? And he has an urge to ask them, an urge to tell them. It's not something he can bottle up forever, but he has a feeling he'll have to. This isn't something to talk about to anyone at all. This is between brothers, yes, but mostly between Elijah and his reflection. And Liam doesn't say a word. He doesn't make a distinct expression to tell Elijah that, yes, he knows Elijah doesn't eat. That his bones become him and he's underweight. That the limelight's blinded not only his eyes but his sense. Because if this makes Elijah happy, then he'd rather Elijah be happy than unhappy. Because he's trying to be a good brother.

And he will let this go on for as long as it must.

Elijah is an autumn equinox, when he lifts himself up from under Liam's arm and goes to sit at the bay window, on the lush cushions that look like giant hunks of green sea glass from broken liquor bottles. He's an equinox because of the way he looks out the window at the sun falling down, the way it casts sleepy golden rays over his face. His face is clean and his hair is down and he's in a plain tee and sweats, and Liam thinks he'd look so beautiful if it weren't for the dips in his face that create obscenely deep shadows in response to the glow. Elijah was always so photogenic—and he still is, Liam deduces ruefully, even though the arms that reach down to rest in his lap are so much skinnier than they used to be. The sun makes them look like goldenrod and he looks almost healthy.

Elijah is too busy looking out at barren tree limbs to notice Liam watching him. He's wishing he looked as beautiful naked as the trees do. He's wishing he was as slender as the thinnest twigs that silhouette themselves in the sun and look so elegant doing it. He's wishing he was a tree.

Weeks later, Liam takes Elijah out to eat and Elijah doesn't order anything except a glass of water with lemon. And Liam offers him something off his plate.

"Are you crazy?" Elijah laughs naturally. "Alfredo is so fucking fattening, so many carbs. I can't eat that." He smiles like it's normal. And then Liam begs him, please, please, just eat the tomatoes at least. And the curve of Elijah's mouth drops, and he shakes his head, sipping his water with the lemon in it quietly. "I'm not hungry anyway."

Liam doesn't even know who's sitting across from him anymore.

That's when he decides to hide the scale Elijah weighs himself on twice a day.

When he does it, Elijah freaks out, just as Liam expected him to. He searches all over the bathroom for it, in the cabinets and behind the toilet, and he even opens the vanity mirror even though he knows it isn't there. But he's already stripped off his shirt and pants for what little weight they all add on and he needs the scale. He double-checks the bathroom and then bolts out, tripping over the shoes he'd toed off.

"Liam?" he calls out, and Liam mutes the TV because he already knows what the problem is.

"Yeah?"

"Where's the scale?" His voice is heavy, afraid, but trying to maintain normalcy.

Liam puts the remote control down on the armrest. "You don't need it, Elijah."

"Liam, where is it?" Liam can hear him becoming more anxious by the second.

He licks his lips, almost feeling sorry. "I took it away. I hid it somewhere."

"You what?"

"You're not getting it, Elijah." He says firmly, standing and walking toward the corridor, and he sees Elijah all stripped down, stripped right to his bones, his knees shaking.

"Liam!" Oh, yes, there's desperation in his voice. But Liam shakes his head. Repeats himself.

"You don't need it, Elijah."

"Yes, I do!" Elijah holds on to the door frame pathetically, his skin so fucking white that it almost blends in. "Liam, give it to me."

Liam shakes his head again, taking a step closer to his brother. Elijah takes a step backward, nudging a shoe again.

"Give me the scale, Liam!"

Liam bites on his lip, and he shakes his head for a third time. And then Elijah slams the bathroom door shut, locking it swiftly, and begins to cry. And he makes no effort to hide it the way he hides the bills for newer, tighter, smaller clothes, the way he hides his constant gooseflesh under feigned calmness, the way he hides the food forced upon him by Liam in his jacket pockets. He backs away from the door, his arms around each other, sobbing and stumbling over his shoes so he slides back against the tiled wall. And Liam's banging on the door now.

"Look at yourself, Elijah! Fucking look at yourself!"

Elijah looks through blurry eyes at his knuckles and jutting wristbones.

"You think I don't see it, Elijah? You think I don't see how you're starving yourself?"

Elijah looks at his ribs and counts them. He plays the piano on them with cigarette butts.

"Let me in, Elijah." Liam's voice becomes weak with emotion. "Unlock the door."

Elijah's feeling his perfectly projecting hipbones, holding on to them because they're so damn beautiful.

"Elijah," Liam's given up on banging on the door now, "please. Please."

Elijah's slumped into a prayer position on the floor, touching all his angles and listening to Liam twisting the doorknob relentlessly. And begging him. Begging him and his clavicles and spine and ankles. His chest is wet from tears, sticking on his exposed skin, and he just keeps telling himself that he's thin and beautiful and thin and beautiful. And then he reaches to the doorknob and untwists the lock. His hand is barely off the knob when Liam jerks the door open and nearly falls into the room. And Elijah can't even bring himself to look up at Liam, not even when Liam kneels down next to him and puts his warm hands on Elijah's cold body.

Liam wraps his arms around Elijah and pulls him flush against himself, running his fingers down every notch in his vertebrae and over every ridge in his rib cage. It's a long moment before Elijah can manage to dare to enclose his arms belatedly around Liam's waist that feels smaller than his own in his embrace. He lets Liam's shirt soak up all his pain. Lets Liam keep telling him that he's sick and starving and sick and starving. Elijah's muffled voice tells Liam he doesn't understand and Liam says that no, he doesn't, and he can't because Elijah was already so thin and so beautiful before and now he's not. Now he's not.

And Elijah screams through his sh-sh-shaking bronchi and larynx to not tell him he used to be thin and beautiful because he wasn't, he wasn't, he wasn't beautiful and he's nevereverever been thin. He's never been thin! And, oh, he needs the scale, he needs the scale to tell him how thin he is now and how beautiful he is now and will Liam pleasepleaseplease just give him the scale. Just give him the scale.

Liam studies Elijah's shoulder blades, his skin and bones. Elijah's crying against him, still, and Liam finally understands his need. Or he feels like he does, feels like it's clicking between the sprockets and cogs in his mind. This need, this desperation and obsession. He can't explain it, but it begins to make sense to him. Studying Elijah's spinal cord and dimples of Venus, he can see that it's easier for Elijah to not admit he has a problem. To act like it doesn't fucking hurt so he can get the satisfaction he needs from his reflection. Elijah is whimpering, his ducts are running out of tears, and Liam touches his Achilles tendons. He murmurs, "I'll be right back," and pulls away from Elijah and stands and leaves. And Elijah's wasted wrists hang limp at his knees, his shoulders slumped, and he sniffles.

A moment later, Liam walks back in with the scale in his hands, and Elijah can only stare at him in a cocktail of hope and incredulity and necessity. And he stands, wobbly, wiry, and watches Liam put down the scale at his feet. He looks between Liam and the scale and Liam and the scale and then he gingerly steps on it. He thinks all the bones in his feet look some kind of gorgeous and he watches the digital numbers flicker for a moment before giving a read-out. He hears Liam's breath hitch but can't look at him. He's too mesmerized by the number, the number that's far too small for someone six foot two. His eyes are tearing again but this time it's in a happy way and he wipes at them with an emotionless mouth because he knows it's good and bad that he's lost six ounces.

Liam looks away from Elijah and the scale. He's less than one hundred twenty-five pounds. Liam feels nauseous. It's sick and unhealthy and malnourished, but Elijah has stars in his eyes and Liam doesn't speak. He doesn't leave, but he doesn't look. He is a stupid kind of wise monkey that is avoiding everything right now because he feels so rigid with disgust and fear and other unnamed emotions. Looking around in the middle of the dream, he just barely sees the taut tendons at the back of Elijah's ankles out of the corners of his eyes. And then he turns and walks out of the bathroom.

Because he will let this go on for as long as it must.

Luke Hodges, 17
Governor's School for the Arts and Humanities
Greenville, SC
Teacher: Scott Gould

Luke Hodges is a native of Columbia, South Carolina, and will study anthropology at Kenyon College. His work is driven by subconscious wanderings and his own nagging questions. He would like to thank his teachers Scott Gould, George Singleton and Mamie Morgan for their help and support.

FOREIGN RELATIONS
Short Story

I hosted a United Nations party for a few of the English as a Second Language kids from school one Friday evening, the same night I found out my father had left for good. Convinced at the age of eight that I was destined to be a diplomat, I donned a pair of spotless penny loafers, a blazer with shiny golden buttons and the finest turtleneck sweater purchased on discount from the department store downtown. Before any of the guests arrived, I sat at the kitchen counter, adjusting and then readjusting my American-flag lapel pin, so it aligned perfectly with my name tag: Grady Wicker, Distinguished Representative from the United States of America. My mother peeked her head out from behind the refrigerator door. She could always tell when I felt nervous.

"Don't be so anxious," my mother said, dropping chunks of potato into a pot on the stove. "You've been over there fidgeting since I started dinner."

I tried to steady my hands. "What are you making?" I asked.
"Traditional Turkish goulash," she said, closing the lid on the pot.

"But goulash is Hungarian," I said. "Not Turkish."

I stared at the hardwood floor. I read most of *Turkey: Life on the Eurasian Continent* in preparation for that night, and compiled a special menu for my mother to prepare, so the distinguished representative from the Middle East would feel welcome. I had met Adnan Pamuk earlier that week at school. He was new and kept walking into the girls' bathroom by mistake, repeating "Not boys', not boys', not boys'." I invited Adnan to the party despite the fact he spoke even less English than his classmates. It felt good to try and speak with someone, even if I knew they didn't understand me.

"Go put a pitcher of water on the table, Grady," my mother said, brushing me up from my chair. "Your friends are going to be here soon."

The dining room table looked smaller than usual, covered with all of the place settings. A light bulb on the chandelier buzzed like a gnat. I stood on a chair and tried to screw it back into its socket, but the hot glass burned my thumb and forefinger. I wanted everything to be perfect.

I heard my older brother stomp down the stairs. Simon was fifteen and liked to wear skinny jeans that my mother said would inhibit his ability to have children. He grabbed the chair I stood on and shook it.

"Cut it out," I said, turning around to knock him on the shoulder. "I could've fallen on the table and stabbed myself with a salad fork."

Simon grinned. "What's for dinner, Baby United?"

I hated his pet names for me. Baby United, Little Jimmy Carter, Mister America. Ever since my father left, Simon and I fought regularly. He didn't appreciate diplomacy like I did.

"Goulash," I said, stepping down from the chair.

"Turkish food, gross," he said.

"It's Hungarian," I said, sounding exasperated.

Simon grabbed a dinner roll from the bread basket on the table, scattering crumbs over the tablecloth and floor. "Fine, Baby United, it's Hungarian," he said, his mouth full.

I gathered up the tiny bits of crust and shoved them in my breast pocket for safekeeping, until I could reach a trash can. "If Dad were here, you know what he would call you?" I asked. Our father ran a used-car dealership, so my vocabulary included numerous dirty words I picked up while eavesdropping on his arguments with customers.

"I don't care what Dad would call me," Simon said. "He's not here. So he's not going to call me anything."

"When Dad comes back," I said, "you know what he'll call you?"

The words *comes* and *back* hung on my ears like sour music notes.

Though my father had been gone for only a few weeks, his distance already felt permanent. I heard a few car doors slam outside, and my mother shouted for me to greet my guests out front. As I stepped out of the dining room, I realized part of me was glad that Simon didn't have a chance to respond. He might have told me what I didn't want to hear.

Dinner seemed to be going well, until the distinguished representatives from France and Vietnam got into a slapping match over the last piece of apple pie. Pham Dung, who instructed us to call him P.D. for short, rolled his cotton napkin into a whip and smacked Jean across the face with it, knocking his glasses to the floor. The representatives from Uganda and Mexico started laughing. I remembered skimming *Croissants to Clemenceau: Life in France* and attempted to divert Jean's attention with a question.

"Representative, is it true that French ladies don't shave their legs?"

"He hit me," Jean said, his voice wavering.

"Sacre bleu," P.D. said, skewering an apple with his fork. I picked up Jean's glasses and looked at Adnan Pamuk, seated at the end of the table, staring at his cold goulash. I wondered what his house must have looked like in Turkey. I thought of huge green palm trees shading the brick walkway to his front door with their fat leaves. I wondered if he missed his old life, if everything felt downgraded now that he lived in a two-bedroom apartment downtown, right beside the university, where his mother studied orthodontics. I'm convinced the two of us would've talked about misplaced parents and homes and real Turkish cuisine, had it not been for Simon, who burst through the kitchen doorway wearing army camouflage and holding a plastic machine gun, eye black shadowing his face.

"I'm here for Grady Wicker," he said, leaning over to examine our faces, as if he wouldn't recognize me outright. "Where is he?"

I knew better than to be afraid of Simon, but Jean and P.D. didn't. The two of them were borderline hysterical, squirming in their chairs like toddlers who couldn't hold their bladders any longer. I tried to pass it off as nothing, tried to pretend Simon wasn't there.

"Adnan," I said. "Did your family own a car in Turkey?"

"There aren't any cars in Turkey," my brother said. "It's a Third World country."

"No, it's not, Simon," I said. "And I think Adnan can speak for himself when I ask him a question."

"No, he can't. The kid can barely say 'Hello' in English."

At this point, a few of the representatives started to giggle. Adnan remained silent. I stood up from my chair. "Would you just leave us alone? We're trying to have a meeting here." I realized the words sounded stupid coming out of my mouth before I could shut them back in. Simon straightened up and crossed his arms.

"Sorry to have interrupted your meeting, Baby United," he said. "I know you have very important matters to discuss. Like your favorite pair of penny loafers, and drawing class after school. You know, those international concerns."

I could feel my face turning red. For a moment, even Adnan seemed to understand what Simon had said. He looked up at me from his bowl of goulash. Embarrassment is a shared language, I guess.

"Father owned a car," Adnan said. "But he is in Turkey, away from us. I ride the bus now. Mother rides a bicycle."

Adnan pressed a napkin to his lips and burped. None of us laughed. The air in the room became still, momentarily silent, save the quiet gurgling of the dishwasher in the next room, which my mother had left running before going to a dinner party next door. We were astonished that he spoke.

"My dad sells cars," I said. "He's away on a business trip, but he'll be back soon."

Simon pulled the trigger on his plastic machine gun. It made a noise not unlike the electric fanfare of an arcade game while the nozzle lit up like a cigarette. "We're not going to talk about Dad, Baby United."

"Why not?" I asked.

"Because, Little Jimmy Carter. Drop it."

"My dad sells Hondas and Toyotas and Mitsubishis," I said. "If we had a Japanese representative here, he might be able to tell us what those names mean."

Simon clutched the gun a little tighter. I heard the trigger snap once more. "Would you shut up, Mister America?"

Right then, I wanted to make Simon angry. So I kept talking. In about one minute, I spilled everything I knew about my father, which was astonishingly little. His failing business, the fights with our mother some nights after dinner, the "extended" trip out of town to see about some cheap deals on cars. I never knew my father beyond a small accumulation of details. I tugged at the collar of my turtleneck.

"Goulash was not a very good meal, no?" Adnan said.

"Dad's not coming back, Grady," my brother said.

Simon stepped out of the dining room, the door to the kitchen closing softly behind him. The distinguished representatives from Mexico and Uganda exchanged glances. Jean wiped a fingerprint off the lens of his glasses and then leaned back into his chair, his eyes darting around the room. I'm no psychologist, but looking back on it, I'm pretty sure I used the United Nations party as a way to deal with my father's absence. Maybe I figured two opposite people could never really understand one another, but it was worth it to at least make an effort.

Adnan Pamuk stayed over long after the rest of the delegates left. His mother called to say that night classes ran a little late that evening, but she had phoned for a taxi to come right over, and it would be there shortly. Adnan and I sat on the screened-in porch that led to my backyard while waiting for his ride. The early summer heat gave all forms of plant life the impression of wilting, and the crickets seemed to chirp extra loudly in protest.

"My father owns a Honda car," Adnan said. "The kind your father sells."

I imagined my father trying to sell Adnan's father a car, the two of them unable to speak to each other.

"I don't even know if my father sells cars anymore," I said. "For all I know, he could be halfway around the world. In Hungary or someplace, making goulash."

I heard the taxi honk out in front of the house. Adnan stood up from his rocking chair and followed me inside, to the front door, where we could see the running car all lit up in my driveway. I liked to hear the sound of an engine humming, even if it meant someone would be going away soon. Sometimes it's nice to fill silence with something other than words.

Mina Seckin, 17
St. Ann's School
Brooklyn, NY
Teacher: Marty Skoble

Mina Seckin is a native of Brooklyn, New York, and will attend Columbia University. She admires the poetry of Allen Ginsberg, Sylvia Plath and Meghan O'Rourke, and notes that, without fail, her poetry always comes back to food.

AN ANNIVERSARY
Poetry

Jimmy with his crushable
wool hat is in the living
room but I can't hear
him making a sound.
Who likes to think that there is a place
in the human mind no one has ever been to
or can go. Who likes to mold the shape of heads
in the exact way they want heads to be.
I can scoop out
with my fingers his
hair from under the soft
wool of his hat. I can tug,
change his directions. Change
the way that water can only slip
between fingers. Change the way you
think that the hole in the living room floor
can't be covered up with a rug, can't be stuffed
with some blankets. Everything has holes, the issue
then is how to fill them with something that will stay.

Haris Durrani, 17
Staples High School
Westport, CT
Teacher: Michael Fulton

Haris Durrani is from Westport, Connecticut, where he observes and writes about multiculturalism, his family and the art of science. He cites Isaac Asimov as a literary influence and will attend Columbia University, where he plans to study applied physics.

JEDI NIGHT
Short Story

Your real name isn't Jedi. It's Geraldo "Jedda" Muñez. Don't ever forget who you are.

Don't ever.

Jedi is the name I gave you when I was ten. This was around the time the new *Star Wars* trilogy, the prequels where George Lucas shit his brains out, played in theaters. For a kid like me it never mattered. It was *Star Wars,* for God's sake.

But this story isn't about Luke Skywalker and Darth Vader or Chewbacca or even Yoda. This is about Order 66. Betrayal.

This story is about you, my favorite cousin in the whole wide world. Mi primo favorito.

You grew up in Washington Heights, the way so many Dominicanos do, and made your way through high school. You did okay and got into college in upstate New York. It's the path of many Dominicans—the path sociologists tell us we follow by nature and the path the media expects us to follow and the path the patriotic citizens of America want us to follow. It is our path. Yours, mine, the path of los Dominicanos. Whether you chose to follow it, to give in, is your own choice.

Not.

Hell no, it's not.

It's the choice of all those other people—the academics and media. It's the decision made by "intellectuals" and "journalists" and "true American citizens." Free will is a joke out of hell. Whoever thinks otherwise es un tonto.

The only way I ever got out was by playing the apple: colored on the outside, white on the inside. When you think like what you're not, you cheat the system. And yourself, I later realized. I always wondered why, when Luke Skywalker had his hand cut off and Darth Vader asked his son to join him, Luke didn't say "Sure, Dad, no sweat!" and then destroy the Empire from the inside. The thing is this: If you follow the set path, whether it's working through the inner ranks or on the cusp of "established" society, you lose your identity anyway. Being a subjugated people means you always lose.

That's what happened to you. By staying true to your path, you didn't stay true to yourself.

I was visiting your campus when the recruiter made his rounds.

"Serve your country."

He was tall and muscular but not domineering. He didn't cast a shadow or look down at you. He looked you eye to eye. Hombre to hombre. Like the guy you'd want to hang out with at the local bar. Like George W. Bush. You know.

You looked at him and nodded absently. He slipped a brochure into your hand. In wide, formal type, type that screamed it knew what it was doing and assured you it understood what was best for you, it read this: HOMELAND SECURITY. You shrugged and slipped it into your pocket, but letters kept coming and more recruiters and more emails. What else could you do in life? Paint houses? Mow lawns? Fix toilets? Run a decrepit auto shop in Washington Heights?

Here the path split. You could go that way. You could also try your prospects at policing or a federal job that really meant something.

But either way you lose, hombre. Either way you're screwed.

You don't decide your future. They do.

***

When you signed up for the Homeland Security job, they gave you a big gun and a shiny holster and a whole new desk to yourself. Of course your work was mostly desk work, but that was how it went. They give you the weapon; you feel the power; you're one of them, end of story.

They had your office in upstate New York, far from family and Washington Heights and los Dominicanos. You left the desk once a month to visit detention centers and talk with illegals. Their holding cells, gray cribs of concrete, stunk of cold piss. You'd go there, cell by cell, and make your rounds. Order of business.

Cell one:

"Jorge Rodriguez…" You paused. "Dominican."

The man looked at you, jaw clenched. His muscles tensed beneath his orange clothes. For a moment he looked like an angry clown.

"Sí," he said.

The illegal looked again at you with his whirling, brown eyes and reached for your clipboard and pen.

"Sign here." You pointed. "You are under federal law to speak the truth and nothing but the truth."

The illegal began to sign. The pen ripped the paper—a gentle shriek of tearing filaments and scratching, like a cat clawing at a door. You made him sign again. He was wasting your goddamn time. You clicked the pen once, twice.

"When did you arrive in the United States?"

He breathed.

"Ochenta y seis."

His voice was like nata, the strong layer of hardened milk that settles over coffee. You know that beneath the nata is flowing milk, boiling liquid that can spill or evaporate or swirl or tremble. Beneath is the chaos of hot fluid. You know the truth about this from all the times Abuelita served us café con leche when we visited her apartment. You know Dominicanos love their coffee so hot it scalds their tongues. It keeps us alive.

"English, Mr. Rodriguez. English."

For the third time, his fiery, dark eyes met yours.

"Why did you come here?"

His eyes swiveled toward the window, where light tumbled through the viscous magma of air saturating the holding cell. This light was a constant light, the light of day, and it did not flicker. This was the lightning without the thunder, the storm without the storm.

"Dinero," the illegal said, then corrected himself. "Money. Oppor-tu-ni-ty. Mi familia." He struggled with the English, but it was more than that.

"And?"

His eyes settled on the window. He didn't want to look at you any longer.

"El Jefe," he whispered, and you heard him curse under his breath. He crossed his shaking index fingers."The Dictator. Trujillo," he murmured to himself. "Veinte años y el espíritu del diablo nunca se murió."

"English, Mr. Rodriguez. English."

Your friends at work said Arizona was hell. Not that they'd ever been there.

"Goddamn Mexicans are everywhere," one of them told you. "The sons of bitches."

The other guy nodded.

"Yeah. It's like *Invasion of the Body Snatchers* or some shit like that. You can't get away from them. Scares the crap out of you."

Veinte años y el espíritu del diablo nunca se murió.

Twenty years and the spirit of the devil never dies.

***

Once I was at your place and we were in your room with a few other cousins and your buddies. You and the older boys were playing Resident Evil.

"Hermano," your brother Pedro said. "Cool it."

"You're on fire."

"No shit, Sherlock."

On screen your character was slaying zombies like mad. One hand wielded a mighty blue sword that decapitated beasts by the dozens. The other brandished some sort of giant machine gun that fired ten rounds a second; each bullet passed through the chests of two zombies in a row, at least, usually it was three.

You finally sliced the last zombie in half, holstered your gun and thrust your sword into its sheath. Now it got interesting. You jogged to the side of the field of dead undead and retrieved a blue, pocket-sized machine from your belt. You pressed a button and tossed the device into the center of the vanquished zombies. It hit the ground, igniting into a frosty, yellow mist. Minutes passed. The zombie bodies began to shift. Arms pulled heads to severed necks at the speed water would turn to ice if you pissed into the freezing air of that snow planet, Hoth, in *Star Wars V: The Empire Strikes Back.*

"Shit no," a friend of yours whined. "No fair." His screen had been the first to fill with dripping red.

"Asshole." Pedro punched you in the shoulder.

You grinned.

Now the zombies stood before you, an unending field of conquered peoples: ZOMBIES UNDER YOUR COMMAND.

At this point my mother popped in to see what all the cussing and yelling was about, and when she saw me doing the doggape like the rest, she said to you, "Geraldo Muñez, you get here ahora. What the hell is this?" She reached over, got you in a death grip, and flung you out of the room. She pried me from the spot where I'd glued myself to the bed and held me like a mother grizzly bear protects her young.

"Geraldo, you playing these violent games with a ten-year-old around?" she demanded of you. She shook her head and began to mutter to herself. "Coño, niño. Hijo de gran puta!"

I tagged along, unsure of what was wrong.

"Tía…" You made your eyes big. "I didn't see him."

"You saw him. You did! Don't lie to me."

"But—" You sighed. "It's just a game. It's not real."

My mother pinched you in the arm. You flinched.

"Who are you to say what's real and what's not? Eh?"

You stood there holding your arm like un tonto as my mother walked toward her bag.

My mother pulled two lightsabers from her bag, put the first in your hand and wrapped your stiff fingers around its warm hilt. She handed the second to me. My face lit, and I squeezed the lightsaber. She didn't have to force me to hold this, oh, no, she didn't. I moved into position, beckoning with my free hand.

"Let's fight!"

You shook your head.

"Oh, hell no, Tía. Hell no. I ain't gonna do some kiddie crap—"

My mother gave you the look. The one every mother's got, the one that burns through your soul and squeezes jugo de naranja from your brains. The one you know you don't want to shit around with.

I turned from her to you to her to you.

"Let's fight!" I exclaimed, not knowing what to do. "Duel!" I extended my plastic lightsaber. It was the green one. My favorite.

You made your eyes bigger and faced my mother, but she wouldn't give.

"You play with your cousin like you ought to, Geraldo. You hear me?"

You shrunk and entered Spanish mode.

"Sí, Tía. Lo que tú quieres, Tía. Entiendo, Tía."

"The hell you do," my mother shot back. She stalked out.

Behind you I could see Pedro and the other boys peeking through your bedroom door, which you'd left ajar.

"Playtime, Jedda?"

You turned once—this would be the only time you would face them again that day—and yelled, "Shut the f--- up." You faced me. "Alright. So how does this work?"

You fumbled your plastic blade out. It was purple, like Mace Windu's. I always thought Mace Windu was hip since he was the only black Jedi, one step from Latino. He was also the first important good guy Darth Vader helped kill, but that's a matter you've got to take up with George Lucas, and George Lucas has got the whole Clone army, remember? You don't mess with him.

I waved my lightsaber about and you followed. Once I saw your eyes spin a little too far to the side, I swung my weapon into your crotch and giggled.

"Jeez, Miguel." You put a hand between your legs. "Don't play rough."

I jabbed my lightsaber at your bedroom door.

"You did." I smiled. Innocent, honest.

You rolled your eyes, dark suns arching over pale skies. Nevertheless, they were soon glowing moons that reflected the brilliant, white light around them. In the space of an instant you'd changed, forgotten your brother Pedro and the rest.

"Shut your mouth," you said, grinning. "You hit me in the nuts one more time, I'm telling Tía."

I flung the tip of my lightsaber toward yours.

"She won't believe you," I teased.

You shrugged it off, and we sparred.

"You're good," I concluded. "You're like a—" I paused, realizing the sheer gravity of what I was about to say. "You're like a Jedi."

***

It was Fourth of July weekend and the whole family was over for a barbecue at Coney Island. A good bunch of us hung around a rough wood table sitting in the hot, white sand, just out of the shade of the boardwalk. I was maybe fifteen. You were in your twenties, still working for Homeland Security. I don't think half of us ever thought much about it.

At this point I'd stuffed myself with enough junk food. I walked off to play with one of our younger cousins, kicking a soccer ball back and forth. The hot sun beat on us like hell from above, and the sand beat on our bare feet like hell from…from hell. It was Tatooine, home of Luke Skywalker, that searing desert planet George Lucas stole from Frank Herbert's *Dune*. The ocean attacked the shoreline in violent, green-brown cascades of foaming liquid and drifting seaweed.

As I plunged a foot into the freezing ocean, I suddenly heard Uncle Enrique's voice, screaming like the crashing waves, and on occasion Tío Héctor's quiet, accented English. The words themselves were impossible to make out at this distance; the air was thick and unforgiving to the hot turbulence of sound.

"Your f---ing culture!" Uncle Enrique was yelling. He sounded drunk."Your goddamn f---ing culture and your goddamn f---ing language! You come here and think you can f--- this country to hell."

I stopped and looked. Uncle Enrique was looming over Tío Héctor, engaged in some sort of argument. More of a brawl than an argument, really. I'd never seen Uncle Enrique like this. He was a quarter Cuban, a quarter English, another quarter white American. Related by marriage. Maybe he hadn't always seemed, you know, Latino, but he was my uncle always and you love your people like they're your people because, well, because they're your people. I guess they'd been talking politics and shit, and Uncle Enrique had probably drunk a little too much beer.

Tío Héctor, on the other hand, usually didn't say much at all. Today, though, he had to say something back. He had to, short as it was. Even that turned into a bad idea.

"Enrique, you're ignorant." Tío Héctor kept it strong on the top, hot and boiling beneath.

"No!" Uncle Enrique's mouth was wide as a dog's, breathing alcohol and hate and fear."No no no no no. You're the f---ing ignorant one, you bastard. You think you belong here. You don't. You belong in the Dominican f---ing Republic. You're infesting this country."

Tío Héctor's eyes weren't narrow or big—they were simply focused, hot, on his furious brother-in-law's face. He didn't say a word. He knew words would do no good. There's always a point in your life when your words don't do shit for you, and you got to act. Silence, that's action. Sometimes that's the best action there is, hombre.

Uncle Enrique stomped off drunkenly, dragging his wife with him. He did his best to make noise in the sand. However, sand isn't the kind of thing that booms; it ain't drums and sticks and goddamn percussion. Sand whispers, sand molds, sand burns, but sand does not ever harden.

As family gathered around Tío Héctor, Uncle Enrique reached his car and sped out. The black pavement shrieked at us. My mouth gaped like a dog's. So did yours.

You sat to the side, at that same spot on the rough wood table, no longer sipping your Coke. You'd run out. You had your badge on the table, and your eyes set on the warm grains of sand churning in the wind, which had gone hot as soon as the family clustered around Tío Héctor to offer him comfort.

The entire scene rotated about an indeterminate axis, as if we sat in a boiling cup of café con leche and someone had stuck in a sugar spoon and spun it around un poquito. There was the family moving hurriedly about, the incoherent banshee wail of Uncle Enrique's car, his cracked Budweiser spinning slowly but surely along the pavement. Even you, who sat so still, seemed to catapult through time. I could see your eyes unmoving one moment and flickering the next.

"Miguel, let's play," our little cousin was saying. He had the soccer ball in his hands.

I breathed for a minute and eventually nodded. He tossed the ball. We kicked to each other along a short distance, as if afraid we'd lose one another across the depth of space. Somehow he understood that something was wrong. Like the Force, a powerful interconnection between all things living and dead, burning and freezing.

The party broke off soon enough, and as I walked to my parents' car I saw your badge there on the table, melting in the silence and in the flaming sun. Screwed or not, you'd decided you could serve your country better by serving your people. Good choice, hombre.

I realized then that I was wrong about a lot of things. In a sense this story was more about me than you. I lived life devoid of any Dominicanos but you guys. I thought I was a hard-knocks intellectual, like so many Latinos and so many whites do when they tough it through the heart of a privileged suburban life in America. Meanwhile, you lived scavenging off the Latinos your friends rounded up like cattle.

In both cases, we got soul-f---ed.

So maybe this is about the two of us, and the paths we can take. And about choices. Us Latinos, we're strong, hombre. We're boiling, we're hot. We burn your tongue and scorch the roof off your mouth. And we don't ever give up. No, hombre, we don't ever. The truth is Latinos always got their Obi-Wan Kenobis and Han Solos. The truth is you can decide your future.

It's just freaking hard.

Andrea Siso, 17
DeBakey High School for Health Professions
Houston, TX
Teacher: Melissa Cox

Andrea Siso lives in Houston, Texas. She feels that in the process of writing her portfolio, she discovered her own voice. Her memories, heritage and family inspire her to write, and she hopes to be a published author someday. She will attend Washington and Lee University in Virginia, where she plans to study creative writing.

PART I: CHILDISHNESS/CHILDLIKENESS
Personal Essay/Memoir

Now you listen to me, buster.

Now you list-

en

    real good :
sing along to my happybells;
And forget abt ur
    Emptyshell;
Leave it alone. Leave—
And take those troubles withya.
we don't need to remind ourselves that
life is an empty
pictcha.

***

I baked a cake for him but he didn't like it, he said that he was allergic to chocolate even though I made him chocolate-covered strawberries three weeks ago for his birthday, but I don't know why he won't eat my cake and why he gave it back because he just said that "I am allergic" and he looked apologetic, but I'm not sure if he meant it. I have the cake now in a white box with a red ribbon, but it isn't tied as nice as before because before the lady from the shop offered to fix my box and I said "Thank you kindly" so she did. It looked all professional, and now it looks all mussed. I don't know how she did it, I already tried to tie the ribbon again. The bows I make never work. They never work. They never work. Because anything I touch doesn't turn to gold. It turns to insufferable silver. Silver but it's not real silver, it is nickel.

The cake smells good. It smells like warm chocolate. It smells like the three hours it took me to bake the goddamn thing. It smells like—

why didn't he want my cake? I baked it for him. Why doesn't he like my cake.

The reckoner is reckoning that my batter wasn't right. Two eggs, two sugar teaspoons or tablespoons? And then of course the chocolate. But I don't really know because I followed a recipe from a book. It's a yellow book.

I ate my cake. It was good.

Why doesn't he want my cake?

***

Frissons of yellow and frissons of gold orange and red but my eyes are closed, they are always closed when something important passes. But I feel dizzy and sick, and I am walking alone along the path in the middle of April, it is 12:12 make a wish. But isn't it 11:11 and 7:11 when we do it? Why the elevens? Eleven me, please.

Nonsense seems to be key in deciphering me. Nonsense seems to be working just fine. Why don't people want my cakes. I don't seem to please, although I am quite eager to, I must admit.

If I take my hands up and if I touch the leaves of the unblooming magnolia tree, will it know that I want it to bloom? Will it know that I want to see those white flowers soon—

White petals are pretty but my mom said she hates the smell of those magnolias, but she also hates the smell of lilies and roses. She just doesn't like flowers. I send her flowers, though, and so does my dad.

She just throws them away.

And I'm sorry for forgetting to water the orchid plant, I've just been so busy trying to live.

Who ever thought that three ice cubes for a potted plant would do just the trick?

***

Peach Blossoms
I picked peaches. They were ripe in my palm.
> They were
>> A child's sweaty hand
>> Sticky with jam.
> They were
>> The two lips on the face
>> Of a lover.
> They were
>> De

Li
Cious.

The juice of the fruit slithered past my lip, sluiced down my neck. Remember when you saw me? You handed me a wrinkled gray hand towel, and I said
> Thank you.
And I thought
> You are a sculptor, and I am a piece of clay.
And you said
> Catch you later.
And then you left.

You came back to the peach tree the next day. I sat underneath it, reading a romance novel concealed with a *Johnny Panic* book cover. First impressions and all. You came and sat beside me. And we did that for the next week. And I started to bring *Johnny Panic.* Not the book cover, but the Real Deal. And you never brought anything. Just your Leather Jacket and your Doc Martens.

Remember that next Monday, when you didn't come to the tree? I sat alone, the small hope budding inside of me wilting after hours of feigning reading. I allowed the rejection to seep into my skin, bathing in caustic waves of self-pity.

Tuesday, though, you did come. You sat. You acted as if you'd never left. And after a while, I started to believe it. And then, we started talking. And then we were a couple.

You told me one morning to Baby, dream your dream, and I said How? And you said

Close your eyes, baby
    Tick, tick, tick
Take your time, baby

And I took my hands out of my pockets and put them on your face. And you put your hands on top. And I did close my eyes then, but I could only see the peachy Opalescent Orange from the sunlight on my eyelids.

You asked me, then, what I saw. And I said I saw a Three-and-a-Half-Bedroom house made out of Ticky Tacky with Three Point Five children and a White Picket Fence and a Border Collie and a Minivan in the Concrete Driveway. And you laughed and kissed the inside of my palm.

And then I asked you

What's
    Yours.

And you said it was what I said. And I asked you what it was I said, then. And you said Don't Be Difficult. And I thought

I wish you would
    F l y|A wa y;
I wish you would
    Fl y|A w ay;
I wish I would
    Fly Away.

And I asked you if my dream would come true. And you said Baby, Dream Your Dream

You came over one afternoon after we met by the peach tree. You came in with your Doc Martens and your Leather Jacket and your Two Peachy Lips that I knew would taste as sweet as the juice you wiped from my mouth on the day we first met. And guess what? They did.

Before you left, we talked. And you said I was treating you as if I were the poster child of remorse. And I saw red and peach and orange and yellow and they were all blended into one and they were all over your head and they were all telling me that you Needed to Leave. And I told you so, but you lingered, and the colors and your voice and the door took me in a viselike grip and they smothered me and they smothered me and they smothered me. And I left you instead.

You followed me down the six flights of stairs because the elevator was Out of Order and the repairman hadn't come yet. You told me to Stop—to Slow Down, but I didn't because the red and peach and orange and yellow were all over you and they wouldn't shut up and they wouldn't leave and you wouldn't leave either. I smelled the colors, and I got sick.

The sun shone through eddies of gnats, and I saw a mockingbird perched on the peach tree. She was singing a song—not hers. Yours.

But the mockingbird was okay with it. She had you in her. And it was okay.

But a creeping dissatisfaction
Riddled the Plain Jane
She bumped and croaked,
With a spirit left to the wind.
A spirit gone from her,
A spirit matching yours.
Left alone—
She would have no song to sing. No song to sing. No Song to Sing.
She would be silenced, a Craven Queen. With no song to sing;
And a kingdom collapsing and a façade crumbling and a book cover concealing her
Romance Novel.
And she would stay with you
Because you gave her a song.
You killed her
Soul—
But it was already half-dead when you met her.

And it was alright with her, so it was alright with you.
And she knew you were Phony,

But she knew she was Phony

And you were Matching Socks.

And she didn't like you, but she needed you.
And you liked to be needed.

Remember that day in July? You said it was hot enough to fry an egg on the sidewalk. We sat at the diner, and Luella served us The Usual. Our glasses of lemonades were rosy, not yellow, and I asked you how they did that and you said you didn't know. When Luella asked us if we wanted any dessert, you said No Thanks, and I said Peach Cobbler. The ripe peach cut through the heat, and you stole a bite with the fork you used to eat your steak.

And then, remember when you tried to take another piece, and it fell on your favorite pair of jeans? You didn't do anything. You left it there, pretended it was gone. And then I started to believe it was gone. And so did you, really. And when we finished eating, you stood to stretch. The piece of peach cobbler toppled to your scuffed black Doc Martens, leaving a creamy stain the shape of Mississippi on your thigh. You kicked the pie off your shoe, and left a twenty on the table. I followed you out the door.

Remember when we went back to the peach tree for Old Times' Sake? I brought a picnic basket. I laid out a red checkered blanket for us to sit on. Whirls of pollen illumined by the summer's late light penetrated the air surrounding us, which smelled of ripe peaches and wet earth since it had rained earlier in the day. You asked me if I had brought food in my basket, and I said "No, it's for the peaches we are going to pick." You started to take some that were resting on the ground, but I told you that those were No Good. I told you to put me up on your shoulders.

I picked the ripest ones from the tree.
And I said, "This is for my fruit bowl."

And you said, "Baby, I'll take care of it."
And I thought then that you were A Good Man?

One day, you soaked yourself in Ego and Pride and absorbed it like a sponge. You thought you were so clever, dropping sentences and names like Hot Potatoes. You said to me one day "If 'we' starts with double-you, what does 'you' start with?" And I stared at the red blotches on your chin that weren't there yesterday. And then you said with a complacent smirk, "Why." And you chuckled, and I could smell the smug on you. You wore it like cheap cologne.

***

I tried to leave a message for you on your answering machine once. Your voice came through the line, radiating self satisfaction, bleating, "I care. I am your acquaintance. One day I may-be your friend. I may already. One day I may love you. I may already. The degrees of care." I felt like saying "You are as deep as a Rain Puddle"—but I didn't, I just hung up.

***

You started waxing poetic idealism once you moved in with me. You started pretending to read Hemingway, and made a strained effort to compel people into believing your illusion. You started wearing your hair slicked back like Marlon Brando in *Streetcar*. You started listening to Count Basie and Miles Davis and John Coltrane. You started smoking cigars every afternoon when I got home from work, ensuring an audience to your act. And our place started to smell of the moldy peaches in the fruit bowl you never Took Care Of like you said you would.

We were sitting under the peach tree
One Murky Morning.
I said—Once, I was broken;
You said—I could fix it;
I said—How?

And the Cat Got Your Tongue.

Remember that day I left before you woke up? I went back to the peach tree and picked peaches. They were
Round. Yellow. Red.
I bit into them. They were
Brown. Dry. Bitter.
And then, I started to read *Johnny Panic.* You came to me, carrying a copy of *Howl.* And then, I knew you were a fool.

You asked me once about my past, and I said
the Itsy Bitsy Spider
crept Up the water spout
Down came the rain and
washed the spider out
out came the sun and
dried up All the Rain
and the Itsy Bitsy Spider
went Up the spout again.
And you said you didn't get it.
I thought you were a man, but you were just a little boy.
Then, remember a month after that when you were watching the Saints play the Packers? You had relinquished your
beatnik phase after grasping your own absurdity. You were lying sideways on the sofa that could swallow you if you let it.
Your feet stretched over the side of the couch, your shoes were kicked off on the floor. I called your name
Again,
        Again,
                Again.
Commercial break.
Then you finally looked up. And I threw the blue stick at you. The one that said I was pregnant. And I got my keys and left.
I went to the peach tree with its bare branches stabbing through the night sky. I sat. I waited:
Your feet broke the backs of resting leaves on the ground.
Your keys rattled on their holder, looped through your belt.

A chill wind carried your smell down to me.
Fear—
Musk
Vulnerable—
Sandalwood
And you said—Hello. How are you?
And you sat next to me.
And you took my hand in yours.
And your eyes were dead and red.
And you got pie on your shoe.
And I said—Peachy Keen.

***

I can be sweet if I want to be and
I can have oodles of charm if I want to ensnare
you and
guess what baby? I can be sweet.
(I can be sweeter than Ben & Jerry's and Italian Ice. And
I can be sweeter than passing a light on Yellow and turning Red in
the middle)
,
and I can be cute and I can have you and I can write notes to you and
put them in your lunch(pail) .
I know you would like that very much.

***

cHangeme and arrrase
the scarS in my pokt are
2mch2bear
In a Game wit youbut
alo. n. ow. e
all can't do this.

***

Sitting still is like
: harboring a criminal in an open cellar, open to the daylight and
God and everyone and open to
Hums of morning bugs. But
: prayforme, prayforme, prayforme:
Dear God, thank you for this food and wine,
and thankyou for making lifesofine.
Je vois La vie en rose thrutheglassof an empty
cup. and "who's gonna mop up this damned
mess?"
He asked me, très abrupt.

***

Don't worry abt
it,
baybee:
Absinthe makes the heart
(grow fonder).

***

Taken from Facebook's Settings page.
"(M)ost of Facebook's
F(eat ur)es
dep(end) (on) the idea that:
There are people in your life that you like to stay in touch and
connect
with.
Whether these
people are best friends, family, coworkers, or
acquaintances,
once you connect to them, they are considered
(Facebook) friends(.)
We've created a few ways for (you) to (easily) find your friends.
Without friends, Facebook (can feel kind of empty.)"

***

(It's Not You, It's Me.)
Dreams are boats
      that never float.

***

(Renovation.)
I touched the wet plaster on the wall.
I touched the wet plaster
      On
The
      Wall.
I touched the wet plaster
onthewall   ;
and I thought of simpler times.

***

Who in the hell do you think you
are—some kind of star?
Do you twinkletwinkle in the bar while
dreamers wonder of your plight:
up above this world so high,
mighty, and bright? and
Don't be cruel to be
kind, it doesn't suit you. but
What are you doing here I haven't seen you in
ages! and
How are the kids and the wife
and the life and the weather outside, is it
frightful? so
Good it pleases us and it pleases you. but
You are strong and silent, and the
voice of reason is
unintelligible.
She said, As she downed another shot.

***

(Do you want to eat dinner now?)
Hot Italian & Reuben on
Rye.
No pickles, please.
I don't understand you.
Can you spot me
        an Aquafina?
And we both drink:
        To us, to us
For our end is nearer
        Than we think.

***

(Let's play truth or dare.)
Girls may be lovely as cranes
        and safe,
but lonely silent hills beg to
        differ:
In the nights when she
        picks truth
            and lies—
Earth's constant thrumming grows
        quicker.

***

As I spoke to
you, and sd—
Danny, I am
tired of
us.

We shrug off
our dead skins,

we silently
pray for
life. What

else can we do
but dream?
Bereavement
envelops, and

Help, you shout,
The world is not
our
oyster.

***

Clandestine hum of the night:
     Tenderly graze our cheeks without
magnificent
Reflections.
Thick as thieves in the late August
     Light, we
Run through Hallowed Hepburn
Puddles,
Splashing about
in
     Distilled countryside
Temptation.

***

your Curly Pleasure seeps into my skin; and
hums in my veins—
     you sigh into my hair. you
     cut the heat
like keylimepie on a sticky July day.
I wear your Curly Pleasure like a dress.

***

And through the cleverly linked words,
utterly evoking a vast lack—
I stumble in my journey for atraso;
but tears and agony at frozen emptiness
make life into an exquisite
nightmare.
I understand my unfulfilled desires; and
am compelled to continue:

I ceaselessly strive to become
Atrasada.

GOLD, SILVER AND AMERICAN VOICES MEDALS

Students in grades 7–12 submit works in 11 writing categories. This year more than 20,000 regional-award-winning writing submissions were reviewed by the authors, educators and literary professionals who served as national jurors. Gold, Silver and American Voices medals were awarded to works that demonstrated originality, technical skill and emergence of a personal voice.

Anne Malin Ringwalt, 15
The Prairie School
Racine, WI
Teacher: Rebecca Wheeler

Anne Malin Ringwalt lives in Racine, Wisconsin, but spent her early years in North Carolina and feels deeply connected to the South. She will attend Interlochen Arts Academy and hopes to someday teach English with the Peace Corps. She would like to thank her family, her church and everyone at Interlochen for their support.

My Southern Accent Used to Be
Poetry

My southern accent used to be:

wild honey boiling on a stove
an old woman standing in a barrel of raspberries
stomping jam to juice
babies rolling around in the mud
their parents speaking in the distance with names
like Rilke and Eliot on their lips
a crown of lilacs.

The birds of my voice migrated to a colder place in winter
froze in the form of candle wax
in summer the wax seeped through with flame, ice melted
my voice longed for honey
my tongue ached like dry clay in a sculptor's hands
digging holes in the Midwest
searching for an entrance-way to a bear's cave
flooding with honey.

Annakai Geshlider, 15
The Urban School of San Francisco
San Francisco, CA
Teacher: Cathleeen Sheehan

Annakai Geshlider lives in San Francisco, California. She writes to salvage and honor moments that she wants to remember, and to find combinations of words that make sculptures when written. In the future, she will roam the world on her Mongolian horse, which she will milk for nourishment.

DRINKING WORDS OUT OF THE CORNER OF MY MOUTH
Poetry

Page for English 2B
Inspired by Langston Hughes' "Theme for English B"

Who is me? I am A (fifteen year old girl), Annakai,
dark brown ratty curls on my head and bracelets on my wrist, a
    backpack that pulls me down when I ride the 24,
hard bones and skin on a scraped hand to hold my pen or tap on
    a keyboard,
ragged eyes after no sleep,
stretching my mouth wide to laugh roar sing sharp
with guitar.
I'm made of me—he, she, the dry lemon tree
behind my house whose trunk is rotting but whose branches hold
    bumpy lemons all year,
Dolores Street, Beale Street, Haight Street, moist grassy parks where
    I slide
onto my stomach and swallow hot naan with sweet cream curry
that lights my throat on fire,
I know who I am in the sun.
Sometimes I look at my eyes and can't believe them,
that I am standing in front of myself, breathe think communicate
    and exist,

that I wave my arms around in the air and rush around like it's
    something trivial
to be here, alive.
I hold a handful from the blackberry bush covered in spider webs
and put my eye almost touching a horse's,
stare at the jogger's flimsy arms,
bend over to pick up coins from the ground,
grind my breath till it's sore
and forget that I am flabbergasted.
I write what I see,
so this is my page for English 2B.

Riding Home From Philo
There are turkey vulture sages resting
on mossy branches in the shade,
heads pink with folds of wrinkly skin atop
charcoal feathers
we whiz by their roost.
Neil Young's guitar and drums clash
when we roll out onto the gold
nasal deep rock while my eyes on dry hills,
glad I'm not touching the searing gray where
black rubber heats like the wet straw on my salty forehead
when we were crunching under the trees
with a dog the same bleached caramel as the leaves
sniffed and sank into them.
Now the sun still glints
on a portable billboard whose driver's beard
is limp on the windowsill braking past the green sign,
Petaluma, next to corn and pumpkins
young and glaucous,
and smells like barbecue smoke too dry for crackling autumn.

Bus Flourishing
It is her daughter who's away,
on a business trip in Wisconsin,
so she must hold the bottle up to her grandson's mouth and perch it

between her fingers until he's suckled the whole thing
down, just as she did when she was twenty and green
for her own daughter
who gorged so excitedly on the milk that dribbled out of the hardy
    rubber nozzle and down her red-pink fatty cheeks,
while they sat rocking together on a bus equivalent
the milk soaked
onto the brown terrycloth bib that is wrapped around his neck now
one of the only things that their two generations share,
the first raised in San Francisco after she arrived when she was
    eighteen
the second is him, the flat baby in her arms, who can gurgle the
    Cantonese she taught him, even though his mother says
English Only
He is confused by all the sounds around him so he arches his perfect
    tiny back,
sliding off her legs towards the rubber ribbed aisle on the 24 Divisadero
where she won't let him fall because she doesn't want him to hit his
    soft and developing head
she doesn't scrunch her cheeks in an angry squint or yowl back at him
because she knows that it won't work,
She holds him
Curls him atop her knee,
Thinking, eerily
about the third day in November far away in the milky future
when she will bond to his baby just the same.

Sunday Morning
Eyes groggy with sleep,
last night's party still on our lashes
gentle, bright sun on
window glass
Seeping through onto our skin
as we attend to the business of doing nothing
I lift a spoonful of applesauce to my lips,
wetting my throat after sleeping so long
My mom fries an egg in a cast-iron pan,

my dad unfolds section after section of the newspaper.
Soon, the morning will move on
we will disperse
to our places in the house
or world,
lazy morning
lingering
inside us.

Sarah Allen, 15
Ladue Horton Watkins High School
St. Louis, MO
Teacher: Patrick Jaranowski

Sarah Allen is a resident of Ladue, Missouri. She draws sporadic inspiration from relationships between people and from her own experiences. A political science enthusiast, she plans to continue to write regardless of her career path. She thanks her brother for his vibrant personality.

A Teenager's Denial of Mortality
Poetry

My little brother wants to die
in a burst of fireworks,
scarring retinas
as he explodes across the sky—
except he didn't say it
quite that poetically.
I try to be amused
when he says,
"I want to die with a bang,"
because it's such a cliche
for a ten-year-old boy
and because I can tell
that he's lying,
even if he doesn't know it yet.

But as we sit there
in a basement illuminated
by fake Hollywood explosions
and shirtless movie stars
beating the shit out of each other,
fear stirs
from where it sleeps
coiled in my stomach,

raising its head and blinking.
My brother is energetic, whiny;
wants to marry his classmate
Rhiannon when he grows up,
and play professional baseball.
The air around him crackles
with dreams, with life.
My brother is so alive
that when he dies,
I want to believe
that the world will die with him.

I decided today
that my little brother is immortal.
Don't try to tell me otherwise.

Anna Kelly, 15
Rowland Hall St. Mark's School
Salt Lake City, UT
Teacher: Joel Long

Anna Kelly is from Salt Lake City, Utah, where she writes as a hobby but admits that it may become a bigger part of her life someday. She is inspired by her teacher Joel Long, who encouraged her to start writing and is a constant source of support.

THE BOOK OF RECURRENT DREAMS
Poetry

After J. Foer

The Dream of Sex Without Pain

You lined the water bottles up on the side of the fridge
It's always the small things in life that I remember
You stirred molasses into the coffeepot when I wasn't looking.

You always left your pillow turned upwards, nineteen degrees
Clockwise from the moon, the indent slightly southward.
It'd stay crinkled from the morning, when you brought the coffee in.

I'd tell you that molasses runs down
The string just fine, thanks. And you?

The Dream of Angels Dreaming of Men

To think that angels would have the need to dream is worthless.
They'd dream of sugarcoated clouds on Jupiter. Call this Heaven.
Call me God.

To think that spinning round in circles twice every morning, and twice
Every afternoon, would keep the world spinning around you, is painful.

To think that dreams are drowned
In dust the color of cauliflower
Is backwards.

Dust is black.
And already angels.

The Dream of Disembodied Birds

The Dream of Flight was the same dream.

The Dream of Perpetual Motion

It was the reason that there were so many bruises
On your arms, that last Wednesday, you looked so brown,
They sent you to work in the fields.

The Dream that We Are Our Fathers

Followed by the dream that we are ourselves.
And hungry
for the dream of disembodied birds.

Marlee Cox, 15
Mehlville High School
St. Louis, MO
Teacher: Mark Gulath

Marlee Cox is from St. Louis, Missouri. She believes that for every moment, there are a thousand non-moments, and for everything that happens, there are countless things that didn't. As a writer, she hopes to explore the possibilities of the things that didn't happen.

SAMSARA
Poetry

She's been chewing the same piece of gum for hours,
Drinking stale-tasting water from a chipped coffee mug,
Wearing his shirt—
Feeling, thought, will, consciousness...
W-w-wearing his shirt,
Over her sweatpants,
No shoes.

He has carved her,
Into,
I-into his own,
Whittled away layers of self and skin,
Uncovering the bone,
Pulling off her—
There are no eyes, no ears, no nose, no tongue—
Pulling off her l-lips,
Her dress,
He is blowing the cigarette smoke in her face,
Watching her cough,
G-g-growing inside her,
Injecting, intoxicating,
Injectingintoxicating her,
There is no attainment of wisdom, and no wisdom to attain

Emptiness,
It d-d-doesn't mean what you think it does,
Empty is interrelated,
A state in which nothing exists purely in itself,
If you were to pick her,
Pluck her from her branch,
S-stop his destruction,
She still wouldn't be safe,
She's from him,
He's in her,
A collar around her heart,
Body is empty empty is body exactly is body and empty,
She's from the mirror she stands before every m-m-morning,
Begging things to be different,
Hoping for a ticket west or just to finally understand the sutra,
Screaming *gaté, gaté,*
Gone, Gone,
Be gone when I get up.

There is no ignorance,
And no end to ignorance.
There is no old age and death,
And no end to old age and death.

When she walks the streets surrounding the apartment,
The young artist sees her,
From behind the wall of g-g-glass,
The window,
The coffee shop window,
He cups the shape of her,
Of her stringy hair,
Of her dingy scarf, fringe fluttering in a wind she doesn't feel,
He cups these things in his hand,
Captures them with his pencil,
Smudges them with the darkened p-pad of his thumb,
Pulls them in tighter.
He doesn't know.

He doesn't know about the other He.

It is the clearest mantra,
The highest mantra,
The mantra that removes all suffering.

And now she's taking a walk out the window,
But she left the mug of water,
S-s-sitting on the table,
Ripples rioting against the curved walls of their enclosure,
Lip of liquid shaking,
S-stuttering,
Eventually settling.
God.
That cup,
That girl.
Both full,
But, God,
B-but,
So empty.

All things are empty:
Nothing is born, nothing dies,

Nothing is pure, nothing is stained,

Nothing increases and nothing decreases.

Elizabeth Yu, 13
Homeschooled
Cary, NC
Teacher: Clarissa Ngo

Elizabeth Yu lives in Cary, North Carolina, where she is currently at work on a series involving her brother being kidnapped by aliens. She admits that the strangest thing about her is that she actually likes vegetables, and hopes to one day make enough money from her writing to buy a dog.

IN KANDAHAR SHE WALKS
Poetry

In Kandahar she walks
Along the ancient Silk Road
Where ancient nomads once peddled frankincense and myrrh
Sandalwood and lacquered bowls for kings
Her eyes are sightless but determined
As her feet stir the parched dust
She is going to school

One day last November
As she had walked beside the mountain Hindu Kush
Craggy and green with coriander
In her best pressed white school shirt and coal black trousers
A sound like a machine gun had devastated
The song of the golden plover that was feathering her nest
In the stream by the road

"It's only a motor scooter," her sister Chaman had chided
Tugging on her headscarf to make sure her lovely hair
Like liquid ink
Did not see the light of the sun
For under the Taliban
No female was allowed to show her flesh or hair in public
To show oneself to a non-mahram male was death

Even to breathe for a woman was a privilege
Under Taliban rule

Paint your nails? Your fingers will be chopped off.
Wear lipstick? You will be cut into pieces and stuffed in a bag.
High heels? Expect to be footless.

No man should hear the footsteps of a woman
Lest he know she exists

And so that day, as the two sisters
Had sauntered down the old Silk Road
Once a road of adventure, now a road of freedom
For knowledge frees the soul
The sound of a machine gun shattered the silence
And the hearts of a thousand girls

Two shadows on motor scooters
Men of the Taliban
Poisoned the eyes of two Afghan girls
With a child's toy—acid-filled water guns
The cheap kind you can get at the corner store
For a few *rupees*

The acid seared her eyes and skin
Eating her flesh
It was like plunging into the heart of a volcano
And being consumed

The Silk Road is empty now
And the swings on the playground are rocked only by the wind
As one girl walks to school
Alone

Catherine Zhu, 13
William Annin Middle School
Basking Ridge, NJ
Teacher: Jill Burt

Catherine Zhu hails from southern New Jersey, where she was inspired to write her poem while gazing into the moonlit night from a city-bound train. She hopes to someday travel the world to find out more about where we have been and where we are going.

TRAINS TO THE AFTERLIFE
Poetry

When we are gazing down at the slowly
    Shifting, blue—
Rimmed, earth
                beneath us
He sings to me;
God is a stargazer
Carving maps
Of where the universe   ends
        Orb in creased palm, he glides
 A solitary ecliptic

Meandering his way down
Through the
       Atmosphere
where memories are scattered like sparrows in the rain—
We are only stardust … he whispers
When we are too tired for sleeping

We are every
       place our souls have never been
Perhaps tomorrow
Folding into our fragile bodies like a thousand canyons
       We'll lie dreaming on trains taking us into the white expanse

Meteors will burn out beside the city skyline
And in the light of a feebly rising sun,
we'll peer into
The hollowed-out   candle-lit place that is your

                             heart

tonight, amidst foreign lands and familiar words
        we'll fall into the arms of strangers as He falls farther away

Zakiyyah Madyun, 14
Pittsburgh CAPA 6-12 (School for the Creative and Performing Arts)
Pittsburgh, PA
Teacher: Mara Cregan

Zakiyyah Madyun is from Pittsburgh, Pennsylvania. She is inspired by the wide spectrum of music that she listens to, and her creativity extends to both poetry and prose.

No Such Thing as Silence
Poetry

My name speaks for me,
when I never asked to be spoken for.
It says it was made up.
It says I'm not from around here, am I?
It says my words will be laced with a thick accent.
It says I speak in foreign tongues,
and foreign tongues are confusing, aren't they?

It lies sometimes,
but what can I say to the assumptions it makes,
when I haven't said a thing?
Then my skin chimes in.
It says that I listen to rap music.
It says my words often come out slurred
and distorted.
It says I don't know much of nothing, do I?

Sometimes it lies.
The book that I'm holding asks for a few words.
It says I'll look down when I speak.
It says my voice will come out high and chiming.
It says I'm a mystery.
It says I want things to stay that way.

Music tells me I'm trying to be something that I'm not.
It tells me to sit down,
and listen to something more appropriate for
people like me, you know.
It asks me why I don't like what they like.
It says I could, couldn't I?
It says I'd like it if I tried.
I don't answer.

My arms and legs revolt against me,
saying that I ought to have some rhythm.
They scold me,
as though talents can be condensed,
and referred to as simply genetic.
I try to make them understand,
but my limbs say otherwise,
taking honesty for modesty.

But the worst liar of all is voice,
warping my words,
making serious sentiments sound lighter.
Morphed by age into something that isn't,
quite,
right.

Rumors are spread,
and the truth lies damaged
in a desolate corner,
because it can't decide whether or not it has anything to prove.
It's used to abandonment.

They see my face,
my skin,
hear my name,
listen to the tone of my voice,
but no one ever sees,
ever hears, or smells or tastes

the truth
that's right in front of their faces,

and it's a shame,
honesty.
So clear, so clean,
you see right through it,
without a backwards glance.

Alex Cuzzo, 17
South Elgin High School
South Elgin, IL
Teacher: Brittany Hennessey

Alex Cuzzo is from Bartlett, Illinois. She enjoys writing about love and what it does to people, but finds that she often has to chase inspiration. In light of this, she is constantly dismantling and reshaping her beliefs. She will study English, philosophy and religious studies at the University of Illinois at Chicago.

MILKY WAY
Poetry

Whenever I think of how it'd be to be together, I see this image:

1. we're always touching
     (palm-to-shoulder, lips-to-wrist, eyelashes-to-thigh, forehead-
   to-belly)
     our hands pour like molasses
     over one another like we're
     trying to cover lunar surfaces.   it isn't sticky.
                                                            it's warm though.

2. we're either in the kitchen or in the bedroom.
     i'm bending over the sink with your voice in my ear—
                                   you're right behind me,
                                   we're dressed crescent moons
                                   bending into each other.
     i'm trying to wash the dishes.
     (i'm trying to wash your mouth out.)
     i'm always turning red so i don't need blush anymore.
             our bedsheets are thick like milk.
             we're clumsy swans,
                     graceful and biting;
     crumbs fall around us and we eat those up, too.

3. we're goofy & always listening,
    waiting for our turns to speak,
    keeping quiet with creased smiles
        shaking heads
        leaning over so our noses fit between neck-and-shoulder
        stifling laughter
            so it can mold around our teeth:
                we're making dentures of one another.

4. it's either up-and-at-'em or lazy daisy,
early morning or too-late night
    (because i think we'd take a lot of catnaps together) (we'd also
  spend most afternoons in the bath together)
             (your call not mine)
    and in these wakeful hours,
    you'd teach me how to be comfortable in my lopsidedness
        how to be dirty and still keep my tongue clean
        how to appreciate a passion i don't understand yet
        how to slow dance without touching
    you'd teach me:
        how to be rhythm
        how to sing loudly
         how to know an honesty so warm it melts in
  my mouth

5. we don't behave or make do.
we grow we grow we grow and then—
        we cut each other down to examine the rings in our
  tree trunks.
      we discover each other over and over again,
    magnify the beauty marks, dust them off,
     place them neatly in glass jars
    and stare at the Shelves of Us:
a whole new kind of milky way.

Will Fesperman, 17
Towson High Law & Public Policy
Towson, MD
Teacher: Bill Jones

Will Fesperman is from Towson, Maryland, where his hobbies include running and reading contemporary poetry. He will attend Wesleyan University.

WIRED
Poetry

We may be, as you said softly,
(one hand on a cup of hot
chocolate in a midnight
November diner)
nothing more than wet,
messy computers—
wet, messy, ugly and
slow.

I mused into the brown
curling mud-flats
at the bottom of my cup.

But maybe,
I wanted to say,
somewhere in the zeroes
and ones of your brain,
in the flawed gray tissue
where all words
shoot to electric life,
you will find the synaptic
language of love,
the chemical pathways
of desire,
the scientific root

(see how
you spark my
ganglia
with your
words)
of all joy.

Lauren Rhoades, 18
Hudson High School
Hudson, OH
Teacher: Virginia Snyder

Lauren Rhoades is from Hudson, Ohio. She finds inspiration in anything and everything, particularly in poetry and rugby. She will be a nursing major at Kent State, where she plans to play on the rugby team and continue writing.

COLLAPSING GALAXIES
Poetry

Keechie was beautiful on Mondays
Especially after swim practice, when
She smelled like pool water and salt.
She was the second-fastest swimmer on
Varsity, but only because of her webbed toes.
I heard she walked across the desert, once
To burn off the webs in the hot sand
But the flesh merely wore through
And was new and soft by the next day.
She liked to wear her hair straight down,
Brown and boring, until I offered to braid
It, and she stared at me, with discolored eyes
And asked why.
That was back in days of summer, though
When she'd stand in her yard all night long
Just to see the big dipper, or collapsing galaxies,
That she swore was happening above our heads
Even though we couldn't quite see it right.
I tried out for the lacrosse team to impress her, but
Got bruises from the Goalie instead,
While Keechie stood on the high dive, glistening,
Concentrated, like a glass of pale wine
Teetering on the edge of my dining room table.
The last time I saw her, was before the prom

She told me she was going in a moon-colored gown
Sprinkled with pool water, or the big dipper,
Or collapsing galaxies, that she swore was happening
Above our heads, even though
We couldn't see it right.

M'Bilia Meekers, 17
Lusher Charter School
New Orleans, LA
Teacher: Brad Richard

M'Bilia Meekers lives in New Orleans, Louisiana, where she will study English at Tulane University. She feels a deep sense of connectedness to her city and to the generations of people who came before her. She would like to thank her mentor, Brenda Marie Osbey.

LOUIS CONGO IN LOVE
Poetry

I.
For you, ma fleur, I toil
on the route of these slaves' escape:
15 pounds a head, planted on pikes
along the levee's edge. I wish the slaves
had chosen another route to follow,
one through the swampland,
one you'd never find;
I hope you don't bring home,
limp in your arms, the lengths of rope
I tied them to the table with
and used to wipe the blood
from the blade after it sliced
through each neck.

II.
Through the window, I watch
you sidestep the rotting magnolias
that mark the path to our home.
I remember then how once you turned
my hands over and over
as though you'd lost something there.
But you never mentioned

the red crust I couldn't clean
from beneath my nails some nights.
You'd just turn my hands over again
and watch them drop to my sides.

Lindsay Oncken, 17
Cypress Woods High School
Cypress, TX
Teacher: Candace Tannous

Lindsay Oncken is from Houston, Texas, and will attend the University of Texas. As an observational writer, she loves to watch people and write about them. Her ultimate goal is to win more Pulitzers than Robert Frost.

GUMBALLS
Poetry

You bought your first gumball machine when you were six. The colors clashed with your plastic heels, making hollow clicks on linoleum—the sound of adulthood, or whatever it is that turns sallow lips red in the mornings that are really afternoons, pale six-foot-two imprints trying to stretch out the other side of the bed. The pantyhose didn't hug your legs like they should have but the skirts always twirled, rising like waves to crash over shoulders that have already broadened to make room for phrases like *She's growing up so fast,* and you stomp through the lousy streets of whatever city you ran to first. That city, the one in the dirty wooden rafters of the attic where you lost your first kiss and tucked it between footprints in the mud, because the past is your favorite to write about. The one where you huddle in the corner chewing the health from your hair and remembering how you used to walk, barefoot and blindfolded on hot asphalt to try and discover the boundaries of being a child. You stumbled over the threshold and landed in a crappy apartment three miles from your eighteenth birthday, inhaling questions like *What's your name, sweetheart?* and holding them in your lungs for an extra second or two. Smoke curls from your lips and leaves stains on the skirt that stopped fitting twenty-three pounds ago, clutching your thighs like you clutched your mother's before someone forgot her in the ICU. That was when doctors told you that you're too tall for candy, but memories taste just fine. You gather them behind your lips and blow, slowly watching everything expand and pop and then you're six again, chewing gum in the backyard and waiting for your mom to take you to school.

Emily Mack, 13
Young Magnet High School
Chicago, IL
Teacher: Alison Stojak

Emily Mack is from Chicago, Illinois. She is inspired by emotional, raw literature. She tries to write about universal experiences in new, unique ways and plans to someday be a reporter.

HUNGER
Poetry

All I taste is hunger
and it's delicious,
is sometimes what I have to say
to get me through the day.

And I can feel you watching me
though I can't see a thing,
and I can feel you wondering
just what the hell I'll bring.

Sometimes I wanna scream out,
but I know my voice is too meek.
Sometimes I wish you'd reach out.
But I know your grip's too weak.
I sure don't wanna slip through
but the road is getting slicker.
I sure don't wanna slip through,
but the cracks are getting thicker.

Sometimes I wish you'd reach out,
and though your grip may be too soft,
then I guess I'll just grab harder—
it's better than getting lost.

Arbil López, 17
Pittsburgh CAPA 6-12 (School for the Creative and Performing Arts)
Pittsburgh, PA
Teacher: Mara Cregan

Arbil López is from Pittsburgh, Pennsylvania. She is inspired by her family, cooking and anything unexpected. She attends the Culinary Institute of America for baking and pastry.

CIUDAD
Poetry

In the morning Pittsburgh moves mechanically,
rises its sun over the rivers and bridges
like our public bus fighting its way over the top of a hill.
The city pulls on levers and lowers the big-top blue sky.
The asphalt rolls by five days a week.

It's not Madrid,
I'll admit,
but when the sun unfurls itself
I feel like it could be.
The light fills the womb
and I bloom like winter's gone for good.

I think I've seen every city,
you think this town rolls into the rest
like you roll your r's.
Downtown they roll hoagies,
on Forbes they roll joints.
Home for us is a nest on the roof of a building block,
chubby hands forming us out of clay.
In my mind, the fountains never dry up.

If I could I would take you home.
If there were something under the dust

I would shake this city out
like a sheet left unchanged
for too many months.
Even in my discomfort
I feel safe in these streets,
even in your discomfort
I reluctantly call this my home.
Pigeons nod good morning every day,
abortion protesters bob their bald heads
even when I don't take a pamphlet.
Nights used to scare me but
mornings scared me more.
One morning I got off at the wrong stop
? and a big man in a parka
called me "honey" and helped me get to school.
I teetered along in heels that day
until I eventually broke them off and threw them
at the pavement.
That day a trash can called me pretty.
A hobo shared his lunch.
I sat down on a park bench and I never got up.

Morgan Garces, 17
Dr. Michael M. Krop Senior High School
Miami, FL
Teacher: Jason Meyers

Morgan Garces is from Miami, Florida, and will study English at the University of Central Florida in Orlando. Her writing is inspired by the emotional insights that she gleans from experiences and relationships. She would like to thank her creative writing teacher, Jason Meyers.

AAA
Poetry

I. I liked it best when
the heater in my
1993 Corolla didn't
have to be on because
our breath left smog
on my windows,
where we drew
smiley faces that
stretched in ways our
faces could never manage.

My radio was dusty,
empty of
our fingerprints.
we didn't need
other people's music
to add a pulse to
an evening where
our fingers tapping upon
one another's hips
was enough to echo
down our spines.
With my bare foot I

could feel the heat of the
engine stroke the pads
of my toes, powered by
the natural resource of
our lost breath,
heavy in the air
like humidity.

II. But now,
my radio won't stop
blaring music
as if it knows
that it is the
only distraction from
me counting your
breaths as they
rhythmically try to
escape from the
cracks in the windows.

And my heater has
been chugging out air
that leaves goose bumps
along my arms like the
speed bumps
ahead of us,
overcompensating for
the icy wisps
that we blow out.

My key is buried deep
in my ignition,
whispering plans to take us
to the tip of our map,
but my wheels
are rusting and
I'm stalled.

Sophia Dillon, 15
Wilbur Cross High School
New Haven, CT
Teacher: Victoria Vivas

Sophia Dillon lives in New Haven, Connecticut, where she is interested in pursuing filmmaking as well as writing. She finds immense beauty and inspiration in words themselves.

MASON JARS
Poetry

Peggy collects beautiful things in mason jars
like crow claws and relief and
a ringlet of her neighbor's hair.
She hoards them under her bunkbed,
stuffed back behind the folds of her duvet.

A man with sweat on his temples once
came in and spoke the word "belligerent"
to her classroom.
Peggy tore off the corner of her worksheet
and copied it down. It went in a jar.

Peggy once took a long route home between
the reds and shingles of Lincoln and found
a stick that had been eaten
away by insects.
She traced her thumb around its grooves
and took it home, beneath her bed.

Peggy's first crush is on a boy with round ears
and rounder cheeks.
His name is Jason and he comes to her house
on Tuesday.
They play hide-and-go-seek and Peggy counts

high and higher until Jason screams and Peggy comes
and sees him picking away at her jars.

"They are what is beautiful."

Jason asks her why there is a rock in her jar
and she tells him it fits, tells
him to feel the grain line of the basalt,
hear the German on the bottle cap,
look at how her lost tooth still has
some pearl to it.

Jason tells her that she is weird.
Jason tells her that she belongs in one of these
jars.
Because she is strange and beautiful.

Peggy wishes now, only
that she could bottle the shade of red
on his cheek, the blush left behind from her kiss.

Kaitlin Jennrich, 15
New Glarus Middle/High School
New Glarus, WI
Teacher: Rachel Ryan

Kaitlin Jennrich is from New Glarus, Wisconsin. Her writing is inspired by symphony music and Wisconsin's beautiful and understated landscape. She hopes to win the Pulitzer Prize every year for the rest of her life and would like to live in London, where she will adopt a British accent.

200 ACRES
Poetry

Mom left on a Sunday,
so it was just you and me.

But it is never truly just
us,
because your cornstalks call,
tall and blonde and resilient
(what I am not)
against a sky blue like the veins
that map the undersides of your wrists
in the half-light of the kitchen lamps.

You believe in all the superstitions
(spit twice
at the beginning of the harvest,
plant the first bloated seed
by hand)
and live by the Farmer's Almanac
and pray to God every day
though we stopped going to church after she left.

When we pass in the narrow farmhouse hallways,
you press yourself against the wall

(we do not touch)
as we squeeze around each other,
as I escape to my teetering tower of books
(waste of space)
and you to the kitchen, where you can pray for rain,
for Jesus to water your cathedral,
watching a sky streaked with black
bruises.

Our sentences are short and declarative.
"I am going to Leah's."
"I'm going to the field."
"I made supper."
"I'll eat it on the tractor."
"The weather's nice."
"It will rain soon. Good for corn."
Your eyes are turning milky with kernels and bushels,
your hands cramp from counting on your fingers
how much faster the corn will have to grow
before you can turn a profit.

The odds do not look good.

The farmhands whisper your craziness,
(obsession)
tell me stories while I sit on the porch, feet bare and dirty
in the sticky August sun,
and you stand in the field, the corn bending toward you,
rustling and tempting,
as you stroke their leaves and plead for deliverance.
(god
forsaken)

You are a waste of wonder;
when I was young enough to be a princess,
Mom and I would watch you pace through your fields,
200 acres that you'd memorized and

every fallen stalk accounted for,
and she would press her lips together until they turned dusky
white
and run a tired hand through her hair
(corn silk blonde)
but I still thought you the strongest, biggest, smartest
Daddy
a girl could have-want-need.

Now I sit alone with faded orange wallpaper,
watching my own veins pulse,
raised ridges against my too-soft skin
as you weep over your silky corn
and blot out the sun on the horizon,
(you were always just a silhouette)
the silo to your right and
dirt bleeding from your fingertips and
200 acres laced through your heartstrings.

Da'Shawn Mosley, 16
Governor's School for the Arts and Humanities
Greenville, SC
Teacher: Mamie Morgan

Da'Shawn Mosley lives in Greenville, South Carolina. The pain, struggles and passions of friends, relatives and complete strangers deeply impact his writing. He strives to be the best writer he can be, and thanks his teachers and grandparents for their encouragement.

I Don't Know
Poetry

i don't know who ratted us out, told our mothers we'd
been smoking weed in the woods behind my trailer.
maybe it was everyone shuffling over to the mailbox
kiosk to get their checks, or maybe mom learned
on her own going outside to watch cars. forget how
i pinned myself to the living room floor when the guy
from the furniture store came on our door. instead, mom
found us. if you had a father, she said, this wouldn't have
happened. she took the belt in her hand and brought it
across my back. from here behind these blinds i've seen
the cops take our neighbor to jail, seen mom wrap
an arm around his wife's shoulder and hand her a t-shirt
that wasn't ripped, tyquan sitting on his steps staring at
the red and blue lights. tomorrow on the bus, he'll curse
at the driver. toss at him weed while everyone sits in
silence. i don't know why tyquan does stupid things, or
why when we get to school and the cops are waiting for
him, he'll smile, like something's funny.

Caroline Lu, 14
Wood Hill Middle School
Andover, MA
Teacher: Karen Parker

Caroline Lu is from Andover, Massachusetts, where she writes reviews of young adult books for the local newspaper. She hopes to use her writing as a way to effect social change. She is grateful to her teacher Charles Gregory, who has been a key influence in her writing.

6:00 A.M.
Poetry

Your legs pump, as you push yourself harder and harder
The sticky track of the treadmill reaches and grabs
The bottoms of your sneakers with every step
With every pounding force against gripping rubber

You struggle to lift each leg, to keep going
Just as you have struggled to remain awake since 5:20
From the treadmill, all appears bleak, life is a struggle
Daily woes and minor issues are ballooned to nightmare size

But, deep down, you know that the day will only get easier
This is the sole idea that keeps you going, your legs moving
The idea that at last, when you finally exit this device of doom
The day will be soft and luxurious, like a lazy summer Saturday

And so when your limbs at last stop pumping
And when your abused sneakers finally touch carpet
You take with you the knowledge that you are merely
At the bottom of the Ferris wheel, as some would say,
You will only rise from now on, and then, of course, eventually
Lower yourself once again, in approximately 23 short hours
But you can't and won't think about that

Maria Brescia-Weiler, 13
Deal Middle School
Washington, DC
Teacher: Kathy Crutcher

Maria Brescia-Weiler is from Washington, D.C. She is most often inspired by her own life and experiences. She plans to continue writing throughout high school and beyond.

MEMOIR IN FULL COLOR
Personal Essay/Memoir

Part 1:

Blue:

I am her dog Lacy. Blue black fur, soft dark eyes, the color of the blue in the center of a fire. Her mother's parents had pushed and pushed for them to get a dog, but the father wouldn't even think of it until, after many phone calls and important family conversations, he announced that they would go and look at the rejected seeing-eye dogs near the little girl's grandparents' house. There were only two dogs up for sale. There was a jumpy, energetic oblivious-to-its-owner's-needs dog who raced around its pen, and then there was me, Lacy, a mellow, gentle wouldn't-hurt-a-fly-unless-it-hurt-my-little-girl kind of dog. And the little girl loved me more than she had ever loved anything else.

Red:

I am her favorite song. I am what compels her father to pick her up and dance her around the room, her feet swinging two feet off the ground. I'm the force that makes her hips sway and her knees bounce as she hops along to me. I am the rise and fall of her voice as she belts out my name. Not red or rojo or rouge but "You can be my bodyguard, I can be your long-lost pal!" Her arms flapping. I am the warmth she feels as her parents dance across the room, the little girl tucked between them clinging to their legs.

PERSONAL ESSAY/MEMOIR

Orange:

I am the rumble of her stomach, the laughter and her sweet dimples. I am strong and serious, gentle and shy, wild and free. I refuse to be confined to whatever it is anyone wants me to be. Except for the little girl; I will be a flying herd of a hippopotami if she wants me to. I have been hers forever, just as long as she has been mine.

Purple:

I am the softness of her hands and the tenderness of her feet, not yet worn or rough. They're little girl hands. Soft and warm and gentle kiss-it-make-it-better hands. Ones that have never slapped or stolen or pulled or grabbed except for when she is really angry, which is not very often, but even when that happens, her slaps are soft and pulls more like a suggestion than an order. Her hands are small hold-only-one-finger hands, ones that rest gently on her parents' hands and wipe away her little my-ice-cream-fell-on-the-sidewalk tears. And her feet are small, tender like the skin underneath your used skin. I am the temporary dents in the soles of her feet as she steps on the stones that lead her to her mother's garden and the blackness of them after chasing her brother around the yard.

Black:

I am the bounce of her hair. Her lively black waves that cascaded down her back. The way it shook when she danced and laughed and the way it seemed to grow a couple inches when she went swimming. Her dad liked to bury his face in her hair, just for a moment when he kissed her good night.

Part 2:

Orange:

Everyone said her laugh was contagious. And it was. But this was not one of those times when it was welcomed. This was one of those put-your-head-down-button-your-lip-and-pretend-you're-not-a-kid-today days. It wasn't the little girl's fault. It was her brothers' fault. It always was, the little girl thought. She liked to sit between her brothers during church. She would look up at them during the service to see if they were singing a certain song or clapping along and follow their lead. One look from her brothers would make her carefully built wall of seriousness quickly drop as the attack of laughter seeped into her little belly. Her shaking shoulders and rumbling belly didn't pay much attention at all to the quiet, serious grown-up faces around her.

She had been so good, so serious and grown-uppity. Her brothers had had to look at her, right when the minister had been singing a particularly high note. The laughter instantly filled the room, bouncing and dancing and colliding with her brothers'. Her parents' heads, along without about a million others, turned angrily to the three smiling children. The girl liked to please everyone. And so she had churned her laugh into a beautiful smile. An innocent smile. One that every little girl has and uses, without hesitation, on her father. It doesn't work on her mother, unless she's in a very good mood; for you see, she was a little girl once, too, and knows all the secret alleys and hidden treasure chests of little girldom.

But it didn't work and soon she was left to wait out in the hall alone. And then she crawled into the world of her imagination, her very own sacred place of worship.

Purple:

Starting when she was about 8, she loved the bumps and scratches on her legs and arms and back. They were her battle scars, the proof of her bravery and strength. She would show them off to everyone. "I got this one in Honduras," she said pulling up the fringed bottom edge of her left pant leg to reveal a small dent, with a thin white scar running through the middle. It was her prized possession, her war medal. "I was playing tag by the pool there. I was winning, of course." She was a boastful little girl. "And someone put a lotta rocks by the pool. They were very jagged and dangerous," she said, repeating the phrase she had heard her parents use so often when telling friends the story. "I was running backwards. I can run backwards really good. And I ran right into those rocks. They dug all the way through my foot. I'm lucky I'm magical, or else I woulda died." She would not have died, nor did the rocks dig through her whole foot. "I got a towel and my mommy held me but I didn't even cry. "I went to the hospital and I barely cried. I just talked to my mommy's friend while my mommy almost fainted. She was lying on the floor yelling *Agua!* I had to make her feel better." The little girl was as dramatic as her mother as they gave her the special numbing shots. "I had to wear a pretty green cast and crutches for six whole weeks. But I was really fast on crutches and they made my arms super-strong." Her father was the one who had gotten the super-strength, well-deserved after carrying her around for six weeks."There's still some baby rocks floating around in my foot, but I'm so brave it doesn't even hurt."

Black:

It seemed I would never stay soft and smooth and untangled. I would somehow twist and gnarl and turn, and she would wake up in the morning with choppy waves of licorice. And the girl refused to surrender to my unruliness.

In first grade, she sat near the supply station. And one day, the little girl could not stand me. She reached into the scissors box and grabbed a pair, dull and colorful, little-kid-proof. Her conscience along with the coldness of the metal scissors pressed to her back threatened to give her away, but she rushed to the bathroom before they could.

Once there, she cut a large chunk of her hair off and tossed it into the trash She returned to her seat, sat down and subtly slipped the scissors back to their place on the shelf.

Her first-grade class shared a bathroom with the pre-K'ers. The pre-K teacher was mean. Her face was always angry and her gray-white hair flew out around her face like an explosion. Her shadow filled the hallway when she walked, and even the big kids were scared of her.

The pre-K teacher walked into her classroom clutching a lock of hair and then she heard the words "I found this in the bathroom and it looks an awful lot like her hair." The teacher pointed toward the little girl and waved the dreadlock. Of course it was the little girl's hair. Ms. Kovin simply suggesting it made it so.

And she stood, shocked that her seemingly impenetrable disguise of regular little girl with a regular haircut doing regular work had been ripped from her. She did her best to hold on to her dignity for the rest of the day, but when she finally reached home, she collapsed into the comfort of the shadowy yellow-pink walls. It was then that the little girl discovered once and for all that she was a truly bad little girl.

Purple:

Toss, catch, toss. Leather and mud and grass stains. Toss, catch, toss. Hard hits and chest bumps and no mercy. Toss, catch, toss. They are the ragged, smiling, down-to-business, hair-ruffling, fist-bumping, pig-piling, spitting, tough, immune-to-pain, lip-biting, leaping and diving heroes that they see on TV. They jump, they catch, they score, they tackle. They do victory dances. Sometimes they might cry just a little if someone tackles them too hard, but they hop back up and tackle back. They climb their father, all three, on his legs, on his waist, on his back. They chase the ball relentlessly, pouncing and tumbling. They call plays, *Blue 42, hup-hup-hype!* They shriek and roll and hand-shake. They rub the soft leather of the ball, hugging it close to their stomachs. They forge through piles of happy brothers and sisters and cousins. They keep the trees and bushes between them, their only defensemen. They run trick plays through the secret path in the backyard. Their legs are stained in streaks of green, brown and bold pride, their own abstract art. They draw plays with their fingers, pushing against their chest. They are correcting all the mistakes those giants on TV make. They are larger than life. They are fearless.

Blue:

It was July 9, 2010. Her brother's 15th birthday. She was only 13. So was I. The little girl had woken up content, tucked in bed next to her cousin at her grandparents' lake house. She had tiptoed downstairs. The summer heat and early-morning anticipation pressing against her back. Her mother, already awake, sat beside her on the little gray-blue couch with pink streaks on it. Her mother's arm hung over the arm of the couch, softly petting me.

Two days earlier, I had transformed into a puppy, leaping into the lake, chasing tennis balls. I had an energy I hadn't had in years. Nothing made the little girl smile more than watching me dive into the water, swim determinedly after a ball, return to shore and bathe in the sand, letting it scratch my back and bottom. And then I would waddle over and rub up against the little girl, covering her shins with rough sand, mixed with unconditional love and loyalty that only her Lacy Lou could offer. The night after, I had changed back. Only worse. I couldn't get in the car, couldn't run, couldn't jump, couldn't swim. Could barely eat. There were enough couldn'ts to furrow the little girl's brow far more than it had ever been furrowed.

They had celebrated her brother at midnight, singing and laughing and hugging. He even drank a sip of beer. But there was too much worry resting in my little corner to make the night birthday worthy. Even so, everyone knew I would get better. Of course I would. I had to. For the little girl.

She woke up that morning and ran down the wooden stairs and into the living room in the big wooden cottage. The air was filled with the usual birthdays-at-the-lake excitement that it had had on that day each year for 15 years. But there was something else. Her mother's usual calm and her father's usual humor had dissolved and the air was heavier. "Mommy, is she okay?" The little girl looked over at the dog that had been her best friend since she was 2.

"I don't know, sweetie." Her mother continued to stroke me as the little girl lay down beside me and rested her head on my belly, gently holding my paws in her hands. She lacked her usual warmth. So did I. She stroked my fur. She had always loved the softness of the fur on my neck. Virgin fur, she called it because it was so hidden, it was rarely touched. She petted and petted, and her pets grew softer until she simply rested her hand on my belly and listened to me breathe as she buttoned her lips and wrinkled her chin and tried very hard not to cry. We were supposed to get married, she thought.

She returned to her mother's side and simply sat as her mother stroked both our hair. Her little girls. It was too hard for the little girl to lie with me. So often she had crawled onto the floor just to rest with me. She loved the way I moaned when the little girl rested her head on me. She used to make space for me on her bed and let me stay there even though it made her uncomfortable. She used to want to grow up to be a dog-dance-and-drama teacher so she could teach me how to dance and we could be in musicals together. She would lift my paws and hold me and try to spin me around. She used to walk me to the ice cream store and sit with me outside as I devoured the vanilla ice cream she bought me, cup and all. She used to sit me on the ground with her dolls and read to us, making sure to show me all the pictures. She used to whisper to me her secrets before she went to bed and explain to me what was going on when she went on a trip she couldn't take me on. She used to jump into the lake and swim out and wait for me to jump in and "save" her. She used to dress me up in a belly shirt and skirt, both covered in sequins, and parade. She had always counted on my being there. We had plans.

It was there, in her mother's arms, that she watched, and heard, and felt that last shuddering sigh as I stretched and released the spirit that hid in the clickety-clack of my paws in the hall and the shaking of my fur after I got out of the water and the way my hips waddled at every movement.

They were all still petting, still hopeful. Her aunt walked over and with one sad glance pronounced "She's gone" in a shaky about-to-cry-voice, which is exactly what she did. What they all did.

"Sweetie, why don't you go wake up your brothers to say goodbye." Her father patted her gently, kissed her and directed her toward the stairs.

She woke up her oldest brother, but couldn't bear to wake up the other, not on his birthday. All she could say to the first was "Can you go wake him up so we can go say goodbye to Lacy?" but all he could hear was crying, which told him enough. He had always been the grown-up one. He shook the other brother awake and, with his arm around both of them, herded them down the stairs.

Her brothers immediately saw what was going on and were crying before they reached the foot of the stairs. They gathered in a circle around me, each crying. The others had always known that I would die, but the little girl was supposed to have me forever. They shuddered and heaved together all seven of them: the little girl, her brothers, her parents, her aunt and her grandmother. After much sobbing, never enough to express their love for me, the little girl's father quietly picked me up and carried me to the car, followed by all the others. Her mother and birthday brother went with him to the vet. The little girl stayed.

A few minutes after they left, her grandmother forced enough hope into her voice that it was audible and said, "We're going to make Timbo a good birthday if it kills us." And they did. They decorated colorful birthday signs. let them dry so the tears that dropped on them didn't show. As cousins and uncles and aunts and her grandpa slowly began to awaken and come to the kitchen, they received whispers from her aunt and grandma that made their faces fall as the little girl and her brother tried to concentrate on birthdayifying the room but still burst into quiet tears every few minutes. The little girl got tons of hugs that day, more than usual, and slowly she attempted to pick up the broken pieces of morning that lay at her feet. The usually chatty little girl was quiet. When her brother and parents returned, everyone sang "Happy Birthday" and smiled and hugged birthday hugs that were really I'm sorry hugs. And for a while the little girl was simply sadder. She still smiled and laughed but lacked something: her honey bubelah, Lacy Lou, wife-to-be, best friend. Me. And she was truly blue.

Red:

Her father had just gotten back from Ecuador. He traveled far too often, for work or something "important" like that, and the little girl did not approve. This trip he had brought her back an orange dress. She loved it. It twirled and twisted and danced with each step she took and she LOVED it! It was soft and it smelled like all the adventures that her dad had when he stepped outside. And so her father and her brother had gotten out their drums and played. And she had danced, pulling her mother along as she hopped and twirled, using every inch and level of the room, dipping and diving and leaping. And her house was filled with laughter and music and dancing and togetherness, their own secret family recipe for happiness.

Jesse Shulman, 17
Upper Canada College
Toronto, Ontario
Teacher: Terence Dick

Jesse Shulman is from Toronto, Ontario. As an aspiring filmmaker and novelist, he is interested in framing small details of life in ways that make them resonate with an audience. After taking a year off from school to write and travel, he will attend Harvard University.

SPLIT ENDS
Personal Essay/Memoir

Yesterday I saw her in the street. Her hair looked slept in, split ends and all.

In another age, when I was eight and she was nine, we wanted to be astrophysicists or inventors. We built a robo-body for Stephen Hawking out of Legos, and a voicebox too, by downloading sound clips from Bogart movies and putting them on a tape recorder, so Hawking could sound like Humphrey. We planned to create guitars that played themselves, so nerds could flip a switch and be cool. We designed connector cords for brains out of USB ports and copper wire, so everyone could open their minds and let others in, so parents wouldn't fight over miscommunications, so old people wouldn't be lonely, too embarrassed to call their children.

Two years passed. Like most girls, she developed fast. I didn't. She raised her anchor, sails unfurled, and I lost her to the horizon; I guess she wanted a new world, and figured it was where I wasn't.

"You're such a boy." She smiled while she said it, which confused me.

You know when you play the same scene over until you're not sure if you've changed the script?

I asked why; she wanted to go. She said she didn't know, that she just wanted to be normal, just regular and boring like everyone else.

"But nobody's boring," I said. She smiled again, which confused me.

Maybe it was when I told her we'd govern an underwater city in a glass dome, where no one starved because of octopi farms and no one was sad, because all the architecture was crisp and colorful, built off blueprints by Haussmann, Hundertwasser and Gehry. All policies would be egalitarian, and there'd be no glass ceilings (except literally, of course).

Maybe it was when I told her: We'd reboot the hot air balloon as the mode of public transport, so everyone could see the world from up high without looking down on one another; we'd be the first reporters to secure an exclusive tell-all with God; we'd start a family in Antarctica, and breed mammoths back into existence to be our pets.

Antarctica is cold, she said.

So we drifted, like jetsam. We split.

When I was seventeen, she was eighteen and heading off for university in Paris. We'd only been talking a few times a month, if that. Sometimes we'd go out: I'd text her to bring running shoes, an attitude for adventure, and always—always—a towel. We'd meet downtown. I'd give us both fake names and fedoras, and we'd pretend to be detectives, asking people on the sidewalk for clues. We'd see tourist sites in our own city, and perform short, silent plays in front of security cameras. Sometimes she'd bring me to her parties, where, ironically, she'd be the one feeling out of place. She'd get jealous if girls crowded me, especially if they were laughing, especially if they had low-cut tops and no split ends.

To me, her imperfections were what made her perfect. I'm not sure if she ever got that.

Usually she'd just come over. We'd cuddle and talk in bed about how the universe was expanding, how stars that burnt out years ago still felt real, how our DNA allowed for 40 billion possible people who could've been born in our place, and we owed it to them to make our lives mean something. We'd turn on a movie we'd never seen, press mute and improvise dialogue.

During her university send-off, we were standing by an intersection and the light went green. She kissed my cheek and whispered something over her shoulder as I walked away; it got lost in honks of traffic. She covered her eyes, turned a corner, and was gone.

Sometimes shoes feel waterlogged, even though they're not.
I felt lost in space. And time. And plain old lost.
Sometimes, reading Stephen Hawking or Richard Dawkins, life becomes microscopic.

I felt like a rocket man because astronauts' tears hang in zero gravity and stay there, like memories, floating, drifting. In space, if you want to get rid of tears before they seep into the wiring and the ship sparks apart, you stick them in Tupperware. You hide them until one day there are too many and the box bursts.

The universe is expanding.

Yesterday I saw her in the street. She was in town for the weekend. Her hair looked slept in, split ends and all. We had coffee on a park bench and watched people pass by like in a Woody Allen movie.

A couple on a tandem bike rolled past on the grass.

I looked at her.

"You can't breed mammoths back to life," she said.

"You can try."

I looked at her, and gave my Humphrey Bogart impression:

"I was born when she kissed me. I died when she left me. I lived a few weeks while she loved me."

She cast her eyes down to the coffee between her thighs. The steam rose and warmed her cheeks. Or maybe she was blushing. She looked up and smiled.

I looked at her.

She looked at me.

"We can try."

Aaron Orbey, 15
Buckingham Browne & Nichols School
Cambridge, MA
Teacher: Althea Cranston

Aaron Orbey lives in Boston, where he draws inspiration from the people around him. He enjoys the work of J.K. Rowling, Stephen King and Sylvia Plath. He would like to thank his school's English teachers for their warmth and their perceptive feedback on his writing.

HUSHED TREPIDATION
Personal Essay/Memoir

Sweltering sunlight beat down upon the Turkish street, reflecting off windshields of dusty cars. Scaffolding gripped the side of the tall building, casting shadows on the nearby sidewalk. A stray cat with opaque eyes leered at the passage of a bicyclist.

I traipsed behind my mother and sister toward the parched apartment complex. My mother's bag rocked slowly as its handle pivoted over her shoulder. I watched as she dipped a fumbling hand into its contents, procuring a set of keys that sent a clink through the musky air. We entered the building, passed up several flights of marble stairs and stopped at the third-floor landing. I followed to a large door whose wearied welcome mat had long been destroyed by prying footsteps.

"Here we are." My mother uttered these words with a hushed trepidation before slipping silently into the dank apartment. Gizem, my senior by nine years, trailed hesitantly. I lingered for a moment in the dark hallway, enveloped by a pair of gritty yellow walls. Cracking my knuckles, I followed over the threshold, shifting to avoid the heavy door that swung back into place with a muffled thud.

And here we were: in the very apartment where, during one of our annual visits to Ankara almost a decade before, my father had been murdered by an intruder. We were enclosed by the doorways between which my sister had been stripped of her innocence, my mother had metamorphosed into a reserved, grieving widow, and my boyish indigence had crystallized into a harsh cynicism. I could sense the thick air, perforated by an acrid, metallic stench, pressing in upon me. A musty green armchair sulked in a corner of the dusty living room. Rows of ancient novels eyed me from a rustic bookcase.

As my mother and sister stepped warily into the kitchen and bedroom, I wandered over to the bathroom and turned on the faucet. The tarnished sink expectorated a torrent of brown water that formed a muddy line of sediment along the rim of the drain. I waited for the pipes to clear of the rust that had accumulated over years of disuse before splashing my face with a handful of water. Raising my eyes to the grimy mirror, I saw my father. The long, narrow face, softened by a blunt nose and protuberant lips, stared back at me. Soft wisps of ashen hair covered two deep eyes.

Emerging, I stole a glance into the kitchen. My mother stood alone, hands clenching the edge of the filthy countertop. I watched as she gazed out of the dusty window at smoke curling languidly upward from the carts of street vendors.

I continued across the hallway toward Gizem's childhood bedroom, where I noticed her crouched in the corner. Upturned rag dolls and a broken magic wand strewn across the faded pink carpet echoed of the times that were. And I saw her holding a photograph, a portrait of our family that had been taken prior to my father's murder. A sole tear developed in the crease of her eye.

I could picture her as the tousle-haired, soulful youth of the photo, pressed against a closed door, forced to listen as a bitter bullet stole the life of her beloved father. I could imagine my mother placing her gingerly on the metal bunkbed as the frantic hum of police cars resounded over outside streets. Without a thought, I glided over and took her hand. She smiled a wobbly smile.

And suddenly, this boy of twelve was the protector—the only one who could fathom the pain, the countless nights spent parsing the paradoxical rashness with which tragedy strikes. I stood over Gizem, gripping her hand in silence, waiting. There was no need to speak: The grateful look in her eyes told all.

When the moment came to depart, I allowed my mother and sister to exit ahead of me. It was time to return to the leisurely swing of late summer, to wallow under the sweltering sunlight while waiting for fall. Stepping over the muddy threshold, I allowed myself a fleeting look back into the abandoned apartment. Gaunt shadows tangled in the midday sunlight, forming grisly silhouettes on the floor of the corridor. The picture that my sister had held stood alone on a nightstand. Light glinted off of the image of my father. I could almost perceive a friendly wink.

A soft call from my family interrupted this momentary lapse. Turning briskly around, I shut the door with a smile.

Lylla Younes, 15
Alexandria Senior High School
Alexandria, LA
Teacher: Laura Helminger

Lylla Younes is from Alexandria, Louisiana. She is primarily a prose writer but is inspired by poetry and enjoys writing about the experiences of growing up. She would like to thank her brother, Abraham, for his example as a writer.

FRUITS OF TIME
Personal Essay/Memoir

Dry leaves and thorny branches crunch under our feet as I lead you through the old, forgotten garden to the lemon tree. It is strange how a simple piece of nature can hold within its branches so much sentimental value, but it can. Four years ago, youthful voices could be heard from under this same tree as my cousins and I played hide-and-seek. Eight years ago you led me to this lemon tree, your wrinkly, callused hand holding on to my tiny wrist as you gave me a tour of the garden. You had walked me over to the apple tree and plucked one tiny green fruit from a branch before presenting it to me. The sweet and sour taste of childhood engulfed my mouth, while its juices dribbled down my chin. I can remember smiling up at you through the blinding sunlight, finally understanding Adam and Eve's predicament. Yes, I can remember a lot of things about Syria—the land of my childhood where, millions of years ago, the ocean carved mountains out of the earth. Nestled among those mountains lies Srajis, a tiny village that contains, among other things, a small store where I bought ice cream; an antiquated graveyard where I scrambled up onto the cobblestones and hid with my cousin Walaa as we painted our toenails bright red; a barn where I helped my great uncle milk his cows; and the home of my grandparents, where I slept on the balcony and listened intently to the coyotes as they sang their melancholy tunes into the inky black night.

Every time I leave Syria, I take a mental picture of it, expecting it to stay the same when I return, but the old saying rings true—

nothing lasts forever. And here I am. Years have passed since my last visit, and the village has changed. My great-uncle has died and the cows have been sold. When I first arrived, I slowly walked through the graveyard that used to seem so huge but now could be crossed with ten steps. And you, my grandmother, the main purpose for my visit, have changed as well. Your skin sags in new places, and your thin hair is unkempt. I can already see how the disease has begun to take over your being. I notice how your dark eyes are sad and confused because you cannot articulate what you are trying to say. I notice how words have become your enemies. You struggle with them.

Yesterday, I watched my feet as I walked along the gravel road to Walaa's house. I was nervous because my Arabic is poor from lack of use. Would the language barrier hinder conversation? But when I got there, we went up to her roof and sat on plastic chairs and talked for a long time. I felt happy, relieved. Not everything had changed after all. She called her brothers and we ate nuts and drink maté and played cards into the night. I arrived back at my grandparents' house late. After showering in cold water, I lay down on the dilapidated couch on the balcony. Unlike previous trips, I had to bend my knees because I was too tall to lie straight. I did not hear the howls of coyotes. I waited for a long time to hear their comforting cries, but then I felt too cold so I went inside to sleep.

And now I lead you through a garden that used to be so full of life—life that has been extinguished by weeds and thorny underbrush and lack of care. The stems of the tomato plants are bent toward the earth in a submissive genuflect, while the fruit at their ends lies on the ground, brown and rotting from within. The corn is nowhere to be seen. And as I approach, I notice that the lemon tree, my big, beautiful lemon tree, is fruitless and sick-looking. I hold your arm with one hand, steadying you, and with the other hand, I carry a bucket. My grandfather has instructed me to take you to the garden to fill up the bucket with miniature apples. You stumble along and I say, "*Yallah, Tata.* Come on, Grandmother." We arrive at the apple tree, and I begin to fill the bucket. You stare at me for a few moments with hollow eyes. Then you try to help. Your arms move in jerky motions as you try to pluck an apple off a branch, but instead you hit it with the back of your hand and it falls to the ground. I stop picking.

I watch you curiously. You bend your head and look at the apple that fell, nestled among many rotting apples that the wind had brought down days earlier. You pick it up and place it in the bucket. Then, suddenly, you are scrambling around trying to pick up every single rotting apple that has fallen. You throw them into the bucket. Your arms are swinging and you are taking short, choppy steps to nowhere.

"No, Tata. Don't put the bad apples in the bucket," I tell you in Arabic. And you are breathing hard, bending over, trying to pick up as many decaying fruit as you can. You look at me, panicked, a strong urgency in your eyes, but for what? I do not know. You stumble, almost fall.

"No, Ta—" The words catch in my throat. Hot tears gather at the corners of my eyes and my mouth is slightly ajar. I cover it with my hand as I watch you, this helpless, confused old woman. Your head swings around and you look lost in your own garden, lost in the land that you had watched grow, lost in the land that you had led me through years ago.

And all of a sudden, you are the apples, all of the apples. There was a time when you grew and when you were plucked and savored. But then you fell and began to break down from within. Now your body is failing you and no one can save you from the dark labyrinth that is your mind. So you try to save yourself. You pick up all the rotting, forgotten, bitter apples fast, as if your life depends on it, and in a way, it does.

"Layla!" My grandfather's loud, concerned voice sounds from the balcony. My head whips around and I look at him, startled. "What is she doing?"

When you hear his authoritative voice, you turn and look from him to the apples, and back.

"Nothing." I hope that he doesn't hear the quiver in my voice.

"We're about to eat," he says.

"Yes, okay, we'll be right there." He turns to go inside.

You and I look at each other, and I hold out my hand. You look down at the brown, gushy apple in your palm. It's decaying juices are already staining your skin. Then, you give up on you. With a soft thud, the apple hits the ground and you walk toward my outstretched hand, knocking over the bucket as you go.

PERSONAL ESSAY/MEMOIR

Ashley Huang, 13
Doerre Intermediate School
Klein, TX
Teacher: Jeannie Boyle-Spears

Ashley Huang is from the perpetually dry town of Houston, Texas, whose climate she considers perfect for writing. She has always felt the need to make straight A's and to share her story with the world. She would like to thank her teacher Mrs. Boyle-Spears.

THE IVORY BLOSSOM
Personal Essay/Memoir

A breeze whipped along the street, rustling the California oaks as the gray sedan raced along. The black asphalt stood out like a blemish against the tranquil periwinkle flowers and yellow-green grass, like a lengthy scar that stretched across the perfect face of nature. As always, the sun blazed overhead, a fiery blot against the soft expanse of the sky, like a giant tangerine flower.

The twentysomething mother exclaimed at the scenery, then continued chatting animatedly. One of her petite, perfectly manicured hands grasped the steering wheel, the other she waved distractedly at the scrawny girl in the back. "I'm telling you, these piano lessons are just what you need. Why, you could be the first Chinese Beethoven!" the driver wondered aloud.

The child perched on her car seat calmly, wispy chocolate hair pulled into a tight ponytail with a halo of flyaways crowning her head. A slight frame, large, luminous eyes and crooked teeth made her seem like a cross between a chipmunk and a fairy. Her gaze was fixated outside her window, she paid no attention to her lecturer. It was as if she was holding a staring contest with the hilly landscape of San Diego. The view whisked by, transforming into dappled olive blurs and light yellow streaks.

"Thank goodness, we're a few minutes early," her mother breathed, relieved that, for once, they weren't tardy. They pulled up to a dark, depressing house, shaded by two twin pines whose tops seemed to poke holes in the clouds. The only color present came from a few birds-of-paradise, whose bright mango feathers and powder-blue bills lit the walkway like a neon glow stick.

The anxious mom wrenched open the door and ushered the minuscule pianist inside, handing the girl her bag and brushing a kiss on her cheek. "I'll pick you up at 5:30, alright?" Smiling at her daughter's shy nod, she got into her car and left.

The little girl had been taking lessons with Mrs. Eugenia for eleven months, but the frigid parlor still intimidated her. A dominating grand piano commanded one side of the room, its black lacquered surface reflecting the glow of the chandelier. Opposite the piano stood a bare coffee table and a classy leather couch, which the girl never sat on for fear of damaging it. There were several glass cabinets filled with delicate china dolls, and a cream vase holding still more birds-of-paradise.

Even though the double doors to Mrs. Eugenia's study were closed, her definitive Russian accent still leaked through, and, as always, it sounded angry. She finally swept into the parlor, followed by a teary teen who kept sniffling. Mrs. Eugenia addressed the girl coolly, "Iris, practice more next time. You'll never be ready for the recital like that." She then spotted her other pupil, and frowned. "Oh, yes. I forgot to tell you, you'll be playing in the recital as well. We'll be practicing on the grand today."

The wispy-haired child stood and approached timorously. She balanced on the bench carefully, feet dangling above the pedals. "I usually have a recital for my students in the fall. It is a formal affair, and only a few may attend," Mrs. Eugenia elaborated, pacing in front of the piano as the so-called Chinese Beethoven stumbled over the scales, "and this year you'll perform. You've practiced your tarantella, yes?" The performer nodded, and winced as her finger slipped and hit a D-flat. Her teacher peered at her from underneath tortoise-shell glasses and motioned for her to play.

It was three measures into the piece when she made her first mistake. The error reverberated through the room, and she could feel Mrs. Eugenia's stare boring into the back of her head, severing the already frayed string that connected her to the music. Her fingers slowed until they almost crawled across the ivory keys and she had to strain to hear the notes. She could almost feel her teacher's disgust; it flew across the room like an arrow and burrowed deep into her heart. The timid child receded into a blank shell, ignorant of every legato, every piano forte, every carefully marked side note. Somehow, she had managed to turn the once lively tarantella into a funeral dirge.

Mrs. Eugenia pursed her lips, inspecting the small pianist like a chef with a piece of unripe fruit. Finally, after what seemed like eternity, she removed her glasses and pinched the bridge of her nose. "I've discovered your problem," she announced.

"You have absolutely no confidence, no passion. Where is your conviction? Your life? You play like a dead piece of wood."

She plucked a bird-of-paradise from the vase and brandished it in front of her pupil's face. "Do you see this flower? See the colors and hues? The extravagant shape? You must play like this flower," she told the befuddled girl, a serious and fierce look on her aged face. "Now, show me your Clementi."

The weeks before the recital were hectic and rushed, and they drove the nerve-wracked child crazy. Every time she even touched the keys her mind revolved around the same statement. The girl had come to hate even thinking about the piano, because she loathed the idea of failing. She had no idea how to play like a flower. It was utterly impossible.

On the night of the recital, sitting in a charcoal dress with too much lace, she watched performer after performer, doubting herself with more and more conviction as she observed a girl playing a perfect Debussy arabesque, a boy running through a fantastic minuet. At last, a familiar face caught her eye, the girl from earlier, Iris. When her name was declared, she rushed up and leapt into a flowing waltz. Her dainty fingers skipped over the keys, chiming out a lighthearted rhythm.

It was stunning, until she hit a wrong chord. Iris gulped, then restarted, only to have the incident recur. She sounded like a broken record, repeating that one stretch of forlorn notes, until Mrs. Eugenia had to fetch her off the stage. To the young girl, this was even worse than the other performances, because she knew that was how she was going to play.

After several more people, the small pupil turned performer finally trotted to the piano, heart pounding and breath shallow. She slowly sank into the solid bench and steeled herself for the coming disappointment. Her mother, of course, would be devastated, her dream of having a talented daughter ripped into pieces. Her father would probably shake his head slowly, a frown stretching the corners of his face. Mrs. Eugenia's advice seemed even more ludicrous now than ever. That was when the flower caught her eye.

It was a single pristine bloom, hidden in a vase near the foot of the piano where the audience couldn't see. The bird-of-paradise was vivid, its colors as brilliant as the sun. Suddenly, everything seemed to click into place. The little girl smiled, and started to play.

Victoria Sharpe, 17
Governor's School for the Arts and Humanities
Greenville, SC
Teacher: George Singleton

Victoria Sharpe is from Columbia, South Carolina, and will attend the University of South Carolina. The process of writing sometimes helps her make sense of things she doesn't understand. She is grateful to her teachers for helping her write.

SIX THINGS I DON'T KNOW
Personal Essay/Memoir

1. I don't know what the Tuesday Special at Lizard's Thicket is.

What I remember most: a grape popsicle melting in my hand. The kind that comes twelve to a box, with pictures of the Flintstones on the wrapper. My fingers turning purple and sticky, my father's suitcases on the floor. He leaves us on a breezy evening in August.

I am eleven that year, a slightly chubby sixth grader. My sister, Kelly, is seven. The same year, the scar from the previous summer's jellyfish sting fades from my ankle. I become known as "that quiet girl" in school. I decide to fall in love with a boy who needs a haircut and can't even spell my first name. That year, my parents separate and later divorce. I see my father cry for the first time.

Two months after he leaves, my dad lives in a trailer in my grandparents' backyard. The trailer doubles as his father's office. My dad takes us to dinner at Lizard's Thicket because of the speedy service. A waitress named Dolly leads us to a booth near the back and gives us menus to look over while she brings our drinks. I sit beside Kelly on the red seat and watch our father run a thumb over his mustache.

He tries to make conversation, but we all know there is nothing to say. He asks us what we are going to order, and I mumble something that he pretends to hear. Kelly replies with a scowl, says that she doesn't want anything. I grip the side of the table and nudge her. Dad tries to coax her into eating, but she won't give in. He suggests all her favorites: mashed potatoes, chicken fingers, macaroni and cheese.

She shakes her head every time, lips pursed. He asks her if she wants ice cream for dinner. She says she hates ice cream.

He looks at me, half-apologetic and half-pleading. I don't look back. My hands clamp into fists under the table. Each sideways glance says what we cannot: You left us.

Later, someone will tell me that anger comes from fear, always. My sister and I—we are so afraid, so scared of what will happen to us. I know families that broke up for good, dads who went away and never came back, not even for Christmas.

I stare down at my menu, determined not to look at my dad. I read and reread all the dinner items, combo platters and desserts. When I finally steal a glance at him, he is staring out the window, watching a family in the parking lot. Two young parents, each holding one of their son's hands. Every few steps they lift him up off the ground and set him back down again. They laugh at his wide, delighted eyes and flushed cheeks.

The waitress comes back and recites the specials of the day. My father nods politely, his lips pressed together. His eyes are red and wet.

2. I don't know how much a woman gets paid per hour to answer phones all day.

My father leaves behind only a phone number. An unfamiliar sequence of digits, not for his cell phone or for his parents' house. My mother doesn't see anything strange about it, or if she does, she won't say so. She tells me I should give him a call. I take the cordless gray telephone into the kitchen and hold it in my hands for what feels like hours until I get up the courage to dial. A woman answers, and my throat tightens. "I need to speak to my dad," I say, choking.

"Room number?" she asks.

I bite down on my lip. My breath catches in my chest. Room number. Like a hotel, or a hospital. Like a cell. Like a prison. The lady speaks again, her voice softer this time. "What's your daddy's name, sweetheart?" I tell her and wait while she connects me to him. I lean against the kitchen counter, listening to the humming noise on the other end of the phone. When my father's voice comes through, my hello sticks in my throat. He does most of the talking, asks me about school and the weather. I answer most questions with "Okay." I don't ask him where he is. I never will. I am afraid of the answer.

3. *I don't know how to keep score in Scrabble.*

Months later, my sister and I sit on the floor of our father's living room, next to a woman we have just met. Her name is Becky, short for Rebecca. She is from England and a novelty to my sister and me. We have to listen closely to understand her sometimes. Her accent rolls soft over her tongue, her speech so superior to my own. When I first meet Becky, she is sitting on the arm of my father's leather sofa. She drinks tea from his blue and green coffee mug. I walk through the front door, and she smiles, tugs down the sleeve of her purple sweater. She greets me like she already knows me. "Tori, how was school?" My sister and I answer her questions politely. My father goes to his room to find a watch, and we are left alone with her.

Becky does not kiss my father in front of us, but they exchange smiles at dinner. They brush thumbs when they reach for the salt shaker at the same time. When my father's lasagna arrives, he offers her a bite from his fork. A year ago, he shared food with my mother.

After dinner, we go back to my dad's house. We spread board games out around us. Checkers, Scrabble. Becky wins every time. In Scrabble, she earns forty-two points for the word "question." I learn that she had never been to America before, that she thinks Columbia, South Carolina, looks like a movie set. Everything is so big. I laugh, and she doesn't understand why.

Becky visits for only two weeks. I've always wanted to ask my father how he knew her, when it was, precisely, that he fell in love with her. He has pictures of her in his bedroom. They have webcams and talk for hours online via video chat. But until now, he knew so little about her. He didn't know how she smelled or the way she folded her hands on her lap. How do you fall in love with someone across an ocean? I don't know.

My mother will ask me about Becky, and I will say only "She was nice." What I won't say: that her eyes are round and big, that her hair is the exact shade of red I envy, that she makes my father laugh. A blush will creep up my face. Burning and burning from the shame of loving this other woman, this woman who is not my mother, the shame of loving her so instantly.

4. I don't know how to fix a marriage in ten easy steps.

Four years later, I am sixteen. My dad lives in a lovely, lonely white house, by a lake. He doesn't talk to Becky anymore. The only traces of what happened between my parents are the whispers of friction between my father and me. The defiance, the "what right do you have?" mentality.

My knowledge of my parents is like a puzzle with half the pieces missing. The portions I have already filled in are made up of strange things: the pills on my dad's nightstand, snatches of phone conversations about counseling and lawyers, the way my mother raises her eyebrows when my dad picks my sister and me up on weekends. The books that sit in stacks on my mother's nightstand and the front seat of my father's car, all with titles like *After the Affair* and *Bipolar Disorder: What It Means for Your Family* and *How to Save Your Relationship in Ten Easy Steps.* Nothing fits together. Nothing makes a complete picture. There are gaps and blurs and smudges. When I try to think about everything at once, my mind chases itself in circles.

We don't talk about what happened. Much of my parents' story is still a mystery to me, and though I know I could ask, I won't. Asking questions knocks all the walls down. The floodgates open, the secrets make themselves real. Where am I supposed to hide?

5. I don't know anything about carpentry.

I am six, small and with perpetually tangled hair. In July, my dad builds the treehouse in my backyard, board by board. He lets me hammer in one of the nails, holds my hands steady over it. He smiles but doesn't laugh at me when I miss the nail completely. When the treehouse is half-done, he helps me climb up the ladder, catches my feet when they slip from the rungs. I call it a palace.

I imagine I can see for miles. I put my hand to my forehead to block out the sun. This treehouse is a pirate ship or a space shuttle. I mimic the whirs and thuds of my father's tools and watch him add the finishing touches.

I am too afraid to climb back down the ladder. He tells me it's easy, but I won't budge. So my father attaches a bright yellow slide to one side. He says he will catch me at the bottom, and he does.

Years later, my father won't know how to explain to me the way a marriage gives life borders, how everything becomes compacted into a glass box. Years later, he will leave and try to tell us in a nice way. Like he didn't screw up as much as he actually did. He will say that he has done something "very bad" and "made your mother very angry." He will use phrases like "a friend I've been talking to." He will leave me with the impression that he has been convicted of bank robbery.

Years later, when he buys his own house, he will build another treehouse for my little sister in his new backyard. My dad knows a lot about how things are put together, and so little about how they fall apart.

6. *I don't know why purple popsicles always melt in your hands.*

In books and movies, parents always say the same thing to their kids when they divorce. "We still love you. We just don't love each other anymore." I never question that my father loves me. The night he leaves us, I ask my mother what exactly he did wrong. She puts a hand on my cheek, says "Oh, honey" and tells me he met a woman over the Internet. He knew the woman for two years. My reaction is strange, something like guilt, the same kind of feeling that will still sneak up on me for years afterward. I'm not smart enough, or I'm not pretty enough. Maybe he wants a different daughter, one who is good at sports and doesn't set things on fire in the microwave. A wife who doesn't nag so much. A house without bats in the attic. A dog that comes when called. We are not what he needs.

My mother feels only the loneliness. She tires easily, naps more than ever. Sleeping gives her something to do. Before the divorce is even finalized, she will date a man who drives the Cheerwine truck. He will drink too much and smell like cigarettes and call in the middle of the night. My mother does not know how to be alone. She clings to what she can, until she knows she will be able to replace it.

We will sew ourselves together well. I will spend the night with my dad every so often. He will take us out to dinner, wherever we want to go. At his house, we will watch BBC sitcoms and make chocolate milkshakes. My sister and I will love our father, even if we don't understand him. But we will see him for what he is. Not the superhero we always imagined him as but a man who bent under the weight of a family, who sought understanding but hurt the women he loved, who knows he will never measure up to his "World's Best Dad" coffee cup but keeps trying anyway.

What it comes down to: a melting purple popsicle. I can wash the mess off my fingers, scrub them until they aren't sticky anymore, but the stain will still be there. I can forget the feeling of something coming apart in my hands, can make myself believe there isn't anything wrong. Popsicles melt. It happens.

India Futterman, 13
M.S. 51 William Alexander School
Brooklyn, NY
Teacher: Kristen Robbins

India Futterman is from New York City. She has been inspired lately by Jack Kerouac's On the Road *and by the work of other Beat-era writers. She writes because she wants to leave her mark on the world, and regardless of where her life takes her, she wants writing to be part of it.*

THE SHAPES OF THINGS
Science Fiction/Fantasy

Manicured fingernails: red. They're shiny, glinting and when at the perfect angle, make the overhead fluorescent light bounce off their curved surfaces, blinding me a little. Sometimes I could even see my hazy reflection in these red mirrors as well.

Fingers: white. Pale skin, smooth and flawless. Snow on fallen logs. I yearned to hold those fingers, to grasp those cold, slender forms. I knew they would be cold. Fingers were always cold.

Envelope: blue. For some reason The Administration always chose blue envelopes—no writing—to send employee notices in. They had an organized yet almost childish way of color-coding their envelopes. It was yellow for greeting—I got one of those on Christmas last year—red for warning, and pure, shining white for importance. I had never received a white envelope. Bill did a couple of months ago after he had sent in a mission proposal. We never saw him again.

I studied the immaculate image before me: red nails, white fingers, blue envelope, connected to an arm, enclosed in a red sleeve, connected to a shoulder—ball and socket joint—connected to a neck that in turn connected to a head, swallowed by puffy yellow tresses and a heavily painted mouth: also red. Red for warning.

I took the envelope from her.

Sofa: mauve. I sat down. It was not exactly a sofa, therefore I should not call it so. Hard. Foam peeking out in various regions where The Administration had neglected to patch up. Discolored, yellow foam.

I did not open the blue envelope just yet. I sat thinking of Judith. Judith, the only woman in the office. Red, red, red, yellow. Judith: beautiful.

I did not quite understand the fundamentals of human affection but I understood that I was in love with her. Truly, deeply, madly, passionately in love with Judith. Judith the secretary.

I held the envelope to my nose. Inhaled. Yes. I detected the slightest hint of her perfume. Lilacs for the office days, expensive French for special occasions. Yes, I knew her perfumes. I had bought her a bottle at The Administration's last Christmas party. I can still recall her wide red mouth parting into a smile.

Oh, David. You shouldn't have. How did you know it was my favorite?

Judith.

My eyes drifted downward to the envelope once more. My thumb and forefinger had formed an indentation upon its smooth blue skin. Darn. I smoothed it out and turned the envelope over in my palm. It was unsealed. I chuckled in my brain. I could tell The Administration intended for me to open it as soon as possible. I had sent my fourteen-page mission proposal into the head office more than three months ago. They said it would take some time to get back, what with all the suggestions and such they get every day, but you'll be alright waiting, won't you, David?

Yes, I would. But I would not open their blue letter directly. Over the ten years of working in the Science Development Department, sitting in my five-by-six cubicle, waiting, waiting for outdated computers to process their virtual meaningless responses…I had learned the art of patience. And I would relish this moment, the moment where I would find out whether I could finally give my life meaning or if I would stay trapped in my cubicle, surrounded by other cubicles I swear are larger than mine. George, I swear yours is larger than mine. Surrounded by people who don't care. And yes. I would relish this moment.

I slid my hand under the unsealed flap. I loved the feel of smooth paper. I peered into the blue depths of the paper enclosure. A single sheet: bright and blinding white. Folded into thirds. I counted the segments. One, two, three. Chuckled. The way The Administration always did it. No, no surprises here. All customary, all uniform. Removing the paper, I glanced at the simple letterhead. Black. Wilson Industries. Science Development Department. A picture of a chemistry beaker, although we never did get to work with substances. I took no deep breaths as I smoothed out the sheet, nor did I wipe my brow of sweat. I read, slowly. Taking in every neat letter of every machined word of every prewritten and reprinted sentence.

Dear Esteemed Colleague!
Yes, that was I. A truly "esteemed colleague."
Congratulations! Your Request for conducting an experimental mission into space has been granted! We will begin the necessary preparatory procedures in a week! We expect the best results from this ambitious project!
Good luck!
The Administration

I realized at that point that my hands were shaking slightly. In an attempt to steady them, I dropped the letter, overused exclamation points and all, where it fell by my sleeping feet. My neck snapped backward and my head struck the wall behind me. I smelled the paint and plaster and air freshener. I loved those smells. It made everything seem like new things were going to happen, like our bathrooms were going to be renovated. In retrospect, it struck me as foolish to get so worked up over a sheet of paper, especially because I had sworn to myself that I wouldn't. But at that point I felt a slight pressure at my retinas, and I comprehended it as crying, crying for sheer astonishment that the thing that lay by my trembling penny loafers was something that I had waited three months for. I could tear it, and I could throw it away, and that would be it. But I didn't. My brain couldn't grasp what was happening, and I stretched my body out on the not-sofa and tried to steady myself. My feet hung off the edge and one of my shoes fell off. I didn't care. My letter was on the floor; my life was on the floor. I hoped to whoever was up in that heaven or wherever that Judith wouldn't walk in and find me in this state. I began to piece the situation together in my mind. I'd do it. They'd let me do it, complete my mission. To blast off with the power of a million stampeding elephants, billions of rabid dogs, my love for my secretary times a thousand, into space, but not even into it, out of it, out of the blackness we all know to be the night sky, past the stars, past the light of the moon, past the unknown. Because I knew it wasn't infinite. There had to be an end and I wanted to know what was on the other side.

It was at that moment that I realized what I was getting into. There could be anything beyond that veil of familiarity. Would it just be better to stay within the known?

A week until we began the mission. I could wait a week. I lifted my head off the purple upholstery and felt the marks it left on my cheek. It was probably high time for me to be heading back to my cubicle. I stepped down the long hallway and into the brightly lit region of cubicles. I squinted at first, my eyes adjusting to the light, and then heard a burst of noise that sounded like bacon being fried in a hot pan. Looking up, I saw the entire office staff standing and applauding. I glanced behind me. No one there. Were they clapping for me? They were all looking at me. This surely couldn't be because of my mission. Lots of people got their proposals accepted by The Administration. Didn't they?

I looked into their sadly cheerful faces and it suddenly all dawned upon me. They all knew it before I did—about the mission. Did Judith seem more friendly than usual this morning? Yes, I think she did. No matter. At least I knew now. My thoughts were quickly interrupted by Boss, the head of the Science Research Branch. No one knew his real name, so we all called him Boss. That was fine with us. He was advancing toward me rather rapidly, and my mind was immediately washed over with anxiety and intimidation as I watched his fat red face with its stiff grin plummeting closer and closer. I took a deep breath and held back my lightheaded giddiness as I saw his green tie with these tiny embroideries of the planet Mars scattered around its surface. Or was it Pluto? You could never really tell with those generic garments. It wasn't their fault that their seamstresses couldn't tell one planet from another.

Boss always seemed to wear festive ties. Bill used to say that he had a new one for each day of the year. We would laugh at that any time he would throw a party.

Christmas party. 1996. Tie: scarlet, embroidered with snowmen in party hats. Atrocious.

Lovely tie, sir.

That was Judith, complete with forced red smile and all. She was really good at doing that.

Why thank you, Miss. What do you think, David? I just bought it yesterday at Bloomingdale's. They were having a sale on holiday ties!

I realized he was addressing me and I quickly averted my eyes from Judith's smile.

Very festive, sir.

Yes! You know, I was thinking of buying you a Hanukkah tie, but I thought a raise might be more appreciated.

He and Judith laugh as someone in a tuxedo hands us all long, slender glasses filled with a yellowish, effervescent liquid. Ginger ale? I hesitate for a moment. I had not touched alcohol since college.

Come on, Davie. It's Christmas! Have some fun for once.

I see Judith delicately sipping from one of the slender glasses.

All right.

I took the glass and swallowed a minuscule mouthful. Choking a bit as the rubbing alcohol liquid stung in my throat and the backs of my eyes, I forced a smile that apparently was not too convincing.

It's only champagne, Dave! Here, maybe a martini will go down easier.

I was immediately handed a bright, unnaturally blue drink in a triangular glass. I took another, more wary sip, and found that this one tasted not only of rubbing alcohol, but of sugar and artificial flavorings as well. But Boss was right. It did go down easier. I did not put the glass down. I sipped until there was not a drop of blue alcohol left, and then someone handed me another. I was beginning to enjoy these violet concoctions. Soon, I had three down. My mind felt foggy, like someone had put a fuzzy blanket over my brain. But I was happy. Judith looked twice as beautiful now. Boss' tie suddenly looked really great on him. I couldn't stand up straight, but I was content with flopping backward onto a plush couch, reclining lopsidedly.

I found myself laughing hysterically in the company of Judith and Boss. About what, I wasn't sure. It didn't really matter. Then I remember a hand, with sharp, cold red nails, pulling me along, then even sharper, colder air hitting my face. Then something else, against my lips. Another martini? No, a kiss. But I can't be sure. I was so intoxicated. For once, the world looked beautiful. I see the wide expanse of sky, poked with blinding white flecks of light. And I'm lying on a cold hard sidewalk and I'm smelling the alcohol all around me and I love it. I hear a voice.

Look at the sky, David. Isn't it beautiful?

The words are slurred. Who is speaking?

Do you think there's anything beyond that, David? Don't laugh at me, I'm being serious. Beyond the blanket of stars, beyond that beauty? Maybe there's something ugly. Or maybe there's something even more beautiful. Tell me, David. Do you know what's behind the sky?

And then I look over and see a red mouth and smell the French perfume I gave her, mingling with champagne. And then I couldn't respond because then there was darkness, but not like the night sky because there were no pricks of light.

That was the Christmas party.

I don't think anyone else at the office remembers it. Too many martinis, I guess.

I realize I'm staring at Boss' tie and I break out of my reverie. His smile has not faded a millimeter but his eyes express the deepest concern. They change as he notices my confusion.

My utmost congratulations, David. We all wish you the best of luck on your upcoming mission.

Thank you.

How are you feeling? Nervous? Excited? Relieved?

I thought for a moment about how to answer this question. I felt it hovering, unanswered, above my balding head. What was I feeling? I couldn't quite place the emotion. So I said the thing that everyone says when at loss for words.

Fine.

Boss was satisfied, and he could tell I was in no state to make lively conversation with him. He beamed again and walked toward the exit, patting me hard on the shoulder as he passed. I flinched and turned back to my coworkers. All had resumed work, not even glancing up at me. As if nothing had ever happened. A relief, really. I hated that kind of attention. I returned to my little cubicle. For the first time in my ten years of working at the office, I felt comforted by my square. There was the picture of my dog. There was my stamp collection. There was my postcard that Jonathan sent me from his trip to Greece. I must have sat in that swiveling chair, staring at the blue, blue water of the Grecian ocean, accompanied by the humming of the computer, for an hour or so, because Frank suddenly approached me, tapping me on the shoulder and out of my daydream.

Sorry, Dave. Time to go.

I rubbed my eyes and cleared my throat in embarrassment.

Right. Thanks. Sorry.

That was one of the longest weeks I had ever faced. I was not impatient, but I could not take my mind off the imminent mission. Yes. I would finally find it. The world beyond the beauty.

I awoke. What day was it? The clock was broken, forever flashing the number 12. I looked at my planets calendar. May was Jupiter. May 22—Friday. Really? The mission began today. I found it hard to believe; nevertheless, I dressed myself, ate my bran flakes, tied my shoes and was out the door, like any other day. The whole morning passed in a blur. I remember getting up to use the bathroom and finding a notice taped to my computer screen upon returning. My, those Administration workers were stealthy. This one was shorter than the previous one. And without an envelope. I read it.

David—

Ah. They addressed me by my name.

Your Boss will call upon you later today, and you will then be taken to your ship to begin the mission. Don't worry about bringing anything; we have your blueprints.

—The Administration.

I removed the notice from my computer screen, crumpled it up and threw it in my wastebasket. My brain was clouded with anxiety, and the notice elevated it to another level. I wasn't processing anything. I spent another hour, or two, or five, staring at my blank computer screen. Gray. Then it was the afternoon. I was hungry. There was an orange on my desk. How did it get there? I hate oranges. I didn't eat it. I would let my stomach growl like an angry dog until I got some bacon into my system. Boss approached me once more. Just like yesterday.

David.

He beckons me near with a sausage-like index finger.

Come. It's time.

I follow him, the office and the faces rushing by in an enigmatic blur. I could feel their eyes grazing my coffee-stained shirt and two-piece suit that didn't even match. None of that would matter when I was in space. I was led through a door I'd never seen into an office that I'd never set foot in. Everything was becoming more and more distant to me as each day, hour, minute, second passed. I felt as if I was blasting out of the galaxy already. But when I looked down at my feet I saw the same colorless carpeting beneath them. I looked up. There they were, like three identical stones sitting erect on identical chairs. One held a suitcase. The Administration. They stood as I lifted my head. For some reason, at that very moment I prayed that they hadn't seen my bald spot. But they obviously had, and as they approached me, their head tops only coming to my chin, I viewed their thick, full tresses with jealousy. I let it slide past. No room for hair envy now. Their shiny gray suits rustled stiffly as they moved. The man in the center, the one holding the suitcase, who was slightly taller than the other two, approached me with an outstretched hand. I stood staring at his emaciated fingers for a moment, comparing them to Boss' inflated protrusions. I grasped them gently for fear they would snap in my firm grip. The tall one said nothing as I shook his hand gingerly. His fingers were cold. He didn't look at me; instead he turned his gaze to the side in contempt. I let go of his clammy hand and turned to Boss.

Follow us, Dave. We'll take you to your ship.

I was temporarily blinded again as I stepped into the warehouse. The first thing I saw was the sheer size of it. It was huge, gargantuan, incomprehensibly enormous. I felt like the entire thing would come crashing in on me in an instant. The next thing I saw was a shiny,

SCIENCE FICTION/FANTASY

cylindrical object very far away, in the center of the room. It glinted and shone, and hurt my eyes when the light hit it at certain angles. Without really noticing what I was doing, I stepped onto a small vehicle and was being propelled closer and closer to the round object. As we approached it, I began to see it looked like a giant can and was impossibly shiny. There was a small door cut away on the side, and a tiny plaque that, as we got closer, I saw bore the words "Outer Space Experimental Mission: Jackson." Jackson. David Jackson. Me. Like James Bond. This couldn't be my ship—could it? It looked nothing like my blueprints. Where were the side panels? The round windows? The pointed top, like they had in movies? Where was it all? I was going into space in a giant soup can. The Administration had warped my plans and I was mad. I felt it all bubble up inside of me, but I swallowed it, harder than containing a sneeze. The vehicle stopped. We all stepped off.

Okay, David. Time to start the necessary procedures. You'll be heading out shortly.

All this time, I hadn't heard the Administration men talk at all. That was Boss, and I looked at the taller man again. He wasn't looking at me. He was gazing at his reflection in the shiny surface of my ship, smoothing his hair out. Bastard. I had a thousand questions that all came out at once.

This is my spaceship? You mean I'm going on it now? There aren't any preparations? Why doesn't anything look like my blueprints? How does this work?

Boss looked at me calmly, and smiled without showing any teeth. The Administration men still didn't lay their eyes upon me.

Don't worry, Dave. Stay very calm. We've handled all of this.

Then one of the men opened the tiny door, and I felt fingers push me hard on my back as I was pushed into the tiny cylinder. My head struck the wall and the world was black.

My eyes opened. The first thing I thought of was Judith. Her fingernails, red, and her smile, also red. I thought of red things. Apples, rubies, blood. The next thing I comprehended was an awful pain in my head. My hand flew up to my forehead and I felt a large bump dwelling upon my skin. I then realized I was lying in an awkward position in a tiny round room, my backside pointing upward, my body in the shape of a triangle. In ten minutes I had deciphered my anatomical puzzle and was sitting cross-legged on the padded floor of the room I knew was my ship. I was facing a tiny screen embedded on the wall, flashing the words "Destination Reached" over and over again. I looked up and saw blue. A sky. A latch had been opened and the entire top of the ship had been flipped off. I was aware of a deafening roar coming from overhead. I was calm. Boss' words rang through my brain.

Stay very calm.

I was. Maybe it was the sight of the familiar blue expanse above me, or maybe I had acquired a concussion and was going mad. It didn't matter. I stared at the opening for a while, that round, empty thing and its roaring noise. I thought of circles and the shape that Judith's mouth makes when she says thing like "Oh, really" and "Oh, my goodness." A perfect, beautiful, red O. I think that was why I stepped out into the unknown so readily. At the time, I hadn't really been thinking of what I would find when I stepped out. But what I found was like no other sight I had laid eyes upon on Earth.

High school. 1981. Michigan Prep, science class, period 4. Teacher: Mrs. Scripp. Lab partner: Michael Fischer. Animal cell paper: due next Thursday. Microscope: silver. Bright, shining silver, shinier than I'd ever seen. My finger was placed on the stage; Michael was twisting the fine adjustment.

Okay, okay...almost got it...okay, stop, Mike. Oh, wow, man. That's incredible.

I peered through the lens, squinting my eyes, and marveled at what I saw. Every single dirt particle, every single pore was absolutely, perfectly clear to me, blown up to epic proportions. I had only a second of amazement, for Mrs. Scripp approached and smacked the back of my neck with her pointer.

Enough goofing around, boys. You'll break the microscope. Do you know how much those cost? It'll come out of our school budget, which is already small, and then we'll have to ask your parents to donate, and then...

And on she would go. But my mind was elsewhere, on my giant hair follicles, on my pink skin, exploded to a million times its actual size...

And I think that was the only way to describe the surface of the land I was on. Giant, black tree-like objects protruded from the pinkish surface and enormous craters dented the surface everywhere you looked. A mind-blowing force was pushing the hairs to one side, then to the other, and I clung on to one as each blow of wind plummeted onto the expanse of pores. Suddenly it stopped. I could see the beginning of a smooth ground near me. Fingernail. I run to it while the finger is still, dodging the elephantine craters and hairs. And then I see red. Shiny, glinting. Am I going mad? No, I already am mad. Mad for even wanting to go on this mission and ending up on a giant finger, which was probably just a hallucination anyway. Mad for trying to approach Judith's triangle heart, sharp from each three angles. But I saw red. I saw the red of Judith's nails, but it wasn't her nails. It was a giant apple. And there were more of them. Apple upon enormous apple, stacked on shelves larger than life. I felt the fingers tense as they gripped the apple. I craned my neck as I was lifted up with the apple, trying to see where I was. A supermarket. I saw huge carrots and tin cans. Tin cans. My ship.

But this wasn't just any supermarket. I recognized it somehow. It was blown to staggering heights, but yes, I'd seen it before. I looked about. The name was on the tip of my tongue. I could barely tell we were moving toward the cash register—everything was so huge that I caught nothing but vague glimpses of color here and there, and the occasional image. Everything else was just a total blur. I could smell the apple from my perch on the fingernail. It was incredible. Stronger than I had ever smelled before. It was placed on a dark, moving surface that smelled of rubber and corn. The conveyor belt. The hand was lifted and the apple was placed gently on the belt. Suddenly I was plunged into a soft, dark, hole. A pocket. My face brushed against something smooth and papery. I was lifted out again, feeling the nauseating tension of a clenched hand yet again. All the sensations were incredible, as if they too, like the objects in this new world, were extended to a thousand times their actual sizes. I saw a glint of black and gold lettering and the letters T...O...M. Tom? Yes. This was Tom, from the supermarket! What was he doing here? I heard a deafening, grumbling noise that resembled talking but was too loud to even be possible to distinguish words. I heard giant's laughter that made my brain rattle. Where was I? I didn't have time to look at his face, for I was whisked off again into a swirl of color, then dunked back into the stifling pocket again, along with the apple and the sound of giant, rattling spare change. I process the sensation of walking, and the huge crunch of rubble under enormous feet. This went on for about five minutes—the rattling, the heat of the cloth enclosure, the smell of apples and lint. I was pulled out of the pocket yet again, and before I was plunged into the scarce hair of my giant human habitat, I caught a glimpse of another red object. No, a person. Red, curvy, enclosed in a tight dress. Yellow top. Judith? But I didn't have time to look again, for I was thrown into a hairy abyss, smelling of shampoo and flecked with giant dandruff bits. As I was taken out into the intense sunlight and shoved back into the stagnant pocket yet again, I saw that the red lady was not there.

Home. I saw the flashing image of a cracked brown leather couch. Identical to mine. I felt beads of sweat from my confusion pooling on my brow. Again I felt the hand tense and take hold of the apple, gripping it firmly. Lifted up again, I was brought to a pair of colossal lips topped with a mustache of epic proportions. It was desperately in need of trimming. Out of habit, I felt my own facial hair. I'd have to trim that as well when I got home. If I got home. I heard a thundering crunch and realized it was the apple being crushed between a pair of yellowing teeth the size of skyscrapers. Massive drops of juice fell onto my head. I smelled the mind-blowing stench of morning breath whose heat and intensity knocked me to my feet. And before long there was nothing but a core, being tossed into a chasm of rotting banana peels, Chinese takeout containers and chicken bones. The hallways and rooms flashed before my watering eyes, undistinguished, until we stopped at a door.

A bathroom door.
My
bathroom
door.
Where was I?

Doorknob: gold. Dulled in some places form constant turning. I had to get mine replaced for the same reason. Smudged with fingerprints and slightly greasy from the oil of hands. I am aware of tears streaming down my cheeks and dripping off. Why? The hand is placed on the knob and it turns. I turn with it. My sink: light blue and chipped about the rim. There was my ever-shrinking bar of soap; there was my shaving razor. And there were my antique mustache-trimming scissors. One of a kind. I travel with the hand to pick them up. I feel their rubbed-down edges and their familiar weight as the hand lifts them. I'm sobbing now. I knew where I was but nothing made sense to me. The hand lifted itself up to the lips yet again, and I threw myself to the floor in madness and desperation. As I feel the first contraction of finger muscles, I look up for a split second at the vast face reflected in the glass before me.

Myself.

Wicy Wang, 16
Hunter College High School
New York, NY
Teacher: Lori D'Amico

Wicy Wang lives in New York City. Although she writes fantasy, her inspiration has always been the world around her; she believes that fantasy changes the world we know and forces us to pay more attention to what we take for granted.

GRANDPA'S KITE
Science Fiction/Fantasy

I.

The flames were not only licking the joss paper but eating it, swallowing it alive. They left almost nothing behind except for tiny glowing ash sprinkles that, buoyed by the heat, floated up to brush by my eyelashes; they clutched at the sky until either I couldn't see them anymore or they were snuffed out by gravity and the night air.

When all the joss paper had evaporated, I put on my coat again—I had taken it off in the heat of the bonfire—and drove home alone. The streetlights and headlights behind me blurred into neon rivers.

I must tell the story chronologically, because that's the way Dee always wanted it told. In our family, whatever Dee says goes.

It was snowing out the first time I flew the New Year's kites. I was five. Grandpa had stayed up all night in his room, perfecting the last touches on our dragonfly kite. In autumn I had held the thin bamboo rods in place as he began work on the frame, but the rest of the kite he insisted on making on his own; sometimes he was so busy he only half-listened as I recited my addition problems to him.

Grandpa had a ferocious concentration I could never break; for one thing, he was too busy using fabric glue to stretch embroidered silk taut over the frame to notice that I imagined eight plus nine to equal one. There was more work after that: He used his favorite calligraphy brush—once my father's—to paint large mournful-looking eyes on the head of the kite and tied red ribbons to the dragonfly's tail.

When New Year's Eve finally arrived, I excitedly tore open the package that contained my new coat and pranced about before the kitchen mirror. Grandpa, in one of his reveries, shoved coals on the fire to warm up water for my bath while patting me on the head absentmindedly. After I had been properly divested of various layers of grime, Grandpa helped me into the coat, and then gave me the honors of fetching the kite; I straightened with pride.

It was dark out by now. Grandpa fished around in the ever-growing junk pile that was our backroom and extracted two large paraffin candles. They were for lighting the path of my parents' souls, he told me, so they could find their way home.

He placed them both in the front window as I watched curiously. The smoke of the twin flames seemed to spiral into recognizable shapes—perhaps that smoke cloud was the mother who always tried to smooth down my hair when we left the house, perhaps that smoke cloud was the father who encouraged me to climb trees and fences, not imagining the many times I would limp home, screeching and clutching at my knee.

But back to the kite: It was time for takeoff. Grandpa and I set off, slowly progressing through the winding roads of the village, although Grandpa was limping along as fast as he could (even then he was getting along in years). The path to the riverbank was well-known to me, since the river was decidedly off limits, which meant that it was the hotspot for all of us five-year-olds to play.

When we turned past the last clump of houses and emerged onto the broad sweep of the riverbank, however, the tableau frightened me instead. The night tide was intruding onto the banks of the river, and a chilly wind blew through my newly washed hair. I huddled down in my coat.

At a word from Grandpa, I held the kite carefully at arm's length, my arm trembling from the effort. I know how to fly a kite, I thought to myself, as I looked at Grandpa for reassurance. But he was gazing intently at the kite. He reached inside his coat and took out a small scroll from an inner pocket, which he tied onto one of the red ribbons dangling from the kite. Now his kite was perfect.

"Time to let your wishes fly, kiddie," he said, looking down at me with a half-smile. I nodded solemnly back and took a few steps as

I unwound the spool. With the kite half-buoyed by the wind, I broke into a run. The string tautened and the kite streamed behind me, tethered only by a string—behind me, then up, then across the river in the direction of the wind.

My knees buckled, and I slowed to a stop. Grandpa caught up with me, and realizing that I didn't have my mittens on, took over the spool himself. "Away," he murmured. Then he turned abruptly, threw me a stern look and said, "Hands in pockets, now!"

As I diligently stuffed balled fists into my coat, Grandpa took out a pocketknife and cut the cord.

The kite string fluttered off at once. I watched Grandpa watching his kite rising and blending into the indigo-black sky. For once, I couldn't gauge his expression. To gain his attention, I asked, "Can you see the mist around our kite?"

"What mist?"

"It's like our kite is being kept afloat by smoke," I explained, trying to point out the hazy halo around the kite. Grandpa didn't reply. He didn't even turn to look at me—he stood as still as the trees lining the riverbank. The moment hung suspended and framed. For that small eternity I was consumed by the fear that Grandpa had left me, and that our world of two had dwindled to one.

When the kite had disappeared from view, we turned back and trudged back home. I'm sure both of us remembered then—but desperately tried to forget—the name of the opposite shore, the kite graveyard.

II.

My hair is littered with pink confetti; I shove my way through the crowds on Main Street, 10 p.m. The stores are brightly lit, and people are shouting and jostling with no regard for either their safety or mine. A perfect New Year's Eve.

The paper box that contains my daughter's favorite strawberry cake miraculously escapes compression by the mob. I give it one last perfunctory glance as I step into the elevator—yes, the icing is unscathed. The elevator doors close, and I rise silently through the stories. But I don't seem to be alone.

As I look at my image in the burnished mirror that is the elevator door, the air behind me turns into mist, contorts and settles into the face of Grandpa. Grandpa smiles. "I'm thinking of you, too," I say aloud, and he nods before sinking back into the floor of the elevator.

When the apartment door is opened, the cake is immediately wrested away to the kitchen, where it will keep the roast beef company until both are escorted to the sacrificial table. Relieved of my duties, I plop myself down on the sofa and yawn. Dee sits down next to me. She's tall for her age, nine years old, and unbelievably bossy to boot. I have to say she reminds me of my younger self.

"Tell me a story," she commands. I lean back and cross my arms behind my head.

"Aren't you too old for this?"

Dee ignores this. "Tell me…you and your grandfather," she says. "How about…you tell me the story about the kite?"

I've told her many times that it's not so much a story as the description of a tradition. What I don't tell her as often is that the tradition died long ago in the past. I reminisce about my grandfather, how he tried to resurrect the traditions and customs of his youth, when Dee brings me back to the present. "Yeah, yeah, I know it's a tradition," Dee is saying. "Speaking of traditions, Nara's parents used to burn money on New Year's Eve." She plucks at her newly acquired friendship bracelet. "Money! How can they possibly be so rich?"

I raise my eyebrow. "It's probably paper money," I tell her, reaching behind her for today's newspaper. I prop my feet up on the ottoman. "Run along and look at the cake. Didn't you want it really badly?"

She leaps right up from the sofa, although my plan to read the newspaper in peace is ruined when dinner is announced. We gather around the table, just Dee and her mother and me. Dee, ever the romantic, fetches candles and a lighter; I light each candle with a thin upside-down teardrop; and each flame flickers like a sprite darting above the shined wood surface. Dee moves to sit down, but her arm brushes against a candle. The flame of the candle tilts over; I am watching it, and in the brief moment before it is snuffed by the quick action of Dee's mother and a kitchen towel, I see smiling faces emerge in the fire to wish me a happy new year.

III.

I revel in the feeling of being the driver, laugh at the wheel, the dashboard, the adjustable seat, the rearview mirror before me. "Hop on!" I grandly declaim.

My only passenger, my grandfather, slowly hoists himself into the backseat, and I berate myself for forgetting his old age. But only mentally, of course; talking to myself would only have confused my hard-of-hearing grandfather more.

We take off. It's a blustery afternoon under an unnaturally calm gray sky that belies the bone-grating cold. The ancient chassis crankily creaks out the first few miles, but as we hit the highway the engine comes to life and we sprint down the road. The sky darkens to a leaden sort of gray. After what seem like hundreds of twists and turns on rocky village roads, we pull up in front of a pair of wrought-iron gates that guard our destination: the cemetery where my parents are buried.

It's a depressing place to be, particularly for an elderly man like my grandfather. And I have no idea why he chose this place for our New Year's Eve bonfire. Not many people like to see evidence of the old superstitions and customs in the city, where we live now, but of all the lonely places to build a bonfire, the cemetery is the dreariest. And gloomiest.

But if there's anything my grandfather's taught me, it's that family trumps all. The cemetery holds my parents' ashes, and my grandfather is, well, my grandfather. I get out of the car and sneak a glance at him still sitting in the backseat, but he just nods at me. So I take out the lighter I've stashed in the glove compartment and build up a small fire with the joss paper on the rock-hard winter soil in front of the cemetery, a dozen or so yards away from the car. When the blaze is sufficiently strong, I add more things to the bonfire: old, frayed leftover ribbons. An old coat I had outgrown. My father's favorite calligraphy brush, that my grandfather treasured over the years.

I add a photo of my childhood home, which we left behind.

A photo of my parents, whose graves we've left behind.

A photo of my long-deceased grandmother, whom I've never met.

Just as I am about to light the incense sticks that officially start the ceremony, however, my grandfather manages to totter over and seize my arm. "The fire isn't strong enough," he frets. I blink. "The smoke is almost eye level."

"No, no, no, they aren't happy, they can't find us," says my grandfather. He puts his hand to the crown of his head, but as he is bald, he plucks a few strands of my hair instead. I am quite shocked into obligingly yielding three hairs, which he tosses onto the bonfire. "Do you see your grandson now?" he asks almost cheerily.

"I'm your grandson," I say, and then it dawns on me that my grandfather isn't speaking to me. "Who are you talking to?" I ask sharply. My grandfather has been behaving strangely all day. Was it Alzheimer's or just plain old age muddling his memory?

"Them." He valiantly tries to bend his knees, but after seven or eight unsuccessful attempts, simply continues gripping my arm. "Now you see them, too."

My grandfather points a trembling finger at the molten photographs of my parents and grandmother. The three people who in this world only he remembers. Although the heat has distorted the photos, their faces seem visible in the flames. The smoke of the fire rises in human-sized columns to form their bodies, so that the fire is encircled by three figures.

Grandpa takes a step forward, and then two, as if to embrace the smoke figures. Perhaps it is the light thrown by the fire, and perhaps it is a deliriousness induced by the heat, but with each step he takes, my grandfather morphs into the younger grandfather of my childhood. He seems half-afraid but half-eager, his eyes fixed on that hazy in-between place of the fire. One step at a time, he lurches toward the images in the smoke, smiles at their welcoming smiles.

"No!" I shout, and yank Grandpa back. For an unexplainable moment I am jealous of the flames, jealous of how easily they have taken over Grandpa's affections. The columns of smoke wobble, look affronted and pull back slightly.

"What are you thinking about—it's dangerous to go so near a flame," I attempt to explain. "Go sit—sit down, inside the car, or something, you don't feel well." I start determinedly in the opposite direction, convinced that my imagination has outrun my reason at last, but Grandpa doesn't respond to my tugging. Instead he gently lets go of my arm.

Tendrils of smoke reach out and take hold of my Grandpa's other hand, and never have I been so angry at a fire. The smoke smiles and holds up a small silk scroll, tied with a red ribbon, inscribed with my Grandpa's wishes. It could have been his will.

Then the smoke curls around Grandpa's torso, legs and feet, and he disappears into the smoke.

I drive home, alone, and the streetlights and headlights behind me blur into clusters of neon stars. Somewhere along the way they coalesce into a half-forgotten picture—a dragonfly kite, silhouetted against a night sky.

Brian Geiger, 17
Manasquan High School
Manasquan, NJ
Teacher: Harry Harvey

Brian Geiger is from Brielle, New Jersey. He is influenced by Joel Stein and Richard Russo, and he admires Shakespeare's symbolism. After he finishes a piece of writing, he puts it on the shelf for a few months (both physically and mentally), then revisits and edits it after he has had time to think it over.

PSYCH 101
Dramatic Script

INT. CLASSROOM—DAY
Bright overhead lights shine on a typical college classroom, where the professor ambles in and the students talk among themselves. Balls of paper populate the floor.
DR. RICHARDSON, a seventy-year-old college professor, clears his throat and adjusts his bifocals. The class settles down.

DR. RICHARDSON
Class, I have your finals graded and in my desk. I will post the grades online tonight. A word of caution: Pop whatever pain killers you've got on you now…the grades are horrendous.

Dr. Richardson smiles and a few of the students in the front row laugh.

DR. RICHARDSON (CONT.)
On a different note, there are a few of you that I would like to see after class. Mr. Barnes.

JOSH BARNES sits at his desk reading from a book. He looks up at hearing his name.

DR. RICHARDSON (CONT.)
Ms. Zhou.

SALLY ZHOU *vigorously pounds away at her keyboard. Upon hearing her name, she looks up in bewilderment.*

DR. RICHARDSON (CONT.)
Mr. Mook…uh…O…Pad…Mr. M.

AHMED MUKOPADHYAY *(sitting next to Josh) idly doodles in his notebook; his full name is written at the top of the page. He scowls when Dr. Richardson speaks.*

DR. RICHARDSON (CONT.)
And Ms. Bolton.

SOPHIA BOLTON *is texting a friend, with her phone obscured by her book. She performs a double take when her name is called. Sally sits in front of her.*

DR. RICHARDSON (CONT.)
Alright now. Why don't we begin—

There is a knock at the door, which reveals a student looking through the door's window. This is JEFFREY. He rattles the handle, as if to show that it is locked. Dr. Richardson stares at the student. The student stares back. A boisterous student in the classroom, ZACH, calls out.

ZACH
'Sup, Jeffrey!

At hearing this, Jeffrey looks away from Richardson and squints into the classroom. He locates Zach. Dr. Richardson strides to the door.

JEFFREY
(muffled) Hey, man, what's—

Dr. Richardson harshly yanks down the blinds, cutting off Jeffrey's sentence. Richardson turns to his class.

DR. RICHARDSON
And that is why you never come late to class. Now, without further interruption, let us begin. If you will be so kind as to open to page 348.

The class flips open their books.

DR. RICHARDSON
Now, what did we think of last night's reading?

In the back of the room, Ahmed is furtively talking to Josh, who reads a book. In the background, Dr. Richardson begins questioning the students.

AHMED
(whispering) What does he want to see us for?

Josh does not respond. Ahmed turns away, then back.

AHMED
(whispering) You don't think he knows, do you?

Josh shakes his head without looking up.

AHMED
What if he does? Then what?

Josh pauses from reading and looks up.

JOSH
We just have to wait him out till five. Then there won't be anything he can do.

AHMED
And what if he already knows?

JOSH
He doesn't.

AHMED
How can you be so sure?

DR. RICHARDSON
Mr. Barnes? Mr. M? You have thoughts on the subject?

Ahmed and Josh look up to find the entire class turned around, watching them. Dr. Richardson looks expectantly from his podium in the front of class. Josh returns to reading his book, leaving Ahmed alone under Richardson's gaze. After a scowl at Josh, Ahmed faces his professor.

AHMED
Thoughts, sir? On what, exactly?

DR. RICHARDSON
You should be paying attention. Absolute truth—does it exist?

AHMED
Good question.

DR. RICHARDSON
Well, I can't claim complete credit...

AHMED
If I did not believe in its existence, I could argue that my "paying attention" to class is inconsequential.

DR. RICHARDSON
Really?

AHMED
If I did not observe the conversation, it did not, as far as I'm concerned, exist. Relative to myself, the only discussion in this class was between me and Joshua here beside me.

DR. RICHARDSON
Fair point, Mr. M. Mr. Barnes, where do you stand on this topic?

Josh looks up from his book and strokes his chin.

JOSH
I'm inclined to agree with Ahmed. If the only events which take place are relative to myself, than perhaps nothing aside from what I personally experience is in existence.

DR. RICHARDSON
And if a topic from our discussion appears on a test, is it existence then?

AHMED
Yes, albeit for the first time.

Ahmed stands up in excitement, pounding the desk as he talks.

AHMED
(shouting) Perhaps, sir, as I stand before you, nothing outside of the scope of my senses is in existence! Everything unseen, unheard, untouched, uh…untasted and…

Ahmed pauses.

JOSH
(whispering) Unsmelled?

AHMED
And unsmelled has no place in MY time or space!

The class stares in silence. Dr. Richardson gives a hearty laugh.

DR. RICHARDSON
That's quite enough. Please sit down, Mr. M. You should consider coming to one of my improv classes.

Ahmed sits down. Josh looks at him with a sly grin.

AHMED
I appreciate that, sir.

Richardson nods.

DR. RICHARDSON
It seems as if we have a grasp of the basic concept. Please turn and read from pages 349 to 356, and keep the volume down. I have a few papers to finish before the grades get sealed in…

Dr. Richardson backs away from his podium and sits at his desk. The students sullenly flip to the new page. Josh returns to reading from his book, and Ahmed sits with his head down.

Sophia leans forward to Sally, who is still typing on her computer. Sally glances back at Sophia, then resumes typing.

SOPHIA
Did you hear what he said?

SALLY
Yes…it does not mean anything.

SOPHIA
What do you mean "it does not mean anything"? He's onto us.

SALLY
No, he is not. I have been very…careful.

SOPHIA
You do realize that if I don't get credit for this class, I might not be allowed to graduate? Do you really think I'm going to let that happen? Do you really think that I want to come back and waste another year here? I mean—are you even listening to me?

SALLY
Yes…what? Yes, I was listening.

SOPHIA
Ya know, I'm the one paying—

SALLY
Listen, I would never have done it if he could have figured it out.

A beat.

SOPHIA
What are you working on, anyway?

Sophia leans forward to look at the text on Sally's screen.

SALLY
Chemistry paper.

SOPHIA
I thought you took chem last year?

SALLY
I did…it's Zach's.

Sophia glances at Zach, who idly tosses crumpled-up pieces of paper at the garbage, missing nearly all of his shots. Sophia looks over to where Josh and Ahmed sit; Josh reads as Ahmed continues drawing.

SOPHIA
What does Richardson want with them?

SALLY
Beats me.

SOPHIA
Well…I didn't see either of them hand in one paper this entire semester.

SALLY
Do you think they are failing?

Sophia shrugs. Dr. Richardson is standing before his podium, and coughs to get everyone's attention. Sally and Sophia sigh and face him.

DR. RICHARDSON
So…what did we think of Dr. Strassman's experiment? Fascinating, no?

We see the clock above Richardson's head transitions from 2:35 to 4:00. Dr. Richardson looks at the clock and claps his hands together.

DR. RICHARDSON
Well, it looks as if we're all done. I'd like to congratulate everyone on a fabulous semester. You truly are an excellent group of students…

The students all look very bored. Most of them take out cell phones, and many walk out as Dr. Richardson speaks.

DR. RICHARDSON (CONT.)
(voice raised) A group whose unending dedication and insightful questions and comments both greatly aided in the learning process and helped me to grow as a professor and part-time therapist.

By now, all except the four students who were asked to stay after are in the classroom. Dr. Richardson strides to the open door, following the last of the students.

DR. RICHARDSON
(yelling) And don't forget to sign up for Psych 102! It will be available in the spring!

Dr. Richardson walks to his desk, plops into his chair and lets out a long sigh. He then notices the four students—Sally and Sophia sit in the front of the room, and Ahmed and Josh in the back.

DR. RICHARDSON
Oh! Right, gather round now.

Richardson gestures for the four to gather near his desk, and they obey. Ahmed shoots Josh a stealthy look as they walk up.

All four stand in front of Richardson's desk, where he sits. Slowly, Dr. Richardson removes his bifocals, showing his advancing age.

DR. RICHARDSON
Now, I suppose you know why you are all here?

Each of the four students looks nervous.

AHMED
No, sir. No idea.

Dr. Richardson stares at Ahmed; Ahmed stares back and then looks off to the side.

DR. RICHARDSON
How about you, Josh?

Josh shrugs.

DR. RICHARDSON
Sophia?

SOPHIA
No clue. We're not failing, are we?

DR. RICHARDSON
Far from it...far from it...

Dr. Richardson briefly picks up a sealed padded envelope from his desk, shows it to the four, and puts it down.

DR. RICHARDSON
Do you know what's in here?

A beat.

AHMED
Missile coordinates codes?

DR. RICHARDSON
No, nothing quite so spectacular. You see—

Dr. Richardson breaks into raucous coughs and then clears his throat.

DR. RICHARDSON
Excuse me, I haven't been feeling so wonderful today. Where was I?

AHMED
Missiles?

Dr. Richardson looks at Ahmed in confusion.

SALLY
You were just explaining why we are here.

DR. RICHARDSON
Right you are, Ms. Zhou. Well, it seems as if, for quite some time now—

Josh and Ahmed exchange glances.

DR. RICHARDSON (CONT.)
—you four have held the highest grades in the class.

A beat.

SOPHIA
Great.

DR. RICHARDSON
Well…this would be great. The only problem with this is that—

DRAMATIC SCRIPT

Dr. Richardson begins violently coughing again. When he stops, it is evident that he is sweating. He stands up and removes his jacket.

DR. RICHARDSON
(to himself) It is hot in here…

JOSH
I'll open a window.

AHMED
You were saying, sir?

DR. RICHARDSON
No, that's quite alright, Josh. I just need a quick drink. I'll be back in a moment…

Dr. Richardson staggers out of the room and into the hallway. When the door closes, the students, who had been perfectly still, become animated.

AHMED
"The only problem with this is that—"…what's that?

SOPHIA
I've got no idea…

JOSH
I don't see what the issue could be.

SALLY
I am unsure as well…

A beat.

AHMED
Well, congratulations anyway—highest grades in class…not too shabby.

SOPHIA
Hey—hard work has gotta pay off sometime, right?

Sally gives Sophia a sideways look.

SALLY
Quite true.

JOSH
Definitely.

SOPHIA
The only thing, how did you guys, without handing in a paper—
(Sophia's voice trails off.)

AHMED
Yeah?

SOPHIA
Ah, never mind.

AHMED
No, go ahead.

SOPHIA
No, really, forget it. It's just—

The door creaks open, and Dr. Richardson staggers in.

DR. RICHARDSON
I think I'm going to be heading home.

Dr. Richardson walks toward his desk.

SALLY
But sir? You had to talk to us?

Dr. Richardson thrusts some papers and the envelope into his satchel.

DR. RICHARDSON
Some other time, Ms. Zhou.

Dr. Richardson hoists his bag onto his shoulder. He coughs again. As he moves toward the door, he swoons and grabs hold of a desk.

JOSH
Sir?

DR. RICHARDSON
Just…a bit woozy, that's all…

Richardson stands up, staggers a few steps and finally collapses. He lies spread-eagle on the floor. The four students stare at their fallen professor for a long moment.

SOPHIA
What just happened?

The four students take a few steps toward Richardson's body, peering down.

AHMED
Is he dead?

SALLY
I think he just fainted.

JOSH
Evidently.

SOPHIA
Weird…

The four gaze at Richardson; no one moves.

JOSH
Should I go get help?

AHMED
Huh. Is that the etiquette for incapacitated teachers?

Sally turns around and looks at the clock; it reads 4:20.

SALLY
Uh…how about we see what we can do first?

Ahmed's eyes move from Richardson to the clock. His eyes linger on the time.

AHMED
Yeah…maybe he just needs some air?

The students look down at Richardson (who has not moved an inch) and then back up at each other.

SALLY
Let me check his pulse.

Sally bends down and places her fingers on his neck.

SALLY
He is breathing fine, and his heartbeat is normal.

SOPHIA
That's good…right?

SALLY
Yes…I think this is just general cerebral hypoxia.

AHMED
Right…exactly what I thought.

Sally looks at Ahmed quizzically, and Ahmed shakes his head.

SALLY
Fainting. If we elevate his legs, blood should return to his head.

Josh pulls up a chair, and he and Ahmed put Richardson's legs up on it.

JOSH
Now what? Is he going to be okay?

SALLY
Yes…

A beat.

SALLY
As long as this doesn't lead to heart or brain trauma. Which it could…

AHMED
But that's not likely.

SALLY
Well…

AHMED
I mean, he's a pretty young guy!

SALLY
He is going on seventy! It is possible—

SOPHIA
Hey! The envelope!

Sophia is picking the envelope up off the ground, a short distance from Richardson's satchel—it had fallen out when Richardson toppled. Sophia begins opening it.

SALLY
What are you doing?

Sophia pauses mid-tear, turning to Sally.

SOPHIA
(innocently) Just taking a peek.

AHMED
Here, let me see it too.

Sophia brings the envelope over to Richardson's desk and puts it down. Ahmed follows her over. Josh, standing near Sally, glances down at Dr. Richardson's body.

JOSH
Should we be opening it?

AHMED
He was going to show it to us later anyway…should be okay…

Sophia breaks open the seal and pours the documents onto the table. Sophia and Ahmed pick them up silently. Josh and Sally look at them.

JOSH
What is it?

SALLY
Sophia?

Ahmed turns around, his face pale.

AHMED
I knew it !

Ahmed strides to Josh and thrusts a paper into his hands.

JOSH
What's this supposed to be?

AHMED
Read it!

Josh looks over the document. His confusion turns to shock.

JOSH
"I have been monitoring students for some time…appears they have electronically altered their grades…request for a full inquiry to be made." Do you know what this means?

Ahmed's head drops to his hands.

AHMED
I told you! I knew he knew!

Josh puts down the paper.

JOSH
This is bad.

Sally and Sophia are looking at a piece of paper near Dr. Richardson's desk.

SOPHIA
He knew this whole time! How?

SALLY
Well… This paper says your "drastic improvement was nothing short of a miracle" until he noticed that…

Sally glances up with a sheepish grin, and continues.

SALLY (CONT.)
…both of our papers were being sent in at the same exact time.

Sophia gives an "I told you so" look. Ahmed and Josh look up at Sophia and Sally.

AHMED
You guys too?

SOPHIA
Yup—what'd he get you for?

AHMED
"Electronically altering grades." You?

SOPHIA
I've been paying to have my papers written.

AHMED
Sally?

SALLY
I have been paid to write papers.

AHMED
Well…it seems like we've got ourselves a Mexican standoff.

A *beat.*

SOPHIA
What?

AHMED
He's got something incriminating on the two of us and we…

JOSH
Yeah. This isn't a Mexican standoff. We've got nothing.

SALLY
Except a lifeless professor.

Sally and Sophia walk to where Ahmed and Josh stand. The four look down at Richardson; a bit of drool is forming at the edge of his mouth.

Ahmed nudges Richardson's feet off the chair. They hit the floor with a lifeless thud. Ahmed shrugs.

AHMED
That's for the many failed attempts at my name. I mean, really—how hard is it to pronounce Mukopadhyay?

Silence.

JOSH
Well, we can get help later, we just have to wait till—

SALLY
Five. After that, the grades are sealed in, unable to be altered.

AHMED
Unless he's willing to go through a ton of paperwork—

SOPHIA
And we all know he's too lazy for that.

The four stare down at Richardson.

AHMED
We've just got…

Ahmed looks at the clock, which reads 4:40.

AHMED
Twenty minutes, and we're free.

The four stand in awkward silence. Josh grabs a chair and sits down. A long moment passes.

SOPHIA
So…how'd you guys do it?

JOSH
What? Change our grades?

SOPHIA
Yeah.

AHMED
Well…it's pretty simple when you're a computer science major…

SOPHIA
Right.

AHMED
…although even easier when your professor has a tendency to write all of his passwords down on a post-it note.

Ahmed nods his head to a brightly colored post-it note sitting squarely in the middle of Richardson's desk.

AHMED
The real question is…

Ahmed spins to Sally.

AHMED (CONT.)
Why are you writing papers? The academic intrigue? Fame? Glory?

Sally laughs.

SALLY
Not quite. The work-study program hardly covers living expenses, and writing papers pays very well.

AHMED
And why were you having papers written for you?

SOPHIA
If I failed this class—and I knew I was going to after about two weeks—I wasn't gonna be allowed to graduate. Honestly, psychology really isn't my thing.

The four resume their silence, and Ahmed whistles. Sally stares down at Richardson.

SALLY
Do you think he will be okay?

AHMED
Well...we've only got fifteen minutes. Then—

There is a sudden, shaking sound; someone is attempting to open the door. The four students stare, bewildered.

AHMED
(whispering) How'd we forget to lock the door?!

The door swings open, and Jeffrey (the student who missed class) strides into the class. He walks to Richardson's desk, oblivious to the four students, who continue staring.

JEFFREY
(to himself) Where'd the old dude go?

Jeffrey turns around and sees Ahmed, Josh, Sally and Sophia staring at him. Richardson's body lies at their feet although is obscured from Jeffrey's view by several desks. Jeffrey does not seem surprised by their presence.

JEFFREY
'Sup, bros.

AHMED
Hey.

SOPHIA
Hi, Jeffrey.

SALLY
Hello.

JOSH
Uh…what's up?

JEFFREY
You don't know where Richardson's at, do you? Gotta get some papers from him…

AHMED
Um…I'm not sure…

Jeffrey jumps up on Richardson's desk, sitting.

JEFFREY
So what'd you guys think of the course?

Sally, Sophia, Ahmed and Josh look at each other.

JEFFREY
I thought it was pretty mind-opening…self-perception theory, cognitive dissonance, all that.

SOPHIA
Er, yeah…definitely.

JEFFREY
I'm signed up for Psych 102. How about you?

The four students are looking down, and quickly look up in the silence.

AHMED
Um—

JEFFREY
Is something wrong? You guys look like you're…like you're bugging out.

SOPHIA
No, we're all fine, really.

Jeffrey eyes her skeptically.

JEFFREY
Are you sure?

SALLY
Yes, we are just here to say goodbye to Dr. Richardson.

SOPHIA
He said he won't be back for a while, though.

JEFFREY
Why are you guys still waiting?

JOSH
We've got some time to spare.

Jeffrey eyes Josh suspiciously, then shrugs.

JEFFREY
I guess that's cool, if that's what you're into. I'm gonna get going…

Jeffrey hops off the desk and begins walking to the door. Ahmed looks at Josh in relief, and Sophia mock-wipes sweat from her forehead.

JEFFREY
Yeah, just one thing—can you tell him I stopped by?

AHMED
(hastily) Sure, no problem.

Jeffrey digs around in his pocket for a moment, takes out a wrinkled piece of paper and begins walking toward the group.

JEFFREY
And could you give him this—

AHMED
Just leave it on the desk!

Jeffrey continues walking toward them.

JEFFREY
Dude, what's up with you? Just take it for me—

SALLY
Leave it there!

JEFFREY
What are you guys—

Jeffrey stops. He has reached the point where he can see Richardson's lifeless body on the ground. His face turns ashen pale.

JEFFREY
Is...is that Richardson?

JOSH
Uh...

Jeffrey looks at each of the four. Sophia takes a step forward.

AHMED
It's not what you think.

SOPHIA
Jeffrey? He just faint—

JEFFREY
Don't step closer! I see what's going on here!

AHMED
No, you don't!

Jeffrey looks wildly from one member of the group to the other. He begins backing away.

JEFFREY
I had you all pegged for a cult the moment I saw you.

SALLY
No, he just fell—

JEFFREY
A man is dead now! Don't you understand this? I'm going to call the police…stay here!

Jeffrey turns and runs out the door. Ahmed looks at Josh and runs out after Jeffrey.

AHMED
Wait!

Sophia and Josh follow. Sally begins to run, looks back, sees the files on the desk, grabs them and then runs out, slamming the door. The door shuts, leaving just Dr. Richardson lying in the center of the room.

A moment passes and Richardson sticks his head up, then back down. Another moment and Richardson stands up, brushes himself off, walks over to his desk and sits down. He picks up a pen and begins to write notes. The telephone rings, and Richardson picks up.

OFFICER (O.S.)
Professor Richardson?

RICHARDSON
Yes?

OFFICER (O.S.)
You're alive, right?

RICHARDSON
Quite so. Why do you ask?

OFFICER (O.S.)
I've got some kid here screaming that he saw you lying dead on the ground, and I got four others saying that you're fine.

Richardson laughs.

RICHARDSON
Oh, no, good heavens. I suppose my improv classes have paid off!

Richardson leans back in his chair, smiling to himself.

RICHARDSON
I was conducting a psychology experiment with some students of mine. Tell them all not to worry themselves over it further.

OFFICER (O.S.)
Alright, professor. Sorry to bother you.

RICHARDSON
Not at all. And officer?

OFFICER (O.S.)
Yes, professor?

RICHARDSON
Tell the students that, relative to myself, nothing happened at all.

A pause.

OFFICER (O.S.)
I'll tell them that.

Richardson hangs up the phone and continues writing. Above his desk, the clock reads 5:00.

FADE OUT

THE END

Rachel Calnek-Sugin, 14
Hunter College High School
New York, NY
Teacher: Daniel Mozes

Rachel Calnek-Sugin lives in New York City, where she is inspired by the array of strangers she sees every day. She writes plays in the hopes that people will find their own truth in her words.

BUBBLY
Dramatic Script

FAYE is standing in the kitchen, doing a rather dramatic reading from a book to her mother, ELLA, who is standing at the stove. There is an open laptop on the table, and it is a rather generic kitchen.

FAYE

It was a morning in late February, and the rain was falling in silver sheets, hitting the ground with that sad rhythm usually reserved for incoming funeral parties. I was wearing Callie's boots, and she, walking next to me, was mumbling on with her rather incoherent morning mumble about ruining the leather. I rolled my eyes, and now I wish I hadn't—now I wish there were a lot of things I hadn't done, but wishes often catch up with you only after it's too late. Bickering away, we crossed the street—or rather, I crossed the street—Callie wasn't so lucky. A scraping of gears, a flash of light, a bang, then a scream. Mine was mingled with hers—but mine lasted much longer. The rest of the traffic came to a halt as I stopped in the middle of the street, rain mixed with salty tears—all falling on her, on Callie, turning her blood pale pink. All I wanted was to lie down next to her and disappear, so I did—I sat down, closed my eyes and gripped her cold hands with mine. Soon, they were stained with blood, just like my conscience—my sister was gone, and it was impossible to speak, or—

ELLA
Darling—

FAYE
Or think, or even stand up again!

ELLA
Faye, honey, I don't want to hear about it.

FAYE
Mom, she goes to Yale now.

ELLA
She's dead.

FAYE
Well, that Callie girl is. But her sister went to Yale—because of that essay. Because her life is actually interesting.

ELLA
Well, lucky girl she is.

FAYE
Yeah, seriously. I bet it was like junior year, and she was all "man, gonna go sit down and write an essay now," and there was absolutely no question in her mind that she was gonna write about that, and then all the Yale people were crying and completely excited to admit her, and—

ELLA
So you want to get in because they pity you?

FAYE
I honestly don't really care. Once you're in, you're in. Do you

want me to go, like, work with you at Walls and Company?

ELLA
Don't be fresh with me, Faye.

FAYE
We could do mother-daughter telemarketing deals. Have you
ever actually sold something that way?

ELLA
Honestly, there was this one time when—

FAYE
Yeah, telemarketers don't actually sell things. They're supposed
to get yelled at, hung up on and then come home with a wad of
cash for doing absolutely nothing. And I'd like to do something
more than absolutely nothing with my life, thanks. I want to go
to Yale, get a job, find a husband, have kids, be successful—

ELLA
And I believe in you, honey.

FAYE
Maybe you're not getting the fact that your beliefs are getting
me nowhere. What, call up the Yale office—"Hi, this is Ella
Denowitz from Walls and Company, I'd like to offer you a wall,
and my daughter, Faye. I really believe in her."

ELLA
Well, what do you want me to do about it, write it for you?

FAYE
No, that would probably be complete crap. Have you ever been able
to sit down long enough to write a paragraph, so much as an essay?

ELLA
I—

FAYE
No, the longest thing that you've ever written was probably a survey at the doctor's office. Took you hours, I'm sure—you'd need a hell of a lot of little check marks.

ELLA
Faye, I'm sorry, I—I know that you can do better than that.

FAYE
Maybe I can't, Mom. Maybe because I was brought up here, by you—because most people's mothers are their role models. Because I grew up in a tortured environment, a tortured environment that isn't quite tortured enough to write an essay about.

ELLA
I don't know what to say. I don't know how to change things.

FAYE
Yeah, that's the problem, you never know. I have to do all the knowing around here, and when there's finally something that I can't figure out, you just sit there and make—what, liver or something? Smells terrible.

ELLA
It's not like I can help you if you don't tell me what you want from me.

FAYE
Well, Johnny, I want my liver back.

ELLA
I—it's chicken.

FAYE
Chicken, just like the rest of America. Yet something else
to distinguish me. Maybe I should just sit down and write
an essay about chicken. Maybe the Yale people would think I
had a mental disorder, take pity on me and admit me, not that
mental disorders have helped people make it—in the past.

ELLA
You are an amazing girl and you're gonna do great things—
whatever it takes.

FAYE
Well, fuck, Mom, means a ton.

ELLA
Watch your tongue, Faye.

FAYE
Fuck.

*ELLA turns off the stove, sighing, popping a pill into her mouth from
a bottle on the counter and downing it with a gulp of water.*

ELLA
I love you, okay? No matter what.

*Faye picks up the book again, flipping through the pages and resuming
her dramatic reading. Somewhere at the beginning of her monologue
Ella exits.*

FAYE

I was hiding behind the wall, eye peeking through a chink when they saw me standing there. There were three of them, and they were each about four times my size, they could have killed me with their hands alone. They taunted me, and I shrunk down, trying to fade away, but it was impossible; I was still solid as I ever had been. They walked towards me, to the point at which I was in full view, and when I closed my eyes, crossed my fingers and pinched my shoulder, I was still awake. The man on the left pulled out a gun. The others sneered as he pushed back the trigger, as if in slow—

Faye is cut off by a loud bang, a gunshot from upstairs. Faye is frozen on the stage. She looks at the book, then back toward the sound, panicked. She speaks as if determined to deny the existence of the gunshot.

FAYE

—motion and I saw the blood before I felt it— *(She replaces the book on the table.)* Hallucinations. I can see why he went to Harvard. Seems as if you're there. Hallucinations. They're probably genetic. I—Mom? MOM? Keys in the lock.

Enter ALLEN, Faye's father, kissing Faye on the cheek as he enters.

ALLEN

Hi, honey. How was your day?

FAYE

Fine.

ALLEN

Fine? Have you reformed into a girl who gives non-obnoxious answers to the questions that she's asked—and if so, should I commend myself on the raising of you, or is something up?

FAYE
I'm fine.

ALLEN
Well, you're not, but I won't press it—where's your mom?

FAYE
Upstairs.

ALLEN
You sure you're okay?

FAYE
Yeah.

He walks toward the door and turns around at the last second.

ALLEN
Nothing you want to talk about?

FAYE
I thought you weren't pressing it.

Exit Allen. Faye sinks down into a chair. You can hear Allen's voice— very soft—from offstage.

ALLEN
Ella—Ella? God no, Ella!

Lights come down and then up. Faye, Allen and a police officer— QUINTON—are in the kitchen.

QUINTON
Do you want me to…sugarcoat it?

Faye and Allen make no acknowledgment of his existence.

QUINTON
Well, uh, she—she's dead. Ella Denowitz, uh—7:04, only a few moments after—

FAYE
No.

QUINTON
I'm, uh, I'm actually pretty sure that—that, yeah—but if you have different stuff—I'm new here, maybe you can tell I hope not—that would be…unprofessional…

FAYE
She's not dead.

QUINTON
I really, uh, I think she is—that's what they told me, I didn't discover it—I'm only telling you what the paramedics told me. I'm just like a messenger, you know, I'm not making this stuff up—if you want me to call them again, I can—

ALLEN
I just…don't understand.

QUINTON
Well, I see you and me are in the same mind here. I don't know about your daughter—if we were thinking the same thing, then the worm certainly would have turned. But yeah, I'm—I'm a police officer. I'm supposed to be finding out what we don't know, but honestly if my wife had just been shot I wouldn't want some scary police officer to come over and interrogate me. Not that I have a wife, but if I did ever get

married then I wouldn't…you know…do you mind? I really don't want to intrude.

ALLEN
No, we—we want to know what happened.

FAYE
We? You maybe. I don't want to know what happened. I don't care what happened.

ALLEN
You—don't mean that.

FAYE
No, no, now you stop trying to put words into my mouth! You and Mom, you're always trying to tell me what I feel, who I am, what I'll be, but I am 17. I can figure that out myself.

Faye picks up the book again and sticks her nose in it, determinedly ignoring both Allen and Quinton.

ALLEN
I'm sorry, officer.

QUINTON
Wow, I was so surprised at being called officer that I had to look over my shoulder before realizing that you were talking to me. You can just call me Quinton. So, uh, Mr. Denowitz—where were you at 7:05—I mean 7:04—tonight?

ALLEN
A few blocks away, driving home from work—do you think it was murder?

QUINTON

Honestly, we think it was suicide. Or they do. Once again I'm just relaying the message.

ALLEN

But she—she wouldn't have killed herself. She couldn't have. I don't—is there a note or…anything?

QUINTON

There wasn't anything, that we, uh, that we know of. We can look more. She was bipolar, though, wasn't she?

Quinton leafs through the papers that he is holding.

ALLEN

She was there—she was almost there. She, fuck, she went to therapy every week. She took her medication. She stopped having hallucinations—or at least she stopped sharing them. She was—almost—okay.

He buries his face in his hands, crying.

QUINTON

Yeah, though, I guess it could have been murder—wouldn't want to think about anyone killing themselves—it could be some ax murderer coming up behind her and—actually no, definitely not an ax murderer, there was a gun, I saw that with my own eyes. Don't look at me like that, I'm not trying to make you feel bad. I told you, we think it's suicide, questioning you is just…just common procedure—I don't think either of you—

Faye looks up, speaking for the first time.

FAYE
You're wrong, then.

QUINTON
What?

FAYE
I did it. I—I killed her.

QUINTON
Oh, very funny—I didn't know that people made jokes like that at times such as these, but then I guess I don't really know much about times such as these, uh, as I mentioned, I am new here and—

ALLEN
Would you just shut up for a minute? My daughter just said that—you're just—what kind of police officer are you?

QUINTON
I told you—it's my first day—I just… *(to Faye)* You say you killed your mother?

FAYE
Yes.

QUINTON
And then you came downstairs?

FAYE
Yes.

QUINTON
So just to be clear, you—uh, you shot the gun, and then you left it there, with her?

FAYE
I—no.

QUINTON
You didn't shoot the gun?

FAYE
As good as. I'm guilty, officer—I—she shot it. Because of me.
My fault. Take me off now, please?

ALLEN
Faye, what the hell?

FAYE
(*choked-up, slightly crazy edge to voice*) Take me to jail—death
penalty, I don't give a fuck, just take me to somewhere where I
don't have to think about this.

QUINTON
I can't just put an innocent girl in jail, Ms. Denowitz.

FAYE
I told you, I'm not innocent! I killed her—I admitted it before,
and I'm admitting it again!

QUINTON
People, er, people often blame themselves for the death of
loved ones—

FAYE
Stop trying to go all school psychologist on me. Honestly, I
don't give a fuck what you have to say, and I'm also not scared
of the fact that you have a badge and you could do shit to me.
I want you to do shit to me. I'm a murderer. A lunatic. I don't

even know what I am anymore.

QUINTON
Well, this has obviously been—very traumatic—I'll just—

FAYE
Leave me here to figure it out? Send me on one of those journeys to, like, find my animal spirit?

QUINTON
I, uh, no—but I should leave you and your father to talk about this—I need to be back at the station—soon...now...I don't know—I'll come back this week, periodically, I mean, you can call me—whenever you need me, here I am, Mr. Reliable Police Officer.

Faye glares at both Quinton and at Allen, sits down, picks up the book and holds it up, hiding her face.

ALLEN
(dismissive) Thank you.

Quinton exits.

ALLEN
Is that it, Faye? Getting into Yale? Is that all that you care about?

FAYE
No.

ALLEN
Then will you put that stupid book down and look at me?

FAYE
No.

ALLEN
Oh, is that all you can say now, no?

FAYE
No.

ALLEN
God, Faye, I thought that you cared. I thought that deep down inside there was somebody who actually wanted to do some good for the world.

FAYE
Yeah, not now, but maybe someday. Maybe when the world wants to do some good for me, then I'll return the favor.

ALLEN
If you just sit around and wait for things to happen, you know they never will.

FAYE
Well, what's the use in trying, then? Mom went through years of therapy! She tried! We tried! We put up with that shit—you chose to, I had to. And look where it's got her now. I don't know where, Dad, but I hope she's happier there.

ALLEN
She didn't have to be there—she could have been here, but no—you had to go and, and push her buttons like that when you knew she wasn't okay.

FAYE
You know, anybody else, in any other family, could have said the things that I said and everything would have been fine, no consequences at all. Just because I wanted to be a normal teenager for a day—

ALLEN
Just because you wanted to be a selfish little kid for a day—

Faye starts to get choked up.

FAYE
Yeah, I did want that, actually.

ALLEN
And so you were forced to grow up—ironic, isn't it? You said it yourself, you're 17. If you don't want other people to make decisions for you, then you have to think before you speak.

FAY
(*quieter*) I don't want any life lessons right now, Dad.

ALLEN
When are you gonna get them, then? What better time than now? Don't you need to be philosophical—won't that help you get into Yale?

FAYE
Dad, I—

ALLEN
You what? Should we throw a party? Postpone the funeral? We could wait until you're done with your application—now you have something to write about.

FAYE

Dad, I don't want that anymore—don't you understand?

ALLEN

I don't, no. I don't fucking understand at all. I don't understand you, and I don't understand why we aren't sitting here, wearing black and talking about her. Isn't that what you're supposed to do when somebody—

He breaks off and there is silence for a moment.

FAYE

There's a fucking lot that you're supposed to do, and you shouldn't be asking me about it, because I obviously don't know. If I did, this whole—this—wouldn't have happened.

ALLEN

We—we can't blame anyone. Not me, and not her, and not—not you either. It was…inevitable.

FAYE

No, it was me. It was my fault. All my fucking fault.

ALLEN

She didn't like when you said fuck, you know.

FAYE

She didn't like a lot of the things that I did, and what good is it to stop now?

ALLEN

I can't do this, Faye. You—go, go make a life for yourself. If you want to forget, then fine, try all you like. I know I can't—but you have a hell of a lot of your life ahead of you, so go. Write the essay. You no longer have to write it about, what was your last idea—some bullshit summer program from when you were eleven. I, on the other hand, have to arrange a funeral.

Allen exits.

FAYE
Dad—Dad—don't…go.

Faye sits down at her computer and, after a moment, begins to type. After a moment, she gets up, looking impatient and frustrated, and walks over to the cabinet.

FAYE
She left them here—didn't she? She—God, fuck this—I don't even—oh? The oblong green ones not to be taken with the spherical white ones?

She swallows a few and closes her eyes, speaking quickly.

FAYE
There's gotta be something in here to medicate this, a pill to reverse time or something, with this many kinds, there should be a cure to, like, everything, God, that's good—I should probably just stop now but—SMTWTFS? I don't know what day of the week it is, I'll just take one from each—I should go do stuff now, no use sitting on the kitchen floor.

She sits back down at her computer and begins to furiously type.

FAYE
Wow, I—shit—nothing really matters anymore, does it? Going crazy now, aren't I, talking to myself, but you know what Mom always used to say, those lists that she made when she was high,

well, she was always high, but—what was it, yeah, the different levels of insanity—

Enter Ella.

ELLA
Talking to yourself, disagreeing with yourself, yelling at yourself and then giving yourself the silent treatment.

FAYE
Mom?

ELLA
Faye—it's me.

FAYE
Mom?

ELLA
Yes—we established, still me here.

FAYE
Mom—I, you're back, are you really here? Am I there? Where are you, Mom? Don't go.

ELLA
You're here, Faye—I'm not there, no, you only exist inside my head.

FAYE
Mom, can you—I am, God, I am so sorry. I didn't mean it, I swear, I didn't mean anything I said, I'm sorry, I wish I hadn't said anything—

ELLA

But wishes often catch up with you only after it's too late.

FAYE

That's—Mom—you listened to that? I'm sorry, all those things I said, I was just—no, honestly, there's no excuse, I was just stupid, a complete and total bitch, and you put up with it, I— Mom, Mom…

ELLA

Yes?

FAYE

Mom, I just want to say it, as many times as I can, Mom—and I want to be saying it to you, Mom, because who knows when—

ELLA

When I'll think about you again?

FAYE

That—yes, that…Mom. I was so stupid, I don't even know why I said that, why I did it—why I've always done it, I—I love you, I do, and I don't remember the last time I told you that. I love you. Can I leave you with that? Did you hear me—I love you, Mom, not just words, I don't say that just to say that, and I don't say that just to gain your forgiveness, either—you can't forgive me, I know, I wouldn't forgive me, hell, I don't forgive me.

ELLA

That's the difference between me and you, Faye. I'm a pushover, and I choose what to believe, and who to believe in—there's no use in holding a grudge, not now.

FAYE
Mom—

ELLA
I should go, your father's coming.

FAYE
Don't leave me, Mom.

ELLA
I'll be back.

FAYE
Mom—can I ask you a question? Is this—are you real?

ELLA
Real? If you want me to be.

Exit Ella. Enter Allen.

ALLEN
Friday—we're having the funeral on Friday, and then we're going out to the graveyard in Jersey to—to bury her…with her mother.

FAYE
Funeral arrangements, Yeah, good, you made them—I, yeah, do you need any help with them or something? Her favorite flowers were sunflowers, I could call the flower people—I mean, the florists, that's what it's called—

ALLEN
Faye, are you…alright?

FAYE

I'm alright. In fact, I'm more than alright, I'm great, why shouldn't I be great, I'm great— *(She pauses and bites her lip.)* No, God, what am I talking about? I'm not alright, I feel like, I don't know, I feel like shit—literally, like shit. Like poop or something.

ALLEN

Faye, what are you on?

FAYE

Oh, Valium, Anafranil, Seroquel, Luvox, Halcion, Suphedrine…

ALLEN

That was…incredibly stupid! What the hell were you thinking?!

FAYE

I wasn't, I think—fuck, I'm still not, and it's great. Really. Thinking sucks. But I feel, you know. I feel something. And I'd rather hurt than feel nothing at all. God, it's great—it's terrible you should try some.

Allen walks across the room and purposefully takes the remaining bottles of pills, tossing each and every one of them into the trash.

ALLEN

Faye, I don't—I don't want to be angry at you right now.

FAYE

Me either, you know, I don't think you should.

ALLEN

In fact, I don't want to be doing anything right now except sitting here with you, crying. It was yesterday, not even yesterday: There can't be a yesterday if you haven't slept since then.

FAYE

So we are, aren't we? We're sitting here—well, you're standing, feel free to join me on the floor—and we're crying, fuck, those are definitely tears…*(touches her cheeks)*…unless it's started raining in the kitchen, and I see some on your face too, Dad. As for the remembering, maybe you're not, but I know I am. It's all I can think about. I don't read minds, though, maybe you've got something else on yours.

ALLEN

Of course I'm thinking about her, but yes, I have something else on my mind, too—my daughter, my living daughter, has just swallowed a hell of a lot of prescription meds, and now I'm even more scared than I was before.

FAYE

Why should you be scared? You have one less person to be scared for now.

ALLEN

I would say I liked it better when you were sober, when you weren't quite so blunt—but I think you were.

FAYE

Well, I'm sorry that you don't like me. I'm sorry that you would have wanted a different daughter—fuck, I would have too. What are you asking me, though, to change?

ALLEN

No, I'm sorry, Faye—

FAYE

Don't be. I'm the one apologizing. I'm sorry, I'm sorry, I'm sorry.

ALLEN
Okay.

FAYE
Okay?

ALLEN
Okay.

Lights off, lights on. Allen is eating breakfast. Enter Faye.

ALLEN
Morning, Faye.

FAYE
Hi, Dad.

ALLEN
I got you that stuff you like—Honey Bunches of Oats, or whatever.

FAYE
Thanks.

She takes out a box of Cheerios and pours herself a bowl.

ALLEN
Those are Cheerios, hon, I got you the Honey whatsits—

FAYE
Thanks, I just—I don't like the pecan kind.

ALLEN
Oh—sorry, I, I didn't know.

FAYE
No, I know, it's—fine.

ALLEN
I like your shirt.

FAYE
It's just kind of…blue…but thanks.

ALLEN
You used to be such the fashionista—what happened there?

FAYE
Don't say fashionista, Dad—and you know what ha—nothing happened.

They go back to eating in silence for a few moments.

FAYE
That's a nice, er *(pauses for a moment),* tie.

ALLEN
Thanks.

FAYE
Very exuberant.

ALLEN
Yes, er, it's—happy, bright, jaunty—perhaps too bubbly—

FAYE
You can stop finding synonyms for exuberant now—we—I, too bubbly? No such thing. We need some more bubbliness in the world. All those men with the somber black outfits at work, you

should put up a sign that says "Bubbly Day" and everyone can wear their yellow ties and sing their interrogations and...and stuff.

There is an awkward pause.

ALLEN
I'm sure our firm would grow immensely in popularity.

FAYE
Right, well.

ALLEN
Right.

FAYE
I should go—I'll be late.

She gets up and puts her bowl in the sink. Allen kisses her on the cheek as she exits.

ALLEN
Have a good day, honey.

FAYE
You too, Dad.

Faye is in the kitchen. Allen enters, holding a pile of mail.

ALLEN
You got something.

Faye says nothing but sticks out her hand to take it.

ALLEN
From Yale.

FAYE
Oh. Oh, God.

ALLEN
Do you—

FAYE
I don't want to see it.

ALLEN
As you wish.

FAYE
What—I was just—give it to me!

She grabs the envelope from his hands.

FAYE
Shit.

ALLEN
What does it say?

FAYE
Generally people can't figure that out until they've actually opened the envelope.

She slides the letter out and reads it in silence.

ALLEN
Faye?

FAYE
…what?

ALLEN
Faye? What does it—

FAYE
Oh, look. They're, they're very regretful.

ALLEN
What?

FAYE
In fact, they regret to inform me that they could not accept me.
I'm sure it was a heart-wrenching experience on their part.

ALLEN
I—

FAYE
Furthermore, they went through careful consideration—seems
like a waste of time, if you ask me—careful consideration for a
girl who was obviously never going to amount to anything.

ALLEN
Faye, you're gonna go somewhere, don't talk like that. Yale
isn't the only school there is.

FAYE
Yeah, it is. It's the only school I want to go to.

ALLEN
You will do great things wherever you go—

FAYE

Precedent disagrees, and so do I. I'm not gonna do fucking anything, and we both know it.

ALLEN

You're 17, Faye, you've got your life ahead of you.

FAYE

Yeah, and so do you. So does everyone. And most people don't
make any mark whatsoever. Tell me this—how many people do
you remember?

ALLEN

I remember your mother—and maybe you don't—but she
believed in you too.

FAYE

Yeah, that's what she said. And I did, too—yeah, I wanted to
change the world, but instead I just, I don't know—I complained,
or something. Didn't try hard enough, I guess. Even if I did, I
don't know if I had the capability to go anywhere.

ALLEN

I remember, when you were a little girl, you used to tell me
that you had a dream—

FAYE

The problem with dreams is that you have to be sleeping.

ALLEN

No, you know, you promised me—

FAYE

And the problem with promises is that they're made to be broken.

ALLEN

No, listen to me, Faye. You didn't get into Yale, so what? There are worse things that have happened to you—and you haven't ever let them stopped you. One cliché permitted per lecture from your father: Every cloud has a silver lining.

FAYE

This was supposed to be the silver lining. Getting into Yale. It was supposed to be the silver lining to Mom—that essay—I thought, I just thought that it meant something—her...her... leaving. That was the cloud—so what the fuck is this?

ALLEN

It's not—it's not the end of the world.

FAYE

Only because the world doesn't revolve around me. 'Cause nobody gives a shit whether I succeed or not, except me, and all I can do is sit here and—and complain.

ALLEN

Faye, everybody's nobody at some point in their—

FAYE

In their life. I know. I know, Dad. It's not a condolence—telling me that I'm...that I'm just like everybody else.

ALLEN

Well, then I don't know what to say to you, Faye. I want to help you—I do.

FAYE

Like shit you do. I don't want your help, though, I don't—

ALLEN
We could take you to Dr. Livingston, Mom's doctor, you know—

She throws the envelope on the floor, closing her eyes.

FAYE
I don't want help from him, either. God, Dad, I don't want help at all. And if you haven't noticed, it obviously didn't help Mom very much in the long run.

ALLEN
Could you stop that, honestly—she's been gone now for a couple months, you—you're still talking about her like that?

FAYE
She's dead, Dad. Isn't it better to admit that, or would you rather be delusional—

ALLEN
I'm not the delusional one here.

FAYE
Well, it's better to be delusional and happy than not happy at all.

ALLEN
Are you happy? Tell me, are you?

FAYE
Do I look happy to you?

ALLEN
I don't know, you said you were happy, and I was kind of hoping to learn the secret to your success.

FAYE

Oh, well, fuck success. I obviously haven't figured it out.

There is a short pause. Allen straightens his tie, and Faye looks glumly at the floor

ALLEN

I have a work thing tonight—I should get going. You can order pizza or Chinese or whatever. I left you money.

FAYE

Thanks.

Allen exits. Faye picks up the phone.

FAYE

Hi, Quinton? This is Faye—Faye Denowitz. I was wondering if you could come over? *(There is a pause.)* I—oh, no, nothing happened—I just *(pause)*—thank you.

Faye sits down, takes a baguette from the counter and absentmindedly bites into it. Enter Quinton.

QUINTON

Hi—you, uh, you called?

FAYE

Yeah, thanks—thanks for coming.

QUINTON

Er, did something happen? Your mother's death—excuse me—was months ago.

FAYE
I know.

QUINTON
I'm sorry to put this so bluntly—but why am I here?

FAYE
Ah, you should be asking yourself that question, shouldn't you?
I mean, you are the one who came, aren't you?

QUINTON
I suppose so, uh, I just thought—you know, you were the first
case that I ever worked on...

*Faye inclines her head and, seeming to realize that she's holding an
entire loaf of bread, puts it down on the counter.*

FAYE
And I see you've grown much more—experienced...since then.
Many less *uh*s going on there.

QUINTON
(visibly confused) Uh, yes.

FAYE
(flustered) There it goes again. Can I—can I offer you a drink?

She gets up and opens the cabinet.

FAYE
Gin?

QUINTON
Er, Faye...

She doesn't wait for a response but pours two glasses, placing one in front of him.

QUINTON
I can't let you drink that, uh—I'm a police officer, Faye, and you're underage—

FAYE
I'm flattered. *(She takes a sip.)*

QUINTON
Uh, no, I actually—I actually know that you're, uh, that you're 17.

FAYE
Indeed. You're not that old either, though…I think.

QUINTON
I'm 30—but the fact remains that I am a 30-year-old police officer who can't just permit a 17-year-old to drink gin in front of me.

FAYE
Can't? I'm not drinking to get drunk—and if you tell me you didn't do this at 17, I sure as hell won't believe that.

He takes a reluctant sip and goes to sit next to her.

FAYE
So—tell me. Tell me about yourself.

QUINTON
Uh—about, about me?

FAYE
Yes, about you, Quinton.

QUINTON
Well, I'm, uh, I'm Quinton Lawrence. I'm 30.

FAYE
That I knew.

QUINTON
I'm, uh, I'm a police officer.

FAYE
That too.

QUINTON
I didn't want to be a police officer, though.

FAYE
No?

QUINTON
No.

FAYE
What, then?

QUINTON
A writer. I, uh, I always wanted to be a novelist. Thought I would be one, too. When I was a kid, I won all sorts of shit, and they all told me I had talent.

FAYE
Yeah, they do tend to say that.

He takes another gulp of gin, more enthusiastically this time.

QUINTON
Well, I, uh, I believed them—and I wrote a novel.

FAYE
That's amazing.

QUINTON
No, it was stupid. I was in college at the time, uh, junior year, it was.

FAYE
College? Where'd you go?

QUINTON
Williams.

FAYE
That's—*(looks pained)*—that's a good school.

QUINTON
Yeah. Where are you—do you know where you're going?

She doesn't respond, just takes a forced gulp of gin, misses her mouth and spills it on her shirt. There's an awkward silence for a minute.

FAYE
So the novel?

QUINTON
I edited it, painstakingly. I, uh, I called it shitty—a sort of disclaimer to any who read it, but I was proud of it...for, uh—for a while. Then... *(He trails off.)*

FAYE
Then?

QUINTON
Then, uh, I realized it was shitty. It never got published, I graduated, and I went to work at, at Shop Rite, spent more than a year with a cheery smile—pretended to be exhilarated by Cottonelle toilet paper and Sombrero brand tortillas. Decided it would all be worth it when something—when something finally happened with my writing.

FAYE
And it didn't?

QUINTON
No, it didn't. I wrote another novel, nothing. It was like at first I thought that the inner editor had got to be worse than the real one—you know, the, uh, the voice inside your head that tells you what you're doing is crap, that you just stop right then and go do something better, like searching random movies on IMDb, or learning exactly how not to be awkward when directing your customers to the aisle with feminine products.

FAYE
So then you decided that you had to become a police officer?

QUINTON
I guess so. It was a—a perfectly respectable job. Something that would benefit other people. Some, uh, some money to make now, maybe some inspiration for the long run—

FAYE
Inspiration? For what? You still—

QUINTON
Write? Yes.

FAYE
But…why?

QUINTON
Write? Yes. Sometimes I wish I didn't. But I—I just can't seem to stop. It's such a twisted addiction—makes me feel terrible, and I hate it, but I don't know how not to do it. It's like I open my computer and it all comes pouring out and I have this, this delusional hope that putting it all down will make everything fall into place, but it just messes it up even more.

FAYE
So then—

QUINTON
But I know that that's preferable to those times when I don't write—and I'm left there, sitting so pathetically on my chair, staring at a blank page—it's the only thing I'm sure about.

FAYE
Quinton?

QUINTON
Yes?

FAYE
I'm sorry.

QUINTON
Don't be—I, uh, I should be saying that to you—you're the one—

FAYE
I get too many empty *I'm sorry*s.

QUINTON
I mean it, though—I am sorry—you going through all this and I come here and, uh, complain to you.

Faye leans forward and silences him with a kiss, which, after a moment, he pulls away from.

QUINTON
Oh, shit, Faye—I'm sorry—that, that is not okay.

FAYE
Shhh.

She moves in to kiss him again, but he moves away.

QUINTON
I, uh, I can't do this, Faye. You're just—upset.

FAYE
Upset? Is that your way of saying that I have problems? Because you could just say it right out, it's not like I really—like I really care.

QUINTON
Look—I, you're a kid—

FAYE
No, I'm not. I'm only 17, but I've gone through a hell of a lot more than most people have.

QUINTON
I know, I didn't mean to—

FAYE
You know? Do you know what it was like for me? Do you know what it's like to find your mother sitting on the bathroom floor—just sitting, no idea why she's there—to find her somewhere like that every day? To come home, have her call out—but not to you, just to her imaginary friend? To have to pretend that you thought that she was really talking to you because you didn't want to cry in front of her—didn't want to set that example, and even though she was the mother, you always had to be the example setter? Do you know what it's like to think that you may have been the one who killed your mother? Do you?

QUINTON
No, I—I don't.

FAYE
Well, lucky you.

QUINTON
When's your Dad coming home?

She shrugs but doesn't say anything.

QUINTON
Well, I, uh, I should be gone. And *(hesitates)* you should probably put away the gin.

Faye nods and Quinton exits. She puts the gin back in the cabinet and then picks up her rejection letter, then sits down at the table, burying her face in her hands. Enter Ella.

ELLA
Faye? Faye—it's me.

FAYE
Mom?

ELLA
Yeah.

FAYE
You're back.

ELLA
In a manner of speaking.

FAYE
What does that mean?

ELLA
I'm not sure, actually.

FAYE
What do you mean? I thought—you knew everything now.

ELLA
Everything? Far from it. Maybe someday, though.

Faye looks up.

FAYE
Someday?

ELLA
The difference, I think, is that I have...forever...to learn

everything. No limits of a lifetime.

FAYE
I miss you.

ELLA
Well, I'm here now, aren't I?

FAYE
In a manner of speaking.

Ella smiles, and after a moment, Faye speaks in a very small voice.

FAYE
What's it like?

ELLA
Dying? It's like waking up. Seeing things in color. Like looking back on your life and laughing, realizing it was just a very, very silly dream.

FAYE
Does it hurt?

ELLA
No. Or at least—not in comparison. Bliss to how you must feel now.

FAYE
But I don't, Mom—I don't feel now. I don't feel like me. I don't feel anything.

ELLA
I do. I feel…almost…bubbly.

FAYE
We need more bubbliness in this world.

ELLA
Which world?

FAYE
I don't know.

ELLA
You don't?

Faye is crying at this point.

FAYE
No, what am I talking about? I do—God, I know exactly, I know—I do, I know.

She stands up, throwing the Yale letter defiantly on the ground.

FAYE
I know, fuck—I know—why did it take me this long to realize that I knew?

Ella begins to exit.

FAYE
Mom—wait.

ELLA
Come with me.

Faye takes Ella's hand and is led off stage. A moment later, a gunshot. Lights off.

Isaac Stanley-Becker, 17
Georgetown Day School
Washington, DC
Teacher: John Burghardt

Isaac Stanley-Becker lives in Chicago, where he writes for his high school newspaper. He is interested in city politics as well as social justice and hopes to pursue a career in investigative journalism, using the written word to uncover issues of local and national prominence.

ANTI-GAY BULLYING AND THE DILEMMA OF A LGBT HIGH SCHOOL
Journalism

Five days a week, Taelor Dorsey takes a bus from her grandmother's home on Chicago's South Side to Harlan Community Academy High School on South Michigan Avenue. A bus ride to school—nothing unusual for most students.

Except Taelor's story is different. From the moment she steps on the bus until the last school bell rings at 2:55 p.m., she confronts bullying and hate speech. That's because Taelor came out as gay two years ago when she was 15.

"I was going to school one time and this guy from my school came up to me and said, 'Hey, you dyke,'" Taelor said. "He followed me all the way to the bus stop and onto the bus, spurting out insults. Every day after that it continued. I was afraid to report it because I didn't want my teachers to know I was gay."

At Taelor's high school, where 99 percent of the students are African-American, the motto is "educate, empower and encourage all students to reach their full potential." But Taelor describes discrimination, disempowerment and discouragement because she's a lesbian.

"I don't think I'm treated very fairly by students at my school. I don't have the chances everyone else seems to have. It's sort of like feeling isolated, like you are forgotten by your own peers. Because once they figured out that I was a lesbian, they said, 'Oh, well, that's the end of us doing anything with her.' Students across the city are facing this exact same kind of thing."

Stories like Taelor's led the Chicago Public Schools (CPS) to propose opening a gay-friendly high school in 2010, the Social Justice High School-Pride Campus. According to its website, the new school would "address the needs of the underserved population of lesbian, gay, bisexual, transgender (LGBT) and questioning youth and their allies."

Awareness of the abuse faced by gay youth is on the rise across the nation. According to a 2009 "National School Climate" study carried out by the Gay, Lesbian and Straight Education Network (GLSEN), nearly 90 percent of gay students, of over 7,000 surveyed, reported being harassed at school. A majority felt unsafe because of their sexual orientation. More than a third had been physically harassed. Last fall, the Associated Press reported a surge of teen suicides linked to anti-gay harassment.

A handful of states and the District of Columbia have enacted "safe school" laws protecting students from abuse based on sexual orientation. Congress has not yet adopted the Safe Schools Improvement Act, a federal bill specifically intended to prevent harassment of LGBT students that was introduced in 2007.

For students of color like Taelor Dorsey, the abuse is more acute. Anti-gay bullying disproportionately affects black and Hispanic youth, according to a 2005 GLSEN report, and is the most prevalent form of harassment in schools.

In planning a gay-friendly high school, the Chicago school system followed the lead of New York City, which established Harvey Milk High School in 2003, and Milwaukee, which founded Alliance, a charter middle and high school, in 2005. Neither excludes heterosexual students; their websites describe the schools' missions as creating a safe environment for all students regardless of sexuality, identity, appearance, ability or beliefs.

The proposal for Chicago's Social Justice High School-Pride Campus is the brainchild of administrators at the Little Village Lawndale campus—four linked Chicago public high schools dedicated to social justice, which were created after community activists staged a hunger strike in 2001 to demand a new high school. According to the Pride Campus' would-be principal Chad Weiden, currently assistant principal at Little Village's Social Justice High School, a design team of school officials from across the city, university education experts and representatives from the mayor's office drafted a plan calling for a school for gay youth.

"On the design team I worked closely with the current principal of Social Justice High School," Mr. Weiden explained by phone. "We wanted to extend the mission and vision of our current high school. We were intentionally including LGBT along with race and gender. It was an act of inclusion, not separating."

Gay-friendly but not exclusively for gay, bisexual and transgender students, the new high school would enroll 600 students and offer a college-preparatory curriculum with requirements in English, math, science, foreign language, physical education and the arts. Citing the absence of an Illinois state safe school law, GLSEN director Kevin Jennings supported the proposal, but stated that no school should be hostile to gay students. It's not "going to change overnight," Mr. Jenkins said over the phone. "In the meantime, these kids aren't going to graduate."

At an October 8 public hearing, Arne Duncan, then Chicago Public Schools CEO and now the U.S. secretary of education, endorsed the design team's proposal for the gay-friendly school. A week later, Mr. Duncan met privately with a group of 11 Chicago ministers, led by Rev. Wilfredo De Jesus, senior pastor of New Life Covenant Church in Humboldt Park. Mr. Duncan then arranged a meeting between the design team and Reverend De Jesus and other Chicago ministers, where the design team agreed to change the school's name to Solidarity High School while amending its mission statement to omit references to sexuality.

"We had a very positive meeting with the design team," Reverend De Jesus explained by phone. "We voiced our concerns about the CPS using taxpayers' money to create a school for minorities. If you're going to say it's really for everyone and not just LGBT students, well, then why call it Pride Campus? We already have schools like that. We wanted to make sure that no one thought we were homophobic."

A Chicago Board of Education vote set for October 22 was postponed to November, as controversy erupted over the gay-friendly public high school, attracting attention nationwide. The Eagle Forum, a national organization promoting conservative values, stated in its journal *Education Reporter* that Solidarity High School was "ghettoizing children based on identity politics." In Chicago, Mayor Richard M. Daley called the school a work of isolationism. The dispute intensified online, on District 299: The Chicago Schools Blog. Responding to statements that the school was not intended for gays only, a commenter in the blog wrote, "Do we really think that pandering to Homosexual extremists is the best use of our educational dime?"

Concerned about school segregation based on sexual orientation, advocates of gay rights also voiced opposition."Instead of enforcing the rights of students to attend the schools their address or scholarship entitles them to attend," a commenter wrote on District 299, "they should just be rounded up and put in a purposely created ghetto?"

In mid-November, the design team pulled the proposal for Solidarity High School rather than bring it to the Board of Education for a vote. The design team now hopes to present a new plan by 2011, after completing further research and holding public meetings, explained Chad Weiden, who participated in the decision to withdraw the proposal.

"We needed more time to reflect and get more community stakeholders involved," Mr. Weiden stated over the phone. "There were a lot of organizations and certain groups of people who wanted to see significant changes to the proposal. But there came a point where the proposal became something that was different from our original mission and vision for the school and what we wanted for the city. That's why we pulled it. The support was still there. But there were misinterpretations that this was a school only for LGBT students, which was not our purpose at all. The school was not meant to be a work of segregation.

"There were religious groups who were opposed to the project," Mr. Weiden said. "We need to do a better job of framing the idea for the school, where all students are supported and welcomed. The Human Rights City Ordinance needs to be included in the matter. We need to use the language of law to ensure that every single person in the city of Chicago deserves education regardless of race, gender or sexual orientation." But according to Reverend De Jesus, any future plan for a gay-friendly high school poses the problem of segregation.

"I think that segregating kids is never a healthy approach,"

Reverend De Jesus explained over the phone. "You don't solve the bigger problem, which is bullying and discrimination. Although people would say that the intent is not segregation, it certainly looks like it to me."

Equality Illinois, a LGBT civil-rights organization, has not weighed in on the gay high school, explained interim executive director Jim Madigan, a former attorney at Lambda Legal, who expressed personal support for the plan and said that it needs a broader base of political support.

"Equality Illinois does not have an official position on the school," Mr. Madigan explained over the phone, "mainly because the plan is being retooled and the design team has not yet come forward on that. We'll wait and see. I have been generally supportive of this school.

"However, not enough was done to secure a broad base of public and political support for it. The decision on whether or not this school is created will not be based on the quality of the curriculum or getting support mainly from gay and lesbian parts of the city. Those are not the type of people you need support from. It's going after the people in government, it's going after community leaders, it's going after the people who shape public opinion."

Addressing the question of segregation, Mr. Madigan said, "There are segments of the city of Chicago that will oppose anything that does any good for any gay people. What's more troubling is that people who were usually in support of gay rights were in opposition. It is the perception by the public that this is something like 'separate but equal.' And this is why a lot of people have not been supportive in the past, why they won't be supportive in the future. So a lot of work needs to be done in terms of explaining what the school is doing.

"There is this crazy mentality that somehow it does people good to be tormented. If students are being treated badly, they should be given an opportunity to go to school and feel secure."

Sources

Interviews: Taelor Dorsey, Kevin Jennings, Chad Weiden, Wilfredo De Jesus, Jim Madigan

Alliance School, http://allianceschoolnet.bbnow.org/index.php

Crary, David. "Suicide Surge: Schools Confront Anti-Gay Bullying," Associated Press, Oct. 9, 2010, http://news.yahoo.com/s/ap/20101009/ap_on_re_us/us_anti_gay_bullying

District 299: The Chicago Schools Blog, http://www.chicagonow. com blogs/district-299/

Eagle Forum, "Chicago Plans Gay High School," *Education Reporter*, Nov. 2008, http://www.eagleforum.org/educate/2008/nov08/gayhighschool.html

Harlan Community Academy, http://www.harlanfalcons.org/about mission.jsp

Harvey Milk High School, http://schools.nyc.gov/schoolportals/02 M586/default.htm

"2009 National School Climate Survey: Nearly 9 out of 10 LGBT Students Experience Harassment in School," http://www.glsen.org/cgi-bin/iowa/all/news/record/2624.html

Victoria Liang, 17
Lakota East High School
Liberty Township, OH
Teacher: Dean Hume

Victoria Liang is from Westchester, Ohio. She would like to thank her friends and colleagues Faiz Siddiq and Tyler Kieslich. She will attend Ohio State University, where, no matter what she chooses to do, she will continue to find beauty and power in words.

NO STRANGER TO THE ELEMENTS
Journalism

Steady hands, just take the wheel/And every glance is killing me/Time to make one last appeal/For the life I lead

Those words pulse out of a pair of earbuds and hold one boy in the art room in a trance while the rest of the students are flitting about sharing petty gossip. His hands reach for a white colored pencil and, delicately, he traces and retraces the same faint white line, a highlight on the edge of a table. His eyebrows are furrowed above his expressive chestnut eyes, his broad shoulders are hunched, and his glasses are slipping down his face while he gazes down at his ghost of a piece. To passersby, it is just an empty black slate with nothing but a few pencil lines meandering around. But East senior Gabriel Crawford is envisioning far more.

His trance is suddenly interrupted by the art teacher passing by.

"Gabriel," she instructs. "Don't outline the shapes. Go from the inside out."

His last twenty minutes of work were essentially a waste, but he does not complain. It does not matter how much effort he has to put in; he is doing what he loves. It is the best time of the day, a cathartic release of all the emotions he has kept bottled up in his 18 years while growing up in the slums with an absentee father or while handling a full course load of schoolwork while supporting his family. It is the fuel that keeps his ambitions burning in the worst of storms.

I was born by the river in a little tent/Oh and just like the river I've been runnin' ever since

In the 19th century, Price Hill was an idyllic hilltop suburb for upper-middle-class families looking for an escape from the cloud of pollution and noise hovering above Cincinnati. Fast-forward a century, and it's festered into a hell. A hell with more trash than trees, more foreclosure notices than street signs. From the confines of his unadorned gray duplex on McPherson Avenue, a street that has had 65 foreclosures since 1999, young Gabriel and his older sister Adedrion learn quickly that violence is the rule. There was the Christmas when they awoke to find their television, PlayStation and all their games stolen. There was the time when his mother Donneice returned home to find their car with a smashed windshield and blood spattered on the bumper.

In her sorrow, Donneice reminisces about how she came up with the name Gabriel. Her faith was waning and she called herself crazy, but before she even knew she was pregnant, she had dreamed that she would have a son named Gabriel. And he would grow up to become a leader.

Here, however, Donneice cannot fantasize for too long about her son's future when she has to worry about his present, sheltering him the best she can from the brutality that encloses them. It is yet another worry that plagues her mind and she is already worried her three tedious jobs are not enough to provide for her family, worried she is clocking too many hours to spend adequate time with her family, worried that not having a strong father figure will drive Gabriel to the streets as it has so many other boys in their neighborhood.

Then again, this decaying area is a place to be grateful for. At least now, while walking home through a torrent of insults about his Goodwill-purchased clothes, Gabriel knows he is going home.

Home. What a strange word for a first-grade boy who has lived as a nomad, traveling back and forth between relatives' homes and a homeless shelter. Now, he will not have to worry about lining up early to enter. He can rest his weary eyes instead of watching out for pickpockets.

To avoid trouble, the family knows to just keep to themselves. After Donneice cooks dinner for her children and rushes off to another grim graveyard shift, Adedrion becomes Gabriel's parental figure and best friend, because even though she is still a child herself, their father is too busy breaking promises.

"Come to my basketball game tonight," Gabriel begs. "Daddy, just this once."

Before heading out to the court, Gabriel looks for any sign of his father. Once again, he is not there. Glimpses of his father are rare, and when they do happen, Donneice tries to supervise the visit, completely aware of his father's poor influence.

"Bad communication corrupts good morals," she sighs.

"He has no respect for me, does he?" Gabriel asks himself every night even though he already knows the answer. He makes a vow.

"I will become the exact opposite of my father."

Back then, it was just childish anger. But it continues to grow into a mantra he embodies, a promise he keeps and a fuel that sustains him when a tide of responsibility threatens to crush him.

It's been a long, long time coming/But I know a change is gonna come.
Oh gravity, stay the hell away from me/And gravity has taken better men than me/Now how can that be?

Gabriel drifts through his next few years as a typical teenager with typical goals after his family moves to the Lakota Local School District, not yet faced with a real chance to prove himself a better man than his father.

This all changes in the midst of a gloomy storm. Two Mormon missionaries show up at the Crawfords' doorstep. After the death of her first daughter, Patanna, Donneice had lost her faith in God, quit attending church, detested holidays and even stopped snapping family pictures. The space where Patanna should have been always left her feeling empty. Still, she is impressed enough that these two teenage girls would trek through this weather that she invites them in and lets them speak.

Gradually, the missionaries' visits become more frequent as they start teaching the kids and neighbors about the Church of Latter-day Saints. Donneice is intrigued and begins attending their services.

They become an extended family, the men of the church treating Gabriel like a son. When Donneice's car breaks down, church members show up at the Crawfords' door promptly at 5 a.m. every morning for a week to take her to work and then drop off her children at daycare. But they also notice the toll working three jobs has been taking on her family and help her find one job that pays more. Then they help her go back to college full-time so her family can escape the slums forever. The church helps with some bills and some transportation, but there is a bigger hole to fill.

As a mere freshman, Gabriel begins dividing a 40-hour work week between Kings Island, a landscaping firm and Kroger to help support his family while his mom is going to school. During this period, his typical day begins at 5 a.m., when his mom wakes him up and practices Scripture with him. Then he goes to seminary and brings his school books with him, using every extra minute to study.

"Can anyone think of a Bible passage that relates to their life?" asks seminary teacher Laurie Hopkins.

There is a silence as other students avert their eyes, either too timid to respond or too apathetic to think of a response.

"'Not that I speak in respect of want: for I have learned, in whatsoever state I am, therewith to be content,'" calls out Gabriel. "Philippians 4:11."

Then it is straight to school at 7 a.m., followed by a four-to five-hour work shift at night. When he finally comes home, he helps his younger siblings and sometimes even his mother with homework before finally beginning on his own pile of honors-level work.

Yet he does not even allow himself a day of rest. Every other Sunday he travels with City Gospel Mission to the outskirts of Over-the-Rhine. In the shadow of the decadent Music Hall, a place where the upper class go to sip champagne while watching world-class musicians perform concertos and symphonies, lies Washington Park, which is also filled with people.

But it may as well be a cemetery. Usually, only the police pay any sort of attention to the hordes of homeless who huddle in the park, but like always, Gabriel is the exception to the rule.

To most, the homeless are just filthy beggars too lazy to work. But Gabriel sees them through an artist's eyes. He knows that behind every solemn face is a story. And he remembers his days of homelessness and how much a simple act of kindness can soothe a tired soul. With each meal he passes out, he also offers his sympathy.

"You know, I used to be a vet," one of the men recalls. "I kept trying new ideas until eventually I just ran out of money. And then to top it all off, my wife left me."

Even though Gabriel has faced his share of hardships, he listens intently to every person who is willing to share and offers his compassion with every meal he serves.

Maybe his grades are plummeting, maybe he is putting everyone's interests before his own, and maybe he is being forced to become more of a man than his father could ever hope to become. But he holds his head high and walks with a smile. After all, he knows he is becoming a hero to his family, his church and his friends.

Just keep me where the light is.

I've become what I can't be/Oh, do you see what I see?

"That Gabriel. Always knows how to make something out of nothing," his grandmother Mary James says.

Not nothing, but pretty close. What other people in his situation use as excuses, Gabriel uses as fuel for his passion.

As a toddler, Gabriel ignores his other toys and picks up a handful of bread ties ready to be thrown away. His grandma assumes he is just being a typical kid until he shows her a whole set of figurines, complete with capes and swords, and then puts them in the display of his aunt's shoe repair store to try to sell them.

From then on, whenever his grandmother comes to visit, he is always hunched over a drawing and asking for criticisms.

"It's gotta be perfect, Grandma," he always says. "I bottle things up and I gotta let it go somehow."

He recalls his latest heartbreak, a former girlfriend who cheated on him. Gabriel is no stranger to betrayal, but this is no ordinary, petty drama—she tries to resume the relationship while pregnant with another man's child.

But also thanks to his father, Gabriel knows that suffocating his problems with self-destructive behavior never solves anything. Instead, he channels them into his distinctive brand of art, marked by a boldness and vividness that are rivaled only by Gabriel himself. This time he wears his emotions across his heart with a T-shirt he

JOURNALISM

designed himself. Two cracked skulls stare out with empty, gaping sockets amid a bed of blooming roses.

"Love is pain," the skulls declare. "How can love be so kind and gentle and then turn around and be so cold?" they ask.

Maybe people will betray him, but art never will, not even in his most difficult times. Even while Gabriel's callused hands are worked to the bone during a dreary shift, they always have the energy to pick up a sketchbook during his brief breaks and channel an idea into a sophisticated work of art.

The inspiration does not have to come from his past. Sometimes it is an everyday object or a song lingering in his mind that will blossom into an idea for his next masterpiece. Sometimes he will even fuse his own style with someone else's idea, like when he designs tattoos for clients.

Gabriel's initiative, in addition to his classroom performance, persuades East art teacher Linda Augutis to give him the rare honor of skipping an entire level of art to take Advanced Placement (AP) Studio Art as a senior, therefore letting him graduate with a grand total of five AP classes in hopes of improving his college prospects.

He plans to make art his career, applying to University of Cincinnati's Design, Architecture, Art and Planning program, as well as Bowling Green State University and Brigham Young University-Idaho to pursue his dream of becoming a graphic designer or the creative director for an advertising firm.

Although his words are usually delivered in soft, measured cadences, when he talks about his future in art, passion tumbles out in unrestrained bursts. While painting, he becomes more than a quiet kid in the corner weighed down by worries. Every stroke captures another unshed tear, another unspoken worry, another unfair responsibility. This release fuels his evolving maturity. Against all odds, he even begins to forgive his father.

"Art is how I can turn something tragic into something beautiful," he says.

Jemma Leech, 13
Pershing Middle School
Houston, TX
Teacher: Julie Bennett

Jemma Leech is a British Texan at school in Houston. She is a poet first, a writer second and a lucky old soul third. She loves to read and write and to go on adventures. She will write until her last breath leaves her soul to fly free, and perhaps she will go on writing even after that.

"Read like a wolf eats," Gary Paulsen Tells Young Readers
Journalism

Gary Paulsen balances his cap on his head. Pulling the peak down over his clear blue eyes, he appears to be shielding them from the glare of public attention as much as from the bright lights of the Pershing auditorium. This man is the author of 200 books and the winner three times of the Newbery Honor, yet he looks more like a cross between Daniel Boone, Captain Ahab and Santa.

Best known for tales of wilderness survival and husky dogsled races, he writes from his own experiences. As a young boy in Minnesota, with a difficult home life, he took to the woods to trap game and to fish, just to get food to live. These skills form the basis of the Hatchet series in which a boy has to learn to survive in the wilderness after a plane crash.

Paulsen said, "I have done everything I wrote about in Hatchet—trapping, fishing, hunting, even two forced landings in planes. In the woods I was cool, I was the man."

He even offers tips to potential survivalists. "Beaver is the best meat of all—it tastes like beef but with 37 percent protein. Beef only has about 25 percent."

He completed two Iditarods, the gruelling 1,100-mile dogsled race across Alaska, and was devoted to one of his lead dogs, Cookie, in particular.

"Cookie was the best thing that ever happened to me; she saved my life several times. I have a picture of Cookie in my wallet, but not one of my wife. Go figure!"

Smiling at the memory, he recalls that it was during his time training and racing the dogs that he wrote his three Newbery Honor books, *Dogsong* (1985), *Hatchet* (1987) and *The Winter Room* (1989). So does he write from the back of the dogsled? Almost.

"I write all the time, wherever I am—on an airplane, in the kennels, on the boat, at my ranch. I carry my laptop with me all the time and when that's not practical, I write longhand on pads of paper. I'm a writer who runs dogs; I'm a writer who sails. I'm a writer—it's what I do, it's who I am."

Jack-of-all-trades in life and in writing, Paulsen writes books ranging from adventure stories like *Hatchet* to historical settings like his newest book, *Woods Runner,* set during America's war of independence. He also writes humor, with the follow-up to *Lawn Boy,* his tale of economic success in a twelve-year-old's lawn-mowing business, published this spring. So which does he prefer, humor or drama?

"Writing is about work and about love, whether it's humor or drama, and I don't find one easier than the other. Alternating them makes for a nice change of pace, but I never decide to write a funny or a serious book. I just start writing and it becomes what it is."

Paulsen is keen to pass on his own wild brand of advice to young writers, too. "Read like a wolf eats. Read everything you can get your hands on and write every single day. The discipline of reading and writing every day will be valuable."

So whether he is running his snow dogs, sailing the high seas or surviving in the wild woods, Gary Paulsen is first and foremost a writer. "I write because I love to write. I would write even if I didn't get published. I will die writing."

His legion of readers hopes that won't be for a very long time. Gary Paulsen gave his readers' talk in the Pershing auditorium as part of the literary organization Inprint's Cool Brains! series. For more information, visit www.inprinthouston.org/cool-brains-series.

Alexandra Warrick, 16
Hewitt School
New York, NY
Teacher: Maureen Burgess

Alexandra Warrick is from New York City and finds that Manhattan is a busy, beautiful borough about which stories can easily be spun. She uses writing as an outlet for her passion about works and causes that move her, and plans to continue exploring popular culture from various sociological perspectives.

HARD EYE CANDY: AN EXAMINATION OF THE TREATMENT OF WOMEN IN ACTION CINEMA
Persuasive Writing

You're strapped to a table inside a locked room, inside a locked grain silo, inside a locked warehouse, inside...another locked warehouse. The facility is surrounded by electrified fences, riddled with automatic turrets and crammed with guards, all of whom are armed to the teeth. The prime minister of Canada is being held hostage and only you can save him—but you've got just eight minutes before the bombs strapped to your legs go off.

Oh, and your only weapon is a broom handle.

Wait! Before you even think of cutting a single wire or picking a single lock, you might want to check your chromosomes. Are you a lady? If so, just lie back and try to relax—the hero will be here any minute now.

Why, you ask? Because, as action movie tropes and constructs frequently indicate, that's just the way it works. Although the days of damsels bound to train tracks are admittedly long since over, treatment of female characters in genres such as action, science fiction and fantasy has remained stubbornly regressive; due to these attitudes, female characters frequently remain writhing, ineffectual love interests and sidekicks. This treatment can change, but only if audiences are vocal about their dissatisfaction. However, are action movies' target audience members, whom studios primarily pander to, really dissatisfied at all?

I decided to interview three members of this target audience. These three interviewees are male and in the 17–24 age range. A large percentage of their disposable income is spent on entertainment and recreation. All three could adequately be described as "fanboys." That is, passionate fans of various elements of pop culture: They trawl popular Internet imageboard 4chan, attend conventions and argue over the merits of their favorite franchises. These three young men are, in short, all members of a demographic that is statistically more likely than any other to spend money on movies. These three ideal consumers, who will be referred to by number to assure anonymity, were first asked a single question: What traits do they feel are important or essential in a good action movie character?

"Action Hank!" One laughs. "Being like Action Hank from *Dexter's Laboratory*. He's all big and buff and and he punches people, and he's macho and he…no, he doesn't punch people, he shoots people…yeah, no, wait, he does punch people."

"Being Bruce Willis," enthuses Two, "in, like, every movie he's ever been in. Abs, pecs, musculature. Knowledge of guns—knows how to use any weapon, uh, can turn anything into a weapon. And he's intuitive…knows how to fight…just like, uh, cunning? Cunning. Yeah."

My third interviewee cut directly to the chase. "Well, it's got to be a guy, for one, because I'm a guy and I identify better with a male character because I'm a male. And I like it if he's funny and gritty. Like Will Smith…with a sniper rifle."

Their answers overlap: All three young men feel an ideal action protagonist is both strong and technically skilled. They also specify, some more directly than others, that the protagonist ought to be male. These preferences shift, however, when I ask the question again with the addition of a single key word: What traits do they feel are important or essential in a good female action movie character?

"Big [breasts]," immediately interjected One. "Really hot. And she basically falls in love with the main character no matter how nerdy or dumb the main character is. And she gives the main character hope that something good will happen"—here he pauses and laughs—"but it won't. It won't. Because he is nerdy and dumb." Three is, as always, blunt. "Obviously I like to see a pretty character—I mean, she doesn't have to be model gorgeous but not…repulsive. I'd say she has to be funny, too. She has to be able to get into cute banter with the other characters."

Two is hesitant before answering. "I'm not gonna say, like, sex appeal, even though that is necessary for females in an action movie…," he says, before trailing off into a quiet mumble in which the name Megan Fox is distinguishable. When pressed for non-physical traits, he continues: "a witty sense of humor…I like that. Good one-liners. She's got to be tantamount in wit to the guy character and she…she dresses nice…like, she has an incredible wardrobe. Oh, and ability to play with the main male protagonist, like, play on his level. Um, example: whoever Rachel McAdams played in *Sherlock Holmes*, because she manages to stay on Holmes' level, even though…" He trails off, but the implicit statement remains: even though she is a woman.

These three moviegoers, at whom action films are primarily and fiercely marketed, all share—with varying degrees of shame, but equal certainty—that what they want in a female action star isn't character development, depth or motivation. They don't even necessarily require genuine competence. In fact, the list of desirable character traits varies wildly as soon as gender is specified.

1. The female action character needs not be physically adroit; if she is, it should not make her physical appearance more "masculine."

2. The character may acceptably display intelligence, but this intelligence must manifest itself in ways that are attractive and/or unthreatening.

3. The character must always be attractive, regardless of whether her male costar is equally svelte or a schlubby, "relatable" everyman. Her sexuality is both her primary characteristic and weapon.

4. The character may function as a love interest, sidekick, supernatural advisor or reward. The character may sometimes serve as a protagonist, but they generally prefer their lead character to be male.

It would be presumptuous to pass off the opinions of these three boys as ones held universally by their peers. However, trends indicate that the attitudes of these young men are held by a large percentage of moviegoers. The message being sent to Hollywood is that action films' audiences wish to see certain gendered "rules" being adhered to; if these films make money, there appear to be no lucrative reasons to challenge these rules. In fact, these rules have often ended up greatly informing studios' output: Warner Bros. president of production Jeff Robinov, after a year in which two female-led films of which much was expected (Jodie Foster's *The Brave One* and Nicole Kidman's *The Invasion*) failed spectacularly at the box office, reportedly issued a moratorium on female-led films of any genre. "We are no longer doing movies with women in the lead," Robinov was quoted as saying; the studio's president reportedly outright refused to read any scripts with female lead characters. Although WB representatives have since denied these allegations and the studio has continued to produce films with female leads, the incident remains telling.

With these concerning stances in mind, can we realistically hope to see a successful, well-written, female-led action film or franchise? Is there potential for a fully developed female Bond or Bourne to capture the zeitgeist with the same staying power as her male counterparts? Why has the mobilization for better portrayals of women in action been so staggeringly unsuccessful? If examined, the current failure of this movement can be attributed to two primary obstacles: audience and characterization.

Action movies offer escapism to audiences. In order for escapism to function properly, a viewer must feel a certain link to the lead character, as the action is primarily experienced through his or her eyes. When the hero takes a punch, you flinch in sympathy; when he takes down a roomful of thugs, you tense in exhilaration. When he goes careening off the side of a building, your stomach drops; when he squeezes past the descending wall in the nick of time, you share his relief.

This identification is the key to an immersive cinema experience. When roughly half of an audience finds it impossible to connect with the protagonist of an action film on a base level, the delicate moments of relatable tension upon which action films hinge are entirely shot. This is the first obstacle in the way of female action characters: the fact that a sizable percentage of men claim they find it uncomfortable, if not impossible, to identify with a female protagonist.

I ask Three why he feels it is difficult to experiencing a narrative from a female point of view when female viewers are asked to experience countless narratives from male points of view. "It's not difficult, per se," he explains, "it's just that I've never seen [a female action narrative]. Ever. Like, not even once." After I mention Quentin Tarantino's *Kill Bill*, "Well, yeah," Three responds, "...but that's like a male perspective because she's killing everyone for revenge." When I bring up that the pursuit of revenge is universal and cannot be attributed to one gender, he asserts that seeing women actively pursuing vengeance doesn't feel natural to him. "I'm just not used to seeing a woman just, like, going in there, guns akimbo, you know?"

The detachment from women felt by male viewers like Three stems from a severe "othering" of the gender in which women's feelings and thought processes are perceived as inherently different. This manifests itself in different ways, such as Three's belief that women are more rational: "I think that, if a woman was the main character, she would have to be more cerebral. The movie would have to show some degree of her thought process...she'd have to be more intelligent than a male character. I just think of women being generally smarter than men." The belief that women are naturally the cleverer gender may appear complimentary, as do assertions that women are inherently calm, emotional or nurturing. However, each serves to make an entire gender seem to intrinsically share a different set of qualities and therefore appear alien. The portrayals of women that result from these misconceptions consequently become difficult to relate to for members of either sex.

This brings us to the second obstacle: the particularly insidious myth of the "strong female character." In light of criticism, Hollywood action writers have recently made greater efforts to strengthen their female characters. In these efforts, however, these writers have made a fatal misstep: By specifically attempting to create strong female characters from the outset, they have successfully dehumanized them through sloppy characterization. Not only have writers tended to strip women of weakness entirely, many slapped skills on them until they resembled "strong" characters and called it a day. Characterization is still treated as a weighing, rather than sliding, scale; rather than balancing out a character's strengths and flaws in a way that is dynamic, three-dimensional and ultimately compelling, many writers simply add more and more positive attributes until the character can no longer be accused of weakness. This may result in an arrestingly beautiful, impossibly agile nanophysicist acrobat expert marksman superspy, but the crux of the character becomes simply that she is a Girl Who Is Good at Things. Another concerning element of this method is the fact that some of these skills (being a crack shot, for instance, or a shrewd military strategist) are given to these female characters because they are considered "masculine" and therefore both atypical and strong. That is, a Girl Who Is Good at Boy Things. Not only does this tacitly promote a dichotomy between strength and masculinity, it also projects that certain useful, gender-neutral traits and skills inherently belong to men. Allowing a woman to competently use a weapon does not make her more "manly." It makes her capable.

However, this gendered delineation of what a woman does and does not do has ingrained itself in audiences, as demonstrated when I ask my three interviewees whether they feel that scenes depicting female characters using "male" skills are believable. They respond unanimously. "No. It's just used as a gimmick because it's unique, because you wouldn't expect it," he rationalizes. "But you wouldn't expect it because it wouldn't happen in real life." Two concurs. "No. I mean…these scenes are really not realistic."

"I think it's believable that a woman, if she tried hard enough, could beat a man into a bloody pulp," concedes Three. "But if she's doing it in heels, or if she's really, really, like, short and skinny…it's just…no, not believable at all. Megan Fox couldn't kick anyone's [posterior], ever."

This brings us to the motivation behind the creation of these "strong female characters." Many action writers may be sincerely trying to challenge gender roles; there are just as many, however, whose intent is less upright. When a character is given certain skills, is it to make her more well-rounded or simply more attractive? Are the leaps and kicks performed by a character meant to show off her skill or her body? Is her facility with a Bowie knife intended to be impressive or solely titillating? Writer Mlawski of popular culture website Overthinking It addresses this in her article "Why Strong Female Characters Are Bad for Women": "…even when [a female character is] being strong, she [is] always doing it in the sexiest way possible. She'd never, say, get a black eye or a broken nose in a fight.... All in all, the 'strength' of her character [was] just to make her a better prize for the hero at the end—and for the horny male audience throughout." A female character of this kind will evade criticism, Mlawski claims, because "she's perfect in every way so the male audience will want to [have sexual relations with] her and so the female audience won't be able to say, 'Tsk tsk, what a weak female character!' It's a win-win situation."

A female character's defining characteristic should not be the fact that she is a woman. A female character's primary weapon should not be the fact that she is a woman. The overall defining characteristic of a female character should not be the fact that she is a woman. Women—surprise, surprise—do not always nurture or provide guidance. They struggle, they outwit, they fight, they kill, and their motives are not only to attract men while doing so. The film industry's adherence to a stringent, outdated gender binary has allowed it to lose sight of the fact that women are human. After all, an action character, regardless of gender, is merely a human being who is placed in situations of incredible danger and must therefore act accordingly.

Speaking of incredible danger, you'd better attend to those bombs—after all, you have only six minutes left on the clock.

Lukas Hadtstein, 18
Governor's School for the Arts and Humanities
Greenville, SC
Teacher: Scott Gould

Lukas Hadtstein is from Isle of Palms, South Carolina, and will attend the Roosevelt Academy International Honors College in the small Dutch city of Middelburg. He thanks his instructors for teaching him that true humor derives from a sense of self-deprecation.

THE DO
Humor

In seventh grade, I stopped visiting the barber and grew my hair so long that it draped over my shoulders. Thick, tousled and feathered at the ends, my locks bounced as I walked. And when the wind blew by, they flailed in the air, pummeling against my forehead. Just envision Fabio's hair on the head of a fourteen-year-old and you'll get the gist.

I can't recall why I did it—this leave of absence from scissors and razors. Maybe I was fed up with bowl cuts. Maybe I wanted to fit in with the Folly Beach surfer scene: the dudes with luscious Simba-like manes cascading down their backs. Maybe I listened to waaaay too much of my father's Pink Floyd, Jefferson Airplane and Jimi Hendrix vinyl. Regardless, I never—not once—expected the dilemma that ensued from my do.

In all my eighteen years, I haven't attended a typical, all-American kind of school. I haven't seen one homecoming game, had my heart broken by a long-legged cheerleader, heard the ear-splitting chants of pep rally, taken a shop class or even been in possession of a single locker. In fact, the closest I've come into contact with these experiences is watching *Grease, Fast Times at Ridgemont High* and *Ferris Bueller's Day Off.*

So, looking back, I can only imagine what would have happened to my long-haired self at a "normal" school. Crew-cut, Nike-clad jocks whistling at me in the hallway. Teachers deeming me "Lucy" instead of Lukas. Goth girls, with bribes of menthol cigarettes, attempting to recruit me to their numbers. Three or four Cool Kids, their faces veiled behind matching Wayfarer sunglasses, seizing me (midstream) from the urinal, bellowing, "This is where you belong!" before shoving me into the girls' restroom. In the spring, a geeky guy touching me on the shoulder, wanting me to be his prom date. Then, dropping his Game Boy after I've turned around and he's seen my face.

School of the Arts, where I went during middle school and the first two years of high school, acknowledged the dirty blond—almost golden—mop on my head in a less shallow, less conceited way. The school, really just a collection of arbitrarily situated trailers, was, after all, the Woodstock of all junior highs. Both my literature teacher and physical science teacher were former Deadheads. My social studies teacher had lived in Hawaii for twenty years, where he chased twenty-foot waves on the north shore. Any given time of the day in the school yard, you could hear the strumming of acoustic guitars accompanied by wailing vocals. After lunch, a sweet, musty smell clouded the bathroom stalls. When they weren't kicking a Hacky Sack, eighth graders got high by suffocating each other with grocery bags. School of the Arts didn't offer football, soccer or even basketball. Just Ultimate Frisbee. Our team's mascot was Pegasus. Although, from time to time, a few people called me a "damn hippie," the public magnet art school was a fairly tolerant place for my do.

And with no one to give me a hard time about my hair, I became cocky. So cocky, actually, that I started the habit of flipping my hair. I'd spontaneously shake my head with a force that sent my bangs lashing to the right. They'd then fall horizontally across my forehead, uneven and ruffled, like I'd been exposed to a Category 5 hurricane. I flipped my hair not because I was nervous, not because I wanted to move my bangs away from my face, but to show off my badassness. My bodaciousness. My brazenness. Looking back, I'm completely humiliated about it. However, this James Dean wannabe phase didn't come without its perks. What I'm saying is: Flipping my hair got the attention of many girls at School of the Arts. On the bus, Noelle Smith and Becca Caulder braided my locks. In math class, Britney Hooper and Lauren Floyd gave me cornrows. Swear to God. At lunch once, Deedee Davis and Greer Ford toyed with my hair for what must

HUMOR

have been twenty minutes. Whatever it is that attracts girls to hairy guys, I should have been more aware of it. I should have been more careful before things got out of control.

Grammar class. I sat beside a girl named Ashlee Youngblood. Freckles, what looked like thousands of them, covered her round cheeks. Every day of the week, she wore the same pair of jeans encrusted with fake diamonds. Even though Ashlee's bowling-ball belly popped out whenever she raised her hand, she wasn't overweight or anything. No—plump seems more appropriate.

Ashlee sat close enough that I could smell her cherry perfume, but she didn't once talk to me. I mean, at least directly. Often during recess, her minions of friends formed a semicircle of interrogation around me. In unison they asked, "You know that Ashlee girl?" And before I could muster any response, they said, "She likes your hair" or "She'd tap that" or "Lukeeee boy." Then, they just laughed and laughed and laughed until a part of me wanted to scream words that would undoubtedly give me a one-way ticket to after-school detention. But these girls were merely messengers. Followers of Ashlee's commands.

Once, while being questioned, I glanced toward the wax myrtle bushes across the school yard, where Ashlee, half-crouched, observed her couriers pin me against a stainless-steel fence. For a split second, our eyes met. She then turned away and, with a loud rustle, vanished into the foliage. I know it sounds like I'm exaggerating, but I swear her braces beamed in the sunlight, making her resemble a pudgy redheaded lighthouse.

I wasn't sure what to make of all this. Ashlee's crush (if you could call it that) puzzled me but was never really a bother. Until she stole my *Writer's Craft* book, I kind of took her affection as a compliment. Fuel to my haughtiness.

Even today I'm not sure when exactly Ashlee grabbed the textbook. During lunch? A field trip to the Charleston pirate museum? While I was at the water fountain? No matter when she performed the heist, though, she must have done so with stealth. Because, for a couple days after, I was convinced the cinderblock-sized book had decided to walk out of my backpack to accompany all of the missing TV remotes, guitar picks and socks.

When I asked my mom if she'd seen my *Writer's Craft* anywhere, she said, "Lukas, you need to keep your stuff together." She suggested I talk to the grammar teacher. I did. The teacher just said, "Sixty bucks," and told me to see the vice principal, Mr. Earl, who shook his head and said, "Sorry, son." I asked the kids I played Frisbee with after school, my brother, the janitor (who was listening to Creedence Clearwater Revival in his closet), even the bus driver—all of whom hadn't seen the book anywhere.

I almost lost hope until the day Ashlee's spokespersons surrounded me, giggling with more intensity than ever. Whatever was funny, they couldn't get enough of it. So I braced myself for some really ridiculous, really off-the-wall question. A girl who blushed more than the rest finally caught enough breath to speak up. But, instead of asking any questions she—giggling in between words—said, "Ashlee has your *Writer's Craft* and she takes showers with it."

I still don't know how I should have reacted. With anger? Frustration? Pure freaked-outness? More importantly, how in the world does one take a shower with a book? I think these are questions I'll never answer. All I know is, right then, during recess, with my back pressed against the cold fence, I was speechless. Had that moment been a cartoon, my jaw would have dropped straight to the asphalt.

The girls, after forever scarring my relationship with grammar, didn't just give me back the book. No—that was too easy for Ashlee. Too simple. When I said to them, "Just hand over the *Writer's Craft,*" they continued to laugh.

"We can't do that," they said.

"And why not?"

"Ashlee wants a ransom." I thought of the late-night cop dramas my parents sometimes watched before bed.

"How much are we talking here?" I asked like the book was not at all a book, but rather the kidnapped daughter of some wealthy senator.

"Not money, silly! Your hair."

"My hair?"

I had no choice. It came to this: By Wednesday, Ashlee wanted a Ziploc bag full of my hair as the ransom. There were, as her friends said, "no buts about it."

That afternoon was the longest I've ever stared at my reflection in the mirror. I tried to picture my hair (which by this time had grown from its Fabio-ish length to a more Tarzan-like look) a couple inches shorter. The first snip was the most difficult, but I soon developed a kind of rhythm chopping the curls and waves. When I finished, my hair had lost a good deal of length and looked like it'd been cut with the lid of a can. I gathered the piles of curls from my bathroom counter and stuffed them into a Ziploc.

On Wednesday, I met Ashlee's friends by the chemistry trailer. There, in the shade, the exchange took place. I handed off the bag and, in return, received my moist *Writer's Craft*. That day, I saw Ashlee down by the wax myrtles again, opening the Ziploc, inhaling its contents. I remember how she closed her eyes and stopped for an instant, like my hair was the sweetest thing she'd ever smelled.

Ashlee Youngblood left School of the Arts after that year, and I haven't heard of her since. A couple days ago, though, when I was watching the news, a report came on concerning the 2010 BP oil spill. An organization called Matter of Trust had collected 450,000 pounds of donated hair from salons, pet shops, sheep farmers and groomers. Members of the organization stuffed nylon bags with the hair and then dropped them in the ocean between the slick and the shore. Apparently, hair is one of the best materials for oil-soaking purposes.

For a moment there, with my feet on the coffee table, I had this gut feeling that Ashlee was out there, with one of those hair-filled nylon bags thrown over her shoulder. Something told me, you see, that she'd still smell like cherries. That her fake diamond-encrusted jeans would be soaked by the ocean. And for a moment, there was a part of me that wanted to hop off the couch and drive south to the coast of Louisiana—to Cameron or Pecan Island. That wanted to find Ashlee. That wanted to shout "Thank you!" at the top of my voice, so loud that it would have disturbed the local pelican rookeries.

Because—man, did I look like a wannabe with that long hair.

Anna Blech, 14
Hunter College High School
New York, NY
Teacher: Kimberly Airoldi

Anna Blech lives in New York City and is an aspiring thespian. Her experience on stage gives her perspective as she writes comic musicals, which, she feels, are funny because they're true. She would like to thank her father, whose song parodies inspire her.

COLLEGE ADMISSIONS: THE MUSICAL
Humor

DAD—A businessman
MOM—A teacher and housewife
MARIANNE—Older daughter, in her twenties
JENNA—Middle daughter, a junior at Harvard
TED—Youngest son, a high school senior
GENIE—A magical being (male or female) wearing long, flowing, dark green robes and a baccalaureate hat
CHASE, LARK and GERTRUDE—Perfect college applicants, wearing all white, except for Gertrude, who also wears a plaid jacket

SCENE 1

SETTING—KITCHEN.
There is a counter upstage with a cupboard and refrigerator. DAD, MOM, MARIANNE and JENNA sit around the kitchen table at center stage. On the back wall hangs a framed vintage photograph of Great Grandpa. There is an open laptop computer in the center of the table. (Lights up. Mom is desperately trying to restrain herself from using the laptop. After a few seconds, she loses control and starts to type. Dad grabs the laptop and pulls it out of her reach.)

DAD
(*loudly*) Wait for Ted to come home!

MOM
I know. I know…but…I can't wait to see the crimson crest and the "Congratulations!!" with two perfect little exclamation points. (*eagerly*) Ted told me his password…

DAD
Listen, Ted will be home in a few minutes. Then he'll check the Harvard website, and we'll find out that we have three kids at Harvard, and we'll break out the champagne.

MOM
(*dreamily*) My three children at Harvard!

DAD
(*pointing to the vintage photograph and singing*)
Great Grandpa went to Harvard in 1893
Grandfather donated the Harvard library
My father was the founder of good old Sigma Chi
So anyway you slice it, we're a Harvard family!

DAD, MOM, MARIANNE AND JENNA
(*singing in harmony like a barbershop quartet*)
A Harvard family
A Harvard family
Any way you slice it we're
A Harvard family

(*Mom extends her hands to the laptop, about to type. Dad pushes her hands away and slams the laptop shut.*)

DAD

(very loudly) Don't check the results! Honey, I've had a long day. I just saved Fannie Mae's butt, and my feet hurt.

MOM

(picks up a book lying on the table and hands it affectionately to Dad) I'm sorry, honey. Here, why don't you read this book and relax for a while...

DAD

What's this book? *(thumbs through it)*

JENNA

I found it in my room. *College Admissions for Dummies!* Guess we won't need this anymore! *(Jenna takes the book from Dad, closes it and leaves it on the table.)*

DAD

No dummies in this family!

MOM

All my children are such geniuses!

Dad stands up and walks toward the audience, singing. One at a time, each family member joins him in song.

DAD

I ran the student council, class of '83

MARIANNE

I was summa cum laude in philosophy

JENNA

Every boy at Harvard is running after me

MOM
Ted's as good as in, he's a sextuple legacy

A door is heard opening and slamming shut, followed by shuffling and the sound of a backpack being thrown onto the floor. Dad, Mom, Marianne and Jenna freeze, glance at each other, then quickly return to their seats at the table. TED enters, tossing a football from hand to hand.

TED
Hey, everybody. Practice ended late. I'm starved. What's for dinner?

Ted puts his football on the counter and goes to the cupboard. He takes out a giant pack of Oreos and shoves four of them in his mouth all at once. As he chews the Oreos, he goes to the refrigerator and pulls out a can of soda. He takes a long swig of Pepsi.

MOM
(*in a dramatic whisper*) The decision is in today…Harvard…

Ted spritzes soda everywhere. He hurriedly wipes his face with a napkin and runs over to the table. Ted logs on to the Harvard admissions website and reads.

JENNA
I wanted to tell you, Ted, that I'll be happy to show you around Harvard Yard.

MARIANNE
Yeah, you can join Sigma Chi! All the hottest guys are in Sigma Chi!

MOM
(*wistfully*) My three children at Harvard.

JENNA
You know, Ted, there's this really great falafel place near campus.
I could take you there during orientation.

TED
(*quietly*) I don't think that's going to work out.

JENNA
You don't like falafel? We could go for pizza.

TED
(*mumbling*) I didn't get in.

JENNA
What?

TED
(*even quieter*) I didn't get in.

JENNA
What?

TED
(*yelling*) I DIDN'T GET IN, OKAY?

Ted puts his head on the table, cradling his head in his hands. Jenna looks at the laptop screen.

JENNA
(*reading from the computer screen, unbelievingly*) Dear Ted Johnson,
(*singing*)
We regret to inform you
The admission committee convened

MARIANNE
(*looking at the screen, horror-struck*)
(*singing*)
And we don't have a place for you
In the class of 2014

DAD
(*looking at the screen, horror-struck*)
(*singing*)
There were thirty thousand applicants
A record number this year

MOM
(*looking at the screen, in shock*)
(*singing*)
We wish you good luck with your college plans,
Your life and your career

DAD
(*looks back to Ted with his head on the table*) Let's give him a few
minutes.

Dad, Marianne and Jenna exit, each patting Ted awkwardly on the
back as they leave. Mom starts to leave, then turns to the audience.

MOM
(*tragically*) My two children at Harvard.

The photograph of Great Grandpa falls off the wall and crashes to
the floor.

Blackout

SCENE 2

Lights up. Ted still has his head on the table. He bangs his fists on the table and groans. He slowly drags himself to stand.

TED
What did I do wrong? I took the toughest courses in school, aced them all, had extremely high SAT scores, played sports, was in the orchestra and even had a miserable summer in Honduras, in 100-degree heat, building latrines for the villagers. What do they want from me? I'm only 17. Maybe Honduras is too common. Maybe I should have gone to Sudan or Chad...I wish I could do it all over again.

(singing)
If I could do it again
Everything would be better
Wouldn't have worn that blue sweater
To my Harvard interview
If I could do it again
Wouldn't have gotten that letter
Saying I'm not a go-getter
And that basically, I'm screwed
No second chance!
Decisions cannot be appealed
The committee met, my fate is set
I thought they couldn't resist me
No second chance!
My entire future's sealed
I'm doomed to be a mediocrity
They didn't even waitlist me
No second chance!

Ted sits down again and cradles his head in his arms on the table, accidentally pushing the book to the floor. There is a blackout and the sound of thunder. Then lights flicker on and off like lightning. Suddenly there is quiet and stillness, and we see GENIE standing on top of the book. He steps down and introduces himself.

GENIE
(with a grand flourish) College Admissions Genie, at your service.

TED
(lifts his head, looks alarmed, shakes his head in an effort to clear his vision) Maybe I'm not getting enough sleep.

GENIE
Of course you're not getting enough sleep. Who is? But that's beside the point. I'm a genie. I know everything about you. I have been watching you since the college process began. And I have no qualms in telling you: Boy, did you blow it big-time with Harvard! What a screwup!

TED
(pulling himself together) Isn't that a little harsh? I worked really hard.

GENIE
Ha! Hard work? Hard work will get you into Harvard like going to church on Sunday will make you the pope. You have to have style, Ted! Flair! Panache! You wrote an essay about how the skills you learn from football—hard work, determination, perseverance—will help you succeed in college. *(exaggerated yawn)* You'd have to be state champion to get away with that! *(Ted looks like he's about to argue.)* But no…shhh…do not worry. *(comfortingly)* That's why I am here. Whenever a kid messes up his interviews, his essays and his transcript in such a colossal

fashion, I appear. I will transform you into the perfect college applicant. A Harvard student.

TED
But it's too late! I've already been rejected!

GENIE
No matter… You think Al Gore got into Harvard without my help? Or George Bush into Yale? Now that was a tough case. I will teach you everything. I will pad your résumé, exaggerate your accomplishments and teach you to conform to the mold of the perfect candidate, one no self-respecting college admissions officer could possibly deny. Then we will go back in time, 18 months to be exact, and you will start all over again. This time, Harvard will come on bended knee to offer you a full scholarship, nay, an honorarium!

TED
OKAY!

GENIE
Are you ready?

TED
I'm ready.

GENIE
(singing)
We will do it again
Everything will be better

TED
(singing)
I won't wear that blue sweater

To my Harvard interview.

GENIE
You wore a blue sweater? Ugh. You have a lot to learn.

TED
(singing)
A second chance!
My Harvard dream can still come true
I just can't wait to matriculate
If I get there, I'll owe it all to you

GENIE
(in a theatrical hush) Excellent. Let the learning begin.

Blackout. Sounds of thunder followed by flickering lights like lightning. When the lights stay on, Genie is standing, with LARK, CHASE and GERTRUDE in a line behind him. There are now three pairs of chairs facing each other.

GENIE
When one is attempting to gain entrance into a top college, the interview is the FINAL NAIL IN YOUR COFFIN! *(Genie laughs. Ted looks alarmed.)* So, Teddy, how was your interview for Harvard?

TED
(enthusiastically) We talked about everything: football, music, politics, how digging latrines in Honduras made me a better person. I thought it went okay.

GENIE
Okay? Okay? Obviously it was not okay, since you got REJECTED! *(Ted looks like he is going to argue.)* Remember when the interviewer

asked you "What is your biggest flaw?"

TED
I remember…I said I daydream about girls in class.

GENIE
(makes the sound of a buzzer on a game show) Incorrect. You're not supposed to give a real flaw, Ted! I know you're an extremely flawed person, but you're not hooked up to a lie detector. You're not supposed to be honest! The question about flaws is an opportunity for you to give yourself sneaky compliments. They correct answer is "I'm too hardworking, and I'm a little bit too much of a perfectionist sometimes."

TED
Well, no one's perfect.

GENIE
You have to be perfect, Ted! If you are going to go back in time with me, I won't have any of this "being yourself" nonsense! Don't you want me to help you?

TED
Of course I do. I'm sorry. I'll try to keep the "being myself" stuff to a minimum.

GENIE
No worries, my dear boy. You forget—that is why I am here. Now watch and learn, Ted, watch and learn. I have brought you three specimens of perfection, three masters of the college process. They will show you how it is done. Behold…Lark! *(Lark steps gracefully out from behind Genie and sits in her chair.)* Chase! *(Chase steps out from behind Genie and sits in his chair.)* Gertrude! *(Gertrude steps out awkwardly from behind Genie.)*

Did I say you could wear plaid?!?

GERTRUDE
(*quietly*) Sorry. I like plaid.

Gertrude sheepishly takes off the jacket and hands it to Genie, who holds it with two fingers as though it smells bad. Genie tosses it off stage, shuddering.

GENIE
Ghastly. You must always dress your best for an interview.

Gertrude sits meekly in the chair, looking upset.

TED
(*reassuringly*) I thought you looked nice.

Becoming animated again, Genie strides back and forth across the front of the stage.

GENIE
Let me begin with a story. One day, I went into a Starbucks to buy a cup of coffee. Being a genie for eternity, I can always use the occasional caffeine boost. As I was walking past the counter, I saw a very attractive young couple enjoying their venti white mocha frappuccinos, when I noticed that the woman's leg was shaking uncontrollably under the table. As I walked closer, I heard the man say (*Genie sits in the seat opposite Lark and faces her.*) "What makes you think Princeton is the perfect school for you?"

LARK
(*singing*)
I've always been interested in foreign policy

I know the Woodrow Wilson School's the perfect place for me
A State Department bureaucrat is what I crave to be
So I'd love to spend the next four years in southern New Jersey

GENIE
(*moves to sit opposite Gertrude*) Gertrude, tell us about your most important awards and achievements.

TED
(*interrupting eagerly*) I'm a National Merit finalist! I took four APs and aced them all. I even got a certificate for perfect attendance!

GENIE
Ehhhh!

Ted looks unhappy.

GERTRUDE
(*singing*)
I set the all-time record of twenty-six APs
Was an Intel semifinalist for research done on bees
I always got a perfect score on all my AMCs
And writing for Scholastic, I won seventeen Gold Keys

GENIE
And most important of all...

GENIE, LARK, CHASE AND GERTRUDE
EXTRACURRICULARS!

GENIE
So, Ted, what extracurriculars do you do?

TED
Well…I'm on the football team. I'm one of the top ten rushers in the league. I carried for eight hundred yards this season.

GENIE
Are you the captain?

TED
No.

GENIE
(*disappointed*) Ehhhh…

TED
Not everybody can be the captain, you know.

GENIE
Spoken like a true loser! At Harvard every student has to be a leader. All sheep herders and no sheep. Do you want to be a sheep, Ted? (*continues before Ted can speak*) Of course you don't! Chase! Show Ted how it's done. Chase started a breakthrough community service program: Tackle Football for the Elderly.

CHASE
(*singing*) The oldest person on my team is Mr. Kominsky
He was in the army back in 1923
He can't see the football, but what is that to me?
I've guaranteed myself a spot in a top Ivy

Chase returns to his seat.

GENIE
What else do you do, Ted?

TED
I'm in the orchestra. I play the drums.

GENIE
Ehhhh… If it was the French horn, you might've had something. Gertrude! Show him how it's done. This girl gave the world its first tuba symphony.

Gertrude plays the melody of the chorus of "Great Historical Bum" on the tuba.

GENIE
And now the pièce de résistance! Lark! Lark saved a small country.

TED
(interrupting) I built latrines in Honduras!!!

GENIE
(yawning) Boooooooring…

LARK
(singing)
I saved a tiny country, not even on the map
What most other students do is just a load of crap
The people of Kazministan are grateful as can be
And every year on Lark Day, there's a big parade for me!

Chase and Gertrude join Lark, all with top hats and canes.

LARK, CHASE AND GERTRUDE
(singing and doing a vaudeville line dance)
Extracurriculars, you'll need them to win
Perfect grades are A-OK, but they don't get you in

So do the most impressive thing your brain can devise
To get into an Ivy, you may need a Nobel Prize

Lark, Chase and Gertrude exit.

Genie takes out a copy of Ted's Harvard application and transcript from a pocket in his robe.

GENIE
Of course you have perfect scores. Everyone has perfect scores…
WAIT! What's this I see? An A-minus on your chemistry final?!?!

TED
(*proudly*) It was the highest grade in the class!

GENIE
You're proud of getting an A-minus?

TED
Yes, I am. Don't you think you're overdoing this a little bit?

GENIE
Haven't I taught you better than that? You get…
(*singing in a lively manner*)
An A-minus on the test, A-minus for the year
An A-minus girlfriend, A-minus career
An A-minus house, with an A-minus wife
And that's the way you end up with an A-minus life!
Do you want that, Ted?

TED
(*borderline hysterical*) NO! But are the only choices to go back in time or to be a loser?

GENIE
Exactly. I think you're ready. Come here, Ted.

Ted walks toward Genie.

GENIE
Now we will go back in time, 18 months, to the day the college process began. You will be the applicant that college admissions officers dream about. I will be behind you, making you sublime. Now close your eyes, tap your heels together three times, and say: "There's no place like Harvard. There's no place like Harvard. There's no place like Harvard."

Ted closes his eyes and taps his heels together.

TED
There's no place like Harvard. *(long pause)* There's no place like Harvard. *(Ted looks stricken. He gulps.)*

GENIE
Well, Ted? One more time.

TED
(quietly) No…maybe…maybe…
(stepping toward the audience and finding his voice, singing melodramatically)
Maybe I don't need to go to Harvard
Maybe I'm okay the way I am

GENIE
That is the stupidest line I've ever heard. You want to be MEDIOCRE? You want to end up at a SAFETY SCHOOL?!?!

TED

I want to be myself! Can't you understand that? *(to audience, with pride)* Hi! My name is Ted Johnson…and I'm a Harvard reject!

GENIE

(to audience) The boy has lost his mind.

TED

THAT'S IT! I'VE HAD ENOUGH OF THIS!

He runs to grab College Admissions for Dummies. *Ted holds the book open in front of him for a moment while Genie watches in alarm.*

TED

GET BACK IN THIS BOOK!

Blackout. Thunder and lightning. We hear the sound of Ted slamming the book shut. When the lights stop flashing, Genie is gone. Ted is sitting alone at the table, with the book shut in front of him. He stands up and walks toward the audience.

TED

(singing)

I won't be studying in Great Grandpa's library
I won't be a member of good old Sigma Chi
You won't find me in Cambridge Square, but I'm not feeling down
I didn't get into Harvard, so I'll just go to Brown

Curtain

Courtney Swafford, 15
Write From the Heart
Indiana, PA
Teacher: Veldorah Rice

Courtney Swafford is from Wilmington, Delaware. Her writing often begins as a single descriptive snapshot and grows into a narrative based on that image. She is grateful to her family and her church for their encouragement.

CRACKING GOD
Short Short Story

Jesus' face fell off a long time ago. I've watched the spidery cracks spread through the paint of the icon from the day I first noticed them in sixth grade, as I pretended to watch the priest. Now the picture hangs in the small recess where the priest stands, at the front of the chapel. The niche is so small that the priest, old, fat and insipid, has to squeeze around the corner to get behind the pulpit. The poor lighting back there hits his crinkled face at odd angles so that it looks like a dress shirt that's been slept in. His sagging, crumpled skin scrunches and creases in an endless maze of flesh as he deadpans the Book of Judith to his audience of lethargic schoolchildren. No one really listens. They just stare, glassy-eyed, while the monotone slogs through the heavy air in the vestry. Who was Judith? Nobody knows, and nobody really cares. The air is too muggy for that.

We used to have a different priest. He was really different. His face was less sagging; his eyes looked out at the students instead of at the words on the page. He was different because he talked to us, instead of down at the podium. When he read, you could think he might actually care about it, as if maybe there was something more to life than the trash we got at home. When he talked, even Jesus, with his dim halo circling his head, seemed to want to hear. Everyone liked our old priest better.

But he died. I never found out how; they just told us that our priest had "passed away," and that a new one would be coming to take his place. I guess they thought we were too young to be worth the bother of explaining. Anyway, that was when I started watching Jesus, hanging directly where he used to hang, above the recess where the new priest stood.

The cracks had started on his outstretched hand, crisscrossing through his scars and down his arm, then they'd spread out in all directions. The first flake to fall had been from his forehead. It had drifted down to the open Bible on the podium, causing the priest's droning voice to slowly trail away as he watched the flake settle. He stared intensely at the fleck, his face scrunching in consternation. The air was clammy and still. Slowly, slowly, he raised a flaccid hand, held it above the pages, and then out snapped his fingers, flicking the flake off the page as if to say "This is what happens to those who obstruct the business of the church." After staring victoriously at the speck on the floor, he dignifiedly lowered his hand and continued reading, as if nothing in the world could disturb him—especially not a bit of paint. Next time we came to Chapel, the picture was behind the priest. It was harder to see it back there.

I squint to see the faded details of the painting. Something moves at the corner of the picture—a moth has found its way into the building. It throws itself against the picture, fluttering up to the blank spot in the canvas. It stops here; the room is too hot for even a moth to move much. In the dimness of the niche, it's hard to see the dust-colored creature. The only light comes from the priest's reading lamp. The moth seems to suddenly realize this, because it lifts its wings and flies toward it. The dusty, fragile insect flies up under the lampshade and disappears, its fluttering wings making the light flicker. The erratic flickering goes on for a few seconds, then stops suddenly: The moth has died.

The priest reads on for a few lines more, then stops and intones, "This is the word of the Lord." Then he steps out from behind the pedestal, and his flowing sleeve brushes some flakes of paint off from Jesus' hair. There's a small heap of these paint chips on the floor under the painting. The priest steps on them every time he goes back there, grinding them into the burgundy carpet.

Down in the pews, all of the students laboriously stand themselves up and pull out their Psalters. The books are old, the tune is old, the words are old, and we can't read music. Our indistinct mumble flounders its way through the meaningless characters on the pages. No one knows the song, and no one really cares. After all, who wants to praise a faceless god?

Colin Powers, 16
Camp Hill Senior High School
Camp Hill, PA
Teacher: Kristie Foster

Colin Powers lives in Camp Hill, Pennsylvania. Like much of his work, his award-winning short story was inspired by music; he is interested in exploring the intersection of music and writing. He would like to thank his friend Liz Laridee for her support.

JOSHUA
Short Short Story

Now that I've seen the life of another unwind, it seems that keeping my own in check becomes much easier. I suppose using my grandfather's life as a moral boundary may seem debasing to his memory, but if it stops insanity from rearing its ugly head, by all means, may he lead by example.

I could've pinned the loss of my grandfather's mind to any number of things. Each day in fall, I would return from my studies to find him perched in his favorite armchair, blaring what my mother always referred to as "amphetamine jazz" and boring a hole in the wall with his wide-eyed stare. It became a habit to turn down his stereo and, with the level of decibels pounding on his eardrums reduced, say something along the lines of "Jesus Christ, Pops, doesn't this crap drive you crazy?" (My Christian tendencies walked out the door after my mother turned the local church's Christmas pageant into a somewhat scandalous Broadway musical.) Most times he gave no response whatsoever. Not a sound would pass between his withered lips, or even a flicker of emotion cross his face. The hole in the wall would continue to grow.

On the rare occasion when it snowed, I would walk in on him silently swaying to a crackling Sinatra record, content, a film reel of memories passing beneath his eyelids. He would not feel my presence at all then.

As spring stretched its life-giving fingers, a strange scene revealed itself in my living room; stark naked, my grandfather lay on the shag carpet, unceasingly tossing a rubber ball against a pockmarked ceiling. I could see his frail body pulsating with the motion of life. The sounds of a string quartet flooded over us, the stereo sharing the same pulsation. He was conducting an orchestra, the repetitive thrust of his elbow driving the music forward. Plaster fell onto the tasteless decor below. Our living space lay in ruins, defaced by my grandfather's naked meditation. But all I saw was beauty.

In the applause that came after the music stopped, he noticed me. I felt like a cub, stumbling upon his elder lion while he groomed. However, the elder was not upset. He rose to the applause, his face unchanged, and walked forward to where I stood. His hand touched my face, feeling my youth, my power. He yearned for what he could not reach, and I could feel his heart breaking before me. A single tear fell onto his breast and revealed his nakedness to himself. Like Adam at the beginning of all things, he retreated in shame, to let the Lord judge him in solitude. That night I read my Bible for the first time in six years.

Yet, in summer there was no music. My Pops spent all of my vacation in the hospital because one morning as we exchanged a rare word over an even rarer cigarette, he decided to plunge his head through a window. Our conversation was about the local minister's arrest for child molestation and his wife's subsequent nervous breakdown. The minister is my stepdad, his wife my mother. Sitting in the waiting room that night, I gave my Bible to the desk clerk, telling her to do with it what she wills; the will of God seemed to have bypassed me.

Now in autumn I watch the first leaves fall through the hospital window. Improvement in his condition is nowhere to be seen, not even among the browning foliage. An unforgiving coma still grips him. I still wonder what caused insanity to grip his mind and wrench it from his control, sending it cartwheeling into oblivion—also known as the panes of our living room window. I have doubts that it was because of the news of his daughter's emotional demise, seeing as the last time they spoke was at her college graduation (in a drunken stupor he had phoned her from a local bar to wish her a merry Christmas). Then was it the seasons? Was he so enraged by the inconsistent weather that he was

266 SHORT SHORT STORY

convinced California lay on the other side of the window? Or did the weathermen bearing ill news drive him to the point of suicide?

Perhaps it wasn't anything to do with climate at all. Could the all-encompassing concept of love be the culprit? Did the hole he's been boring in the living room wall for 50 years begin with the death of my beautiful grandmother? Upon his return from the Vietnam War, he found her hanging by a wire over the very shag carpet where I learned how to pray and how to sacrifice. Was his immediate reaction a deadpan stare into the adjacent wall? Or was it to lie naked and bounce a ball next to her limp body?

Asking these questions, upon the brink of a revelation, the constant beeping that has been with me for the past several months has stopped. The monitor is at peace, just as my grandfather is now. My mother at my side buries her shaking head into the chest of the minister, who, upon seeing death for the umpteenth time, stomachs his guilt. Benny Hinn is flooring people with the power of Christ on the television. As my stepfather retrieves a leather-bound Bible from his pocket and begins to recite Scripture, I can smell the brandy on his breath. Flakes of plaster float down from the ceiling to land on my Pops' face, covering his path to heaven with cheap snow. A tear blurs my vision. Amid this cacophony, this recurring dream, I see beauty in front of me again, naked and ethereal. Beauty's name is Joshua.

Simone Braunstein, 13
The Dalton School
New York, NY
Teacher: Carolyn Karp

Simone Braunstein is a native New Yorker and a budding robotics engineer. She wrote her winning story as an assignment for English class; she would like to thank her teacher Carolyn Karp for her help and encouragement.

ESTRANGED
Short Short Story

I never thought I would attend a funeral. Especially in a church. Being here seems to make people believe that my family had actually come before. As if we had sat here in the pews, staring up at the preacher while he told us how great God was in too many words. Going to church was just never something my family was interested in. It is certainly more interesting now, to say the least. Not necessarily in a good way, either.

I step down, walk out of the building. I turn, looking up at the tall, gray stone of the church. Ha! A church. As if Daddy would have ever gone. He says (well, I guess said, now) that churches are for people who want to be there. I don't understand why he has to go now that he is dead, especially because he never wanted to go while he was alive. I turn, walk down Fifth Avenue in my black dress, my black hat, black shoes. Mom does not follow me, not that I am surprised. She does love me, I know that. It's just that she can never punish me, never thinks anything is my fault. Mom was raised with finger-shaped bruises covering her body. She doesn't want that for me, doesn't want me to feel her pain. So she never says no.

I walk into the park, near the children's zoo, and sit. Look up. The whole in my chest gapes, something empty. I can't think of much else to do, so I cry. I have never had someone close to me die before, much less someone I love more than anything. I know crying can't help; if nothing else, I have learned this in my fourteen years. I can't seem to stop, though. I can't see, which isn't all that bad right now.

That means I can't see the other people staring at the strange, pale, stringy-haired white girl sobbing her heart out with a confused look on her mascara-stained face. The thing about death isn't that it is unfair, like everyone says. It just surprises you, trips you up. The last thing I said to Dad two days ago was "Have a good day." Yeah. Sure. That was a really good day for him. I do wish that Daddy hadn't died, of course. All of my wishing, though, won't change anything. No matter how much I love him, or how much he loves me, nothing I do can bring him back to me. Mom loves me too, I guess. She just doesn't know how to say no to me. She thinks everything that I do badly is her fault. She can only comfort me, not punish me. This might seem great to some kids, and, yes, it is in the beginning. Then it gets hard to do anything without trying to push her boundaries. I am always trying to find a "no" inside of her weird sort of love.

I get up from my spot of mushed-down grass. My hands are still able to lift my body from the ground, helping my legs do their job as well. It is a comfort to me that my body still works, still does what I ask of it. I rise, and start to run. Blindly I shove through the crowds of people in the park, ignoring their jabs of sharp protest. My feet slap the pavement, hurting in my high heels. I am running as fast as I can go. I run to my house, not knowing where else I can go. I slip my fingers under the "Welcome!" mat, grip the key so hard that when I check later there is an indent in my palm, twist the key in the lock, open the door and slam it closed soundlessly. Then I stop, still and rigid. Across the hall, I can see my blotchy red face in the mirror. I choke out a sob, the usual one that accompanies the sight of my own ugly reflection. Reaching to the table, pressed up against me in the confided space, I grasp my plate covered with remnants of lasagna from last night's dinner and throw it with all of the strength I can muster at the mirror. The plate falls to the floor with a bang, shattered, the undamaged mirror still showing an ugly open-mouthed girl staring in horror at the damage and mess she has created. I sigh heavily, and turn to the couch. Within minutes I fall into a troubled sleep.

I push myself up from the stained brown and green couch, and hear the springs breathe a sigh of relief. The floor creaks under my bare feet. Everything in my house talks, as if it wants to share secrets with me. As if a flood of words, like a great windstorm or a swollen river bursting with sound, needed to escape from their confines.

Here comes Mom. I can feel the vibrations of her feet on the brown-carpeted floors. Here she comes, as always, dressed in her blue flannel nightgown with nothing underneath. Her fuzzy blue slippers, which she still has from college. Her hair, black brown like mine, up in one of her messy ponytails, frizz shooting out in every direction. This time, though, her step is different. More like my Dad's, trudging slowly down the hall. Almost as if it's too hard to support her own weight, and she has to slide her feet on the floor to avoid falling. But today she is holding the world on her shoulders, supporting herself along with me. I didn't think she could do it, didn't think she could take care of me too. But the sounds of her steps seem to transform her into my father, or at least a part of him. Tall and strong, holding the world up like Atlas. Different, though. He, and she now too, don't do it because they have to, because they are given no other choice. They stand, taller and stronger than Atlas, holding up the world so I won't have to. So I don't have to shuffle down the hall quite yet.

She comes into my tiny, blue room. Everything presses in on us, and she groans, like she can feel it. She sits on my bed, pushed up against the wall, a good two inches from the door. Other than the dresser, there isn't much else in my room. She squashes next to me on the bed and opens her arms. I settle into them and sob. I can feel her body shaking with the pain, the emptiness of it all. I know she has the hole in her too, and like me, she can't figure out how to make it go away. I feel myself slipping into the safety of sleep, wrapped in the cocoon of Mom's arms. As my eyes shut out the pain in the world, I hear her murmur, "Sleep safe, baby. My little girl," and my eyes are closed and I am falling.

Ava Tomasula y Garcia, 16
Adams High School
South Bend, IN
Teacher: Becky Folk

Ava Tomasula y Garcia is from South Bend, Indiana. She cites Samuel Beckett as a major influence on her work. She can't imagine not writing, because she is fascinated and inspired by the ways that people communicate.

TERRA OBSCURA
Short Story

A land. A house. My house, *my* house; my father built it. We say.
We say, *my* mother, *my* brother, *my* wife. This is *my* daughter. *My* son. This life—mine—I bought it. Mine, mine—ownership.
But this house is not mine. This land.
Whose?
And so the story crumbles here, like an unkempt house, no longer a home—caving in on itself—falling in on its my ownself, leaving only chips and splinters to mourn silently in corners, erasing and so also hiding themselves from the, corrosion of constant ice form, ice melt. It is unimportant. It is cold, covered with ice and neglect.
"That house belongs to—" A catch in the throat. A tangle of loss. Welcome.

So to think about the *mine* of the house, my (your) little son and father, you have to reconstruct the house yourself. But only part— don't finish it. Make it *mine* (yours) only halfway. Then picture that catch of the throat, that intake of breath, that *about to,* that *almost*— cracking through the ice, and you will *have* them. *Yours.*

There is a photograph. A very famous photograph.

Yours?

His father—your father—was his *hands.*

Have you ever held a photo
of a house or person,
up to the same house or person,
now much older,
dilapidated,
almost melting?
Transposing the now in the photograph
to the now *staring, cracked-windowed*
and glassy-eyed, at you?

Everything he had came from his hands, but like everything, everything he lost was because of them.

He comes up through the ice with hands held open, in front and first.

The father had built the house, house through will alone although it's still a home, with his hands. Ice blocks. He had tanned skins and picked grasses. He had held his son with the hands, had made dolls and slaughtered animals and bandaged cuts. He had spoken with the hands, translating his thoughts, and feelings of thoughts, into the outside world of rough and garbled words. He had even thought with the hands, had run them through his hair and let them finger what they might as he prayed silently to himself.

He had *seen* himself with them, seen himself in his son. The father had watched himself not himself; a him that has so little to be sorry for, when he stroked his (child's) sleeping face.

Soft, child hands, unhardened and quiet with the certainty of ice form, not having seen ice melt.

His hands were young when he did these things, lived those little lives. Fine, unsullied by years of sun up, sun down. Ice form, ice melt.

But now he is old.

Your fingernails grow about
The same amount

As the continents
Move
Every year.

If he had lived here, today (not yours anymore, too complex), he might have known how many birthdays he had had (68), or how much his brain had shrunk since he was about 26 (roughly 8 percent), or even that he would be laughed at by people younger than his son, because he didn't know what F-A-T-H-E-R spelled. Or that, years and years from his now, the ice shelf that held his home and son would break apart and melt away, helped along by those grown, laughing readers who don't know and maybe shouldn't know how to begin an apology.

A single snowstorm
Can drop 40 million tons
Of snow,
Carrying the energy equivalent
To 120
Atom
Bombs.

But he is in his *now*. He knows that he will live here on the sleeping shelf with his son and the caribou that breed there for many tomorrows.

The hands first held his son just before the caribou fawn began appearing as fawn pin pricks next to larger mother-tears on the shelf. Just before the exhausted bodies of new mothers began falling into the snow and freezing.

At that time, he taught his son how to use his own baby hands, how to keep them soft and young for now, because the father—his son's—was there to bear the age for both of them, to hide the dead mothers and bury them in the snow at night before his son could see and be sad, before his son's veins bulged under his soft hands' skin as well. Instead, the father guided his son's grasping hands in making tiny villages out of snow and ice, in drawing with burnt sticks, making patterns with wool and color and telling stories with the sons of their hands—shadows—becoming now a bird, now a man, flickering on the warm walls.

But this *prehistory,* this lineage of their lives, is not history worthy of making.

To the world, to the *nows* around them, not on the shelf, they are nothing, until a photographer that is famous in a now of cities, magazines, conferences and books comes to the shelf and captures their image.

They are a sub-story, or just storyless. Handless.

They are a family on their way to vanishing, an instant trapped in a photograph, a now that has since disappeared, or changed into disappearance, no longer there for the photographer to return to, if he ever did, which he did not. He had his prize.

As they are farthest away
From the heart,
Hands tend to become
Frostbitten quicker
Than any other
Part of the body.

Once, when the son had seen caribou young born on the shelf six times, he sat on top of his father's shoulders and pointed at the pin pricks miles away on the flat shelf. He is laughing, at least, in the memorized image of the day he is laughing, clinging to his father's neck and upheld hands, and the father is too, saying, "Not so tight, not so tight!"

Is it love to want to die there, inside that image? That photograph in the son's memory, him, with his father, not knowing about mothers and buryings deep in the night?

Caribou
Can smell lichen
Up to three feet beneath
The snow.

The story is about animals.

Across the shelf, a caribou mother is walking with her son, already delirious and weak from (ice form), but she is still leading him (ice melt), growing more and more tired, until she lets slip that tiny life, and it falls, falls onto the already cracking shelf and stays there while the mother keeps walking until she too collapses like a something that falls all at once.

The father puts his own son down on the ice and snow, and runs ahead to the little life lying there near the already freezing mother, running and forgetting his son's eyes and hands for a moment, for he is caught up in doing here what he does at night on the shelf bury mothers and kill already dying sons. He has to do what he does when he leaves his son to happily dream about sons and fathers and caribou inside their warm home.

He can tell there is nothing to be done, nothing hands can do for the little caribou son now, except hold it. And he does, he holds its head tightly and sings a very old song with his eyes closed while his human son sobs, standing there, on the shelf by his father, growing veins and wrinkles.

Then, the animal dies.

Camera comes from
Camera obscura,
Which means "dark chamber."

The son would continue the story, continue his memory from there. He would think, if it were him lying there in the snow, if the last thing he saw was his animal mother falling down in the snow and the ice, and if it was the image of the father and his son that found him at the cracking edge of the shelf, maybe his leaving took a home with him forever. Like a photographed house that has since been demolished.

And since it was the son and the father who found the animal there on the cracked ice, maybe the difference between them melted away, hand gave way to hoof and hoof gave way to hand.

No matter. The son loves this story. This photograph. He loves this fatherless, handless, motherless, storyless story of a created time before the fawn son died, before the crack his father is sitting on gave way beneath him and his caribou son and they disappeared forever in the cold, shadowy water pulsing beneath the shelf.

It is a story he loves to death, and loved before the house and the shelf and the son melted into another *now,* a *now* that *could,* and had sons and daughters, they're *my* son, *my* daughter, *my* mother, *my* father. *A my now* that cherished the photograph of the son and father, liked to think from warm museums and houses of them alone on the shelf, with howling winds and savage animals. Liked to think of them breaking through the ice, mangled hands first.

Tatiana Dubin, 15
Hewitt School
New York, NY
Teacher: Maureen Burgess

Tatiana Dubin is from New York City. She is interested in Nietzsche and other existentialist writers, and she explores similar themes in her own work. She would like to thank her best friend, Francessca Caracci.

CUTTING THE STRING
Short Story

That old piano elegantly stood in the corner of your, or should I say his, Victorian living room. You were beautifully singing as you tapped your white hands on the glossy keys. You've had that piano for as long as any of us could remember. You had it in your parents' modest house right outside of town, you had it when you moved into that dusty little one-room studio overlooking a trashed parking lot when you were in your rebellious phase, and now here, in your new husband's house, whom I know you don't love. "What is love, anyway?" I remember asking you one pale afternoon, seated on a chipped green bench eating grilled cheese with tomato sandwiches. "An old Roman sculpture, an apple, a hammer, a rusty old watch." You responded with complete indifference. I stood there, dazzled, surprised, enchanted by your response that for some reason made so much sense to me. Love is and was a bunch of random, inanimate objects. You don't love him, Lucy.

That piano once held a lovely, shiny glaze that covered the deep brown, almost black mahogany. It seemed so perfect back then, so gentle and delicate, so simply ordinary that in its simplicity it was especially beautiful to me. Whenever I would go over to your pretty little white house, which was basically every day after school. (I don't know if you remember this anymore, or if it even matters, but remember when your mama's rose patch was destroyed one Tuesday afternoon and I claimed a raccoon came and jumped into it? It was me. I stepped on it by mistake as I was in a hurry to get to you. I'm sorry.) Anyway, when I would go to your house, I used to purposely walk through your living room (even though the hanging, bloody-looking Jesus above your fireplace scared the shit out of me) to stare at your piano. I don't really know why (I know it seems rather creepy, now that I look back on it) but it reminded me of you. It still does. Even though the glaze is chipped and the wood has lost its legendary gleam, it's still you.

I recall that one year you hated your piano, despised it with every bone in your body, wished for its disappearance. You were about ten at this point and your mama decided that in order to make you a "good Christian" you had to swear to celibacy, attend all church events and do all that other bullshit "good Christians" do. She made you take piano classes three times a week in two-hour sessions with an evil Russian lady who would slap your sweaty little hands as you cried. She said the discipline would make you more aware of your religious duties; she even claimed you were going to hell because when she would come into your bedroom at night to recite prayers with you, you would question the power of God and if he was really there in the first place. You never understood how someone could just believe in something so demeaning, so abstract. I loved you for that, Lucy. I loved how you went against your mama when no one would go against her, not even your dad.

My mom would drop me off at your house after your lessons and we would plan master plots to run away to Coney Island together and live underneath the carousel. What ever happened to that plan, Lucy? It all was ruined when you met Gregory Goldfarb. (That obese ginger. Sorry, that was kinda obnoxious, I just hate that bastard. That fat, red-haired, freckled loser with a huge trust fund and thin little deceiving lips.)

I bet you he doesn't love your piano as much I did and still do (yes, I still love your piano). I'll always love your piano, Lucy.

Why did you invite me over to your house last month? We hadn't spoken since college, since that night you called me, your voice shaking so badly that, even though I was pissed as hell, I asked if you would be alright. That night you took my metaphorical heart and ripped it into a million different little pieces. (Just to let you know, Lucy, ever since that bone-shattering, sleepless night I've been trying to find the pieces you made me lose. I can't find them, though. Do you have them by chance? If you do have them, I'd appreciate if

278   SHORT STORY

you gave them back because it's not exactly easy to live with missing pieces. It's very, very hard, Lucy.)

You told me about Gregory that night, and I fucking died, Lucy. Did you know I hit my dorm wall so hard, so angrily, that my knuckles started to bleed? Did you know you indirectly made my knuckles bleed? You should feel absolutely horrible, Lucy.

I'm getting a bit carried away. I'm sorry, Lucy, I really am, but I've just gotta know why you called me. I almost started to forget about you at that point, there was even this girl named Persephone. (I know what you're thinking: "weird name, weird girl." We used to make up funny names and laugh about them together—do you remember? She is weird, but you always told me that being weird was a compliment. Do you still live by that motto? Did you tell Gregory? Does he agree? I always agreed.

That image of you from last month won't leave my mind. You, seated in a light pink, silk (I'm sure very expensive), fitted suit. Your skirt went down to right below your knee, the translucent tights covering your still exquisite, perfectly proportioned legs. Since when do you wear long skirts? I remember you at sixteen years old, skirts that ended just above your pink Rolling Stones underwear, belly shirts that held offensive statements, lipstick so black that it made your skin look like the shell on an egg. (I loved it, though. I loved you throughout all of your phases, even when you told me you were a nihilist and nothing mattered, I loved you.) Back to that image I was telling you about, the image of you sitting there with giant (also, very expensive-looking) pearl earrings that made you look like my Granny Ann. Clear nail polish covered your once-bitten nails. (what's the point of clear nail polish, anyway? It has no color…it's a waste of money if you ask me. Does Gregory think it's a waste of money? I bet he does but he just doesn't tell you.) Your perfectly manicured hair was held tightly within what looked like a bird's nest (you called it a "French bun"). How fucking pretentious.

Our conversation was really quite awkward; I didn't want to ask you why you asked me to see you. I thought it may seem rude, and the last thing I wanted was for you to be insulted and kick me out. You've always had the tendency to leave when you had a problem— for example, when Jane told you I cheated on you with that blonde waitress over at Princess Diner, the one who always wore bright red lipstick and those blue fake eyelashes, and you believed her right away and didn't call me or talk to me for two weeks. In school you would glare at the walls with a chilling coldness that drove me crazy, it was so very hard not speaking to you for that long. Finally, Jane admitted it was an immature, annoying rumor that she started in order to get revenge on me from the sixth grade, when I made her cry by making fun of her ponytails. (She only admitted it because my anger took the best of me and I followed her one day after ballet and I shook her so hard she started to cry. I forced her to call you. I never told you, and she never told you about that because, I mean, I threatened her. I do know how much my anger management problem freaks you out. After that incident I even saved up the money from my piggy bank—250 dollars—to see a therapist to help me figure my shit out. I would do anything for you, Lucy.) You should've known I would never cheat on you. I wonder if Gregory has ever cheated on you with those Russian prostitutes I've heard rich men use when they get bored of their wives. No, Lucy, I'm not calling you boring. You know I could never think you're boring. If you had married me instead of that fucking sack of tomatoes, I would have slept with you and only you for the rest of my life.

You lost your virginity to me. Do you remember? I was so nervous with my pale, scrawny body. You were so very beautiful. (Not model beautiful, but girl-next-door beautiful. I wouldn't work well with a girl who looked like a model anyway. Too many expectations.) I recall every detail of this night perfectly within my mind, your black lace bra, me hitting my head on the headboard of your bed, a tear scrolling down your flushed face as I stared deep into your eyes and whispered that I loved you. It was the type of night that poets attempt their whole lives to record, that movies are based on. It wasn't a poem or a movie, it was real life. We were real and so close to perfection I even felt like I touched it sometimes.

Why did high school have to end so soon? What the fuck am I doing with my life? Thirty-two years old and still living in a one-bedroom piece-of-shit apartment. Why aren't you seated here with me instead of sitting with that man you don't love? You once told me that "you can tell love by the way someone looks into your eyes." I saw a picture of you two on Facebook looking into each other's eyes. (You were on some perfectly groomed, Hallmark-card-worthy beach somewhere in the Caribbean. You were wearing matching Ralph Lauren polos and your hair was in that bird's nest that I hate. He held this evil smirk, his face so conniving I would've punched him right then and there.) There was nothing in your eyes or his eyes, Lucy. Do you hear me? Nothing. It was posed bullshit, the type of picture that we would've made fun of back in high school, we would've titled the photo something like "Constipated Couple" or "Giant Ginger with Mistress."

I think I'm done, Lucy. No, I don't think I'm done, I know I'm done. I know I'm done loving your piano, I know I'm done thinking of you every day, I know I'm done with this stupid letter or whatever this damn thing really is. You don't have to answer. Actually, you do have to answer.

I'm not going to pretend I don't care what you have to say, because I always will care what you have to say. I emphasize that fact that my entire life was crafted, planned, constructed around you, Lucy! Fuck, Lucy, I even envisioned us as old people, our satisfying smiles pleasing each other, our deep wrinkles signifying the joyous years we spent together. (You'd be such a beautiful old woman, so poised, so dignified.)

I am not resilient, Lucy, I have never had that quality, I have never been able to say "Fuck it, I'm moving on." I hope that after this letter I may finally learn to put you behind me, to merely think of you as a part of my past, a pretty memory.

Think of yourself (or, more accurately, your memory) as a string that hangs off of me, follows me everywhere, almost like a tail. What I have just written, Lucy, this release of past anger, this liberation, this final realization has given me the strength to pick up a pair of scissors (my bravery) and snap the haunting string off of me.

I now take back the fact that I will always love your piano, because I realize now that love cannot last, nothing that beautiful can ever last. You gave up our potential, our life together, for some vacations to overly expensive hotels and maids to pick up your shit. You're just like the rest of them. Fuck this. Fuck you. I'm moving on.

James Rode, 13
Charleston County School of the Arts
North Charleston, SC
Teacher: Francis Hammes

James Rode is a resident of North Charleston, South Carolina. He finds inspiration from the work of songwriter Serj Tankian, and much of his work is a fictionalized account of his own experiences. He is currently writing scripts for YouTube videos, which can be found at www.youtube.com/user/mediabyv.

GROWING AWAY
Short Story

See, I was going home with my family after dinner, when me and Ken decided to see who could run faster. We checked both ways down the street, but there was only one car, and it looked to be a long way off. I sprinted out as fast as him. We had gotten to the end of our little race when we turned around to see that our parents weren't behind us. Ken pulled out the knife our dad had given him— Shreveport isn't exactly the safest city—and crept back to where our parents should have been walking, I only a couple feet behind him. Even though the moon was far waning, I could still see Ken's haunted face as he turned to look at me, hand motioning for me to get back; his eyes were lit up like the moon that illuminated them. He was as pale as ice; his usual smile was replaced by the atypical grimace, and his skin was leeched of all hue. I never truly understood my brother until I saw this, and when I had first understood him, I had known something was wrong. He snapped to reality and sprinted toward the road where we had started running. I stayed back, knowing Ken didn't want me up there, but still looked at Ken's feet. There were two lumps that looked strangely like...

"Our parents," I breathed. There was Mom, petite and innocent-looking. And Dad, too, strength etched in every pore of his body. I see the car we had spotted earlier, but this time it was a couple hundred feet down the L-shaped road. It was moving too fast and swerving from side to side. Drunks probably. Then it connects: the swerving, speeding car and my parents lying on the ground.

I rush forward to see them, but Ken comes at me and restrains my yelling, shoving body.

"Leroy, you don't want to—you don't," he says in a weak voice.

I believe him. It's a good thing, too; Ken hasn't been the same since that night…he left me that night. He went down a separate path. Growing away.

***

I remember the good old days before Ken isolated himself from everything living. Me and Ken would head down to the arcade and spend all of our allowance on the games, especially Ms. Pac-Man, which we would play in turns until one of us admitted defeat. We didn't play by the rules, though; we pushed each other around, jokingly, while trying to hit the knob in the direction of a ghost so the other's Pac-Man would lose a life. Then, after we finished Pac-Man, we would play some air hockey. Ken may have always beaten me at the joystick games, but I was an air hockey master. I could smash the little disc into Ken's goal before he realized it was coming in his direction. This isn't to say he wasn't any good; it's just that I was better. For the finale, we would head over to the Ghost Recon game. He let me be first player, choose my character first and let me snipe. We would fly through the level, always trying to beat our record on that game. People would gather around us to watch our fingers fly, our guns point at enemies that stand there, getting blown away by our reaction time, accuracy and the ability to fire more rounds in semi-auto than full-auto. On our way back from the arcade, we would stop at the ice cream parlor and get two large cones. I got a Swiss chocolate and strawberry mix, and Ken got a peanut butter and vanilla mix. We would walk back to our house, empty-pocketed and drained from all of the trigger-pulling, puck-smashing, button-mashing and ice cream licking.

Of course, that's how he used to be. But not anymore. Not anymore.

***

Only moments after the bell rings, signaling the end of the school day, I am at my locker, unloading and loading textbooks, binders, loose sheets of paper and the occasional love note. Well, scratch the love notes; no girl wants to go out with a guy like me. It has to do with the stereotype of kids who lose their parents, I guess. Supposedly, we are all demons who are out to get revenge on living people because all those people killed our parents, and we plan our revenge by sitting in isolation, sketching out the worst pain and ways to get others to feel it. By the way, untrue.

Anyway, this stereotype had gotten me unwanted attention for a time, while I recovered as best I could. After that, I fell back into my usual—albeit with some variations—routine. By that time, everyone had come to think that depression was my permanent state. They left me alone and treated me like an outcast—no invitations, no one to sit by, just me, myself and I. And Ken of course…at first.

***

I wait patiently outside the school building for Bettina, the eighty-year-old woman who walks me home every day. It's not because I need someone to hold on to—I'm sixteen, after all—but because we are just the best of friends. We aren't related in any way, except for the fact that she lives near me and Ken. She was also the person who came calling when me and Ken started screaming for help that night my parents got killed; she took in these two random kids, one who only knew his parents were in grave trouble, the other who was in tears, screaming out in the night, screaming for a person who was never going to touch him again. Bettina sat down and comforted us, told us it was going to be alright. She had lost her parents too, she told us. Her mother died while giving birth to a boy who would have been Bettina's baby brother, had the boy not caught a deadly virus only days after he was born. Bettina had been ten then. It took six years before her father caved in to the pain of losing two loved ones, the debt from getting drunk every other night and the pressure of being unable to support the both of them. Bettina told me that he bought a gun from someone in the city and shot himself, leaving her to fend for herself. She went to live with an aunt for two years and then moved back to Shreveport. She said she couldn't leave all of the memories—both good and bad—behind: her first kiss, her first boyfriend, her father killing himself in front of her. She always said, "Without memories, we have no past, and therefore, no future."

Bettina looked as strong as always: mildly gray hair, not obese or underweight, 20/20 vision, as tall as me or Ken, perfect hearing. Really, she could have been a thirty-year-old woman if it weren't for the couple of wrinkles here and there. Otherwise, she and her brown eyes, angular face, tight pursed lip and a cop-like personality toward disobedient kids all made her seem like she stopped aging a long time ago.

Today, we talked about girls; just from my body language, she said, she could tell I was in love. I admitted there was a girl. So we spent most of the walk just talking about her, about how she was beautiful, about how to flirt right, how to get her in my grasp. Like, when flirting, to give a quick smile and turn away real quick and blush (according to Bettina, I'm very good at the blushing part). Or to get her to fall for you, write a simple, short extended-metaphor poem, one that portrays the girl through the view of an innocent animal.

When Bettina talked to me, she sounded like the friend I never had. Sure, Ken had been good until the incident, but after our parents got killed, he had never been the same. When he recovered from his depression, he changed. He did not trust Bettina at all. He failed classes. He sat with known gangbangers at lunch instead of with me. He did not come home until midnight, and when he did, he would roll cash into wads as he entered the apartment. I didn't know if he was dealing, if he was mugging people or what he was doing. All I knew is that he was changing. Locking the door between us shut. Growing away.

***

Bettina and I walk up to her apartment. She thanks me for the company, I thank her for the girl advice, and we part. I jog to the little apartment me and Ken inhabit. It's messy, filthy in some places, but we can live in it. Ken looks at me as I enter. "You're late," he comments. I just nod and drop my book bag on the floor, waiting for his remark. "Don't tell me you were with that Bettina woman," he says.

"What's wrong with her?" I ask.

"I don't trust her."

"You say that about a lot of people."

"That's 'cause I don't trust them, either."

Of course he doesn't. When we go to the grocery store, he inspects every can, bag, carton, whatever we are going to get, for a puncture. "Poison," he claims. "People can poison these things by sticking an aerosol-tipped needle and spraying antifreeze." I personally think he's losing his marbles, but then again, his crew, as he calls it, is like that too. I'm almost certain he's in a gang, but I don't want to say anything because he will take offense. I may think he is a bit crazy, but he is my brother.

***

Watching R-rated movies is a little game for me and Ken. It's about trying to watch one without the other noticing. Before the "incident," we would play the same game, but with PG-13 movies instead. Now, however, I was sixteen, and Ken was eighteen, so I figured R-rated movies would be alright. Only, when I finished *Tears of the Sun* and tried to tell Ken about it, he wouldn't listen. He was busy playing with his knife: flipping it, spinning it, popping the blade out, all with one hand. Sometimes he would spin it on one finger, and it would spin around and the hilt would make contact with his other hand. The knife would transition over, and without a cut—not even a nick—he would keep it rotating. Later that day, when Ken ran out to grab some grub, I slid my switchblade out of my mattress (I had slit it down the side, and used the new sandwich-type storage as a secret hiding place) and tried to re-create some of the tricks Ken had done; tossing it up and catching it by the blade with the other hand had been successful, but when I tried to spin it around my index finger, it sliced off a large chunk of skin down my middle finger. I dropped the knife and ran to the bathroom; blood poured out of the wound, and my hand did next to nothing to prevent the maroon liquid from hitting the floor. I ran cold water over my finger while grabbing a Band-Aid from the medicine cabinet (which was really just a shelf on the wall with ibuprofen, cetirizine and bandages). I pulled off the wrapper with my teeth and slapped the Band-Aid onto my cut (who cleans their wounds with rubbing alcohol first, anyway?). After a couple of minutes cleaning up the sink and the carpet of our apartment, I pull up the fitted sheet of my bed and stick the knife into the slit of my mattress.

Yet another thing Ken can do that I seem to be incapable of doing correctly.

***

Once, ten years ago, when I was six, Ken had tattled on me, and in return, he said he would show me how to swim. So the next day we went to our backyard pool, Ken telling me how much fun it is being able to go for a dip without "swimmies," as he called the rings that wrapped around our bodies and kept us above the water. He told me to put down the towel but keep the swimmies on. Then he pointed toward an ancient oak at the corner of the yard. I turned my back, and no quicker than I had set down the towel Ken had pushed me into the pool. I landed on the surface with a belly flop, cracking the sound barrier with the flab I used to have. I flailed my arms and legs out, everywhere, thinking I was going to sink to the bottom. I found a way of flinging my limbs that kept me up, and I performed that maneuver while shouting gibberish at Ken. But he was already paddling beside me, ready in case I did indeed sink. Gently, like a mentor, he said, "Try keeping our arms more outward." I did this, and instantly, I sat on top of the water, dispensing less energy than before, yet getting a more favorable outcome. I smiled and yelled "I did it!" to Ken. He just grinned back. "You did it, bro. You're swimming."

***

Bettina arrives on time, as usual. She knows something is wrong by the way I don't respond much to what she says, or not have anything to share. I just walk in silence alongside her. Thinking to cheer me up, I guess, she takes me to get an ice cream. She even offers to get me a large cup, and I graciously accept. We continue up the line, her licking a vanilla kid's cone, me spooning mouthfuls of rich Swiss chocolate and strawberry into my mouth. The cash-register lady looks new, as she is smiling and messing things up at the same time. When we get to her, she says, "seven dollars, eighty-eight cents, please." But as Bettina pulls a ten-dollar bill out of her pocketbook, a hundred-dollar bill falls out onto the floor. I try to act like I don't notice it, but, really, I want it. I want it bad. It reminds me of those days of Ken telling me how I'll never be like him, with all of his riches and street cred, and getting all the girls and respect that come with being like "him." It dawns on me that a hundred-dollar bill is usually followed by better things: more money, bank cards, credit cards, checks, all of this great stuff.

Bettina and I leave the ice cream parlor with our treats, chatting happily about how teachers can be so dim-witted about things like pop culture while knowing the middle names to every British heir since the 1200s.

"I know!" Bettina laughs. "I had this one teacher in my freshman year who, believe it or not, still rode a horse to balls and vacations." I laugh nervously, trying to cover up anything suspicious. "What's wrong?"

My mind flashes back to when I was twelve, and me and Ken were playing on our little Nintendo DS, which had just come out. We were on the little chatting program, PictoChat, at midnight. It was so much fun, just sending little, badly drawn smiley faces to each other. We would try and outdo each other, making some smiley faces with their tongues sticking out, some with goofy ears. I remember Ken sent me one with a Mohawk. I thought that was just so cool! A black circle with dot eyes, a curvy line for a mouth and then a sort of triangle for a Mohawk.

I remember when he would sit there with his jacket partly open, hat backward, talking about his "girlfriend." I remember that. And I miss it. All of it.

Jessie Li, 17
State College Area High School
State College, PA
Teacher: Kate Hoffman

Jessie Li is a resident of State College, Pennsylvania. She is interested in writing about people and their connections to each other and to the world. She will study English at Davidson College, which has named her the recipient of a Patricia Cornwell Scholarship, an award for students with exceptional promise in writing.

LANEY
Short Story

I was the prettiest girl in the third grade. I had skin as soft as butter and thin, graceful arms, and my hair was chopstick straight, bearing no resemblance to the mess of curls and waves of the other girls. My hair was ebony black, like Snow White's, my mother used to say, and sometimes the boys in art class would try to put their inky hands in the hair of all the girls in my class and I would be the only one left unmarked.

Sometimes even you would try to muss my silky hair, but it always stayed the same, and I would run away before you could try again. Not only was I the prettiest girl in the grade but I was also the best sprinter, and most of the boys, including you, couldn't even catch me. One time the librarian read the story of the goddess Atalanta to our class, and I could feel everyone's eyes glance back at me at least once in the story, because I was just like her. She was a running beauty, the librarian read, and when I told my mother I was one as well, she told me I had something called overconfidence.

You were the cutest boy in the grade, and everyone knew it. All the girls whispered your name in the mornings, when we hung our coats by the doorway and glanced back at you. You had hair like caramel and eyes like chestnuts splashed with a hint of olive when you smiled. Your mother dressed you in clean polo shirts every day, and sometimes the girls made a show of pretending to grab you by the collar when you weren't looking.

He is so dreamy, Laney said one day as we were lacing our sneakers for recess, when you turned to grin at your friends. *He rides my bus,* I bragged. We sit across from each other. Laney whipped her golden head around and looked at me. *What bus,* she gasped, *do you ride? Bus 2,* I replied, smiling sweetly before running off to play foursquare.

I was dashing toward the ball, which had flown high over my head, when I ran into you. Our bodies clashed together, and the moment before we fell to the ground, I could have sworn I felt your heart beat against mine. Oh! I cried, as the jagged sediments of the pavement dug into my skin.

It's your fault, you scowled, pushing yourself off the ground, and before I could catch myself, I blurted, *Wanna play?*

I felt my cheeks grow warm, and sweat seemed to gather around my nose. This wasn't right. I hadn't meant to say that. I was the prettiest girl in the grade, and boys were suppo sed to ask me to play with them, not the other way around. My palms began to moisten, and I glanced at you, pretending I didn't feel the turbulence of a thousand butterflies and bees and moths flitting around in my stomach.

Eventually, you began to nod. Sure, you said, and without thinking, I grabbed your hand and began to run. *Where are we going?* You shouted as the breeze, light as the touch of summer cotton, brushed against my skin and pushed back the hair covering your forehead.

Did you know that sometimes I used to imagine you holding my hand, just reaching out and clasping my hand with your sun-kissed fingers? Sometimes I even wondered what it'd be like to kiss you, just a peck on the lips, and I wondered if you tasted like chicken or beef stew or whatever it was that Laney told me she tasted the first time she kissed Roger Delillo. She was the first one in our grade to have a boy kiss her, smack dab in the middle of the playground, during a game of truth or dare, and I still think she's probably more of a grown woman than the rest of us. She even wears a bra.

I don't mind, really. Apparently boys like boobs, but my chest is as flat as the cover of our history book. It's kind of gross, I think, when girls have big things hanging inside their shirts. I mean, doesn't it get uncomfortable?

You and I continued running toward the foursquare ball, which had landed near the woodsy area next to the playground. When we finally stopped, the first thing we noticed was the writing on the tree. Scrawled on the trunk of the tree was the word fuck, in big letters, F-U-C-K. The indentation was deep and around the edges of the etching I could see frayed pieces of wood coming out of the rough letters. *Fuck?* you asked. *What does that mean? Fuck,* you repeated, over and over, as though the mere sound of the word could reveal its meaning.

I had heard it once before, on the side of the road walking home from the grocery store. That day, an old man was holding a sign up, in the middle of the road as though he was invincible. "Fuck 4 Bucks," it read, and he was screaming that over and over, his raw voice escalating into the frigid air. I remember him because he had the strangest look about him—rotund and dwarfish, grotesque yet well dressed. There were several women walking about him in different colors of lace and lots of makeup. I remembered they were beautiful and I asked my mother if they were getting ready for a dance performance. My mother quickly grabbed my hand and we turned in another direction. That day we had to take the long route home so we wouldn't have to cross the street where the man was standing.

Fuck, I said. *I think that's…that's when you want something you can't have. Or maybe when you see someone beautiful and—*

Like her? You asked, looking at Laney, your eyes widening. Without thinking, I rushed in front of you, hiding her from your probing eyes, trying to decipher what your words meant. Like her? Those two words reverberated in my mind later that day, over and over, and when I finally turned to look at her, it was as though I had seen her for the first time. Suddenly I noticed the slight rise of her chest, and I remembered the time our class ran the timed mile and she claimed she ran slowly because she was now a woman and had to deal with all that bouncing. No wonder Roger wanted to kiss her.

Why is your face in my face? you whined.

Did you know, I started, *I have a line of freckles on my face?*

Everyone has freckles, you said, *who cares?*

But mine are in a line. A perfect line. A diagonal line and you can barely see them, I replied, but you were already looking back at Laney, who was jumping rope double-dutch and singing, her voice mellifluous and full. I asked my mother for fifty cents, to see the elephant jump the fence—

Look! I was yelling at you now, *Look at me! I'm going to tell Laney you liiiike her if you don't come back!* But you were running already, running toward Laney, your hands waving wildly in the air.

Wanna play tag? you shouted to her. Out of the corner of my ear, I saw you turn toward me, and then you screamed, *Hey, Laney, she thinks you're beautiful! She thinks you're beautiful, and she won't stop telling me how beautiful you are. I think she has a girl crush on you.* You pointed at me and burst into laughter, and for a moment I forgot about how smoothly our hands linked together or how exhilarating it felt to have the pulse of your heart against mine.

Stop, stop, stop, I shouted. *Laney, that's him! He told me he thought you were beautiful. I never even said that. Why won't you believe me?* I could feel the tears well up in my eyes and my skin grew hot and my hands began to sweat. I began to cry—I didn't mean to—and then the teacher came over and scolded you for laughing at a girl. From the corner of my eye, I could see Laney's blurred face twisted in a smirk, her thin rose-colored lips sweet with vengeance. *Girl crush, girl crush, girl crush,* they cried.

I stopped playing with you after that, and I didn't talk to Laney, either. I could feel her pitying eyes on me whenever she was near, and the whispers that followed from her friends. I didn't care. I was still the prettiest girl in the grade, and it didn't matter what anyone thought. I rode the bus with you every day and sat across from you and played with the lace adorning my cotton dresses and I knew you were still watching me because the bus driver didn't like people to talk and what else could you do?

But secretly I watched you sometimes too, after the seat across from me became empty, after you got off the bus. You'd stumble down those steep steps a little, turning right, down Falconer Street, across the length of the bus, shrouded by the clouds of dust the bus left behind. I watched you sometimes—you used to wave to Jeremy, who was cute but didn't have your smile, and sometimes you just turned around and grinned at all of us. I liked to think it was me you were looking at. After all, I was the prettiest girl in the grade and didn't you like my yellow dress? The one with the soft petals and no flowers at all, just floating velvet petals soft like the silk of your hands, like that one time I touched them and almost didn't let go?

I watched you sometimes, even after that day I saw your eyes on Laney's face, on her porcelain skin, on her thick yellow hair, on her eyes sparkling like a picture book's cerulean sky. I watched you sometimes even after I saw your eyes move over the angles and the curves and the contours of her body and for the first time I believed you might have thought of that word, fuck, even if you didn't know what it meant then. I watched you sometimes and I wished I'd never taught you that word or asked you to play or shown you the line of freckles across my face. I watched you sometimes and wished you would disappear, fuck, gone, into quicksand, and I would be the only one there to save you.

Acknowledgments

The Alliance gratefully acknowledges the thousands of teachers who annually encourage students to submit their works to The Scholastic Art & Writing Awards and the remarkable students who have the courage to put their art and writing before panels of renowned jurors. Our mission is greatly furthered through special partnerships with the National Art Education Association and the Association of Independent Colleges of Art and Design. In addition, we would like to specially recognize the National Writing Project for its continued commitment to our program and for its far-reaching effects in the writing community. Our ability to honor creative teens is also made possible through the generosity of our supporters: Scholastic Inc., Maurice R. Robinson Foundation, Command Web Offset, Jack Kent Cooke Foundation, The New York Times, Ovation, Amazon.com, Dick Blick Co. and AMD Foundation.

Regional Affiliate Organizations

The Alliance would like to thank the regional affiliates listed for coordinating The Scholastic Art & Writing Awards.

NORTHEAST

CONNECTICUT
Connecticut Art Region
Connecticut Art Education Association

DELAWARE
Delaware Art Region
Delaware State University

MAINE
Maine Art Region
Heartwood College of Art

Southern Maine Writing Region
Southern Maine Writing Project

Pittsburgh Arts Region
La Roche College

South Central Pennsylvania Writing Region
Commonwealth Connections Academy

Southwestern Pennsylvania Art & Writing Region
California University of Pennsylvania

RHODE ISLAND
Rhode Island Art Region
Rhode Island Art Education Association

VERMONT
Vermont Art & Writing Region
Brattleboro Museum & Art Center

SOUTH

DISTRICT OF COLUMBIA
DC Metro Writing Region
Writopia Lab

FLORIDA
Broward Art Region
American Learning Systems

Miami-Dade Art Region
Miami-Dade County Public Schools

Miami-Dade Writing Region
Miami Writes

Palm Beach Art Region
Educational Gallery Group (Eg^2)

Palm Beach Writing Region
Blue Planet Writers' Room

Pinellas Art Region
Pinellas County Schools

Sarasota Art Region
Sarasota County Schools

GEORGIA
Georgia Art Region
Georgia State University Ernest G. Welch School of Art & Design

KENTUCKY
Louisville Metropolitan Area Art Region
Jefferson County Public Schools

Northern Kentucky Writing Region
Northern Kentucky University

South Central Kentucky Art Region
Capitol Arts Alliance, Inc.

LOUISIANA
North-Central Louisiana Writing Region
Northwestern State University Writing Project

Southeast Louisiana Writing Region
Greater New Orleans Writing Project at the University of New Orleans

MISSISSIPPI
Mississippi Art Region
Mississippi Museum of Art

Mississippi Writing Region
Eudora Welty Foundation

NORTH CAROLINA
Eastern/Central North Carolina Art Region
Barton College

Mid-Carolina Art & Writing Region
Charlotte-Mecklenburg Schools

Western North Carolina Art Region
Asheville Art Museum

OKLAHOMA
Oklahoma Art Region
Tulsa Community College Liberal Arts Department

Oklahoma Writing Region
Daniel and Kristen Marangoni

SOUTH CAROLINA
South Carolina Art Region
Lander University

TENNESSEE
East Tennessee Art Region
Maryville College

Mid-South Art Region
Memphis Brooks Museum of Art
(Serving parts of Tennessee, Arkansas and Mississippi)

Middle Tennessee Art Region
Cheekwood Botanical Garden & Museum of Art

TEXAS
Harris County Art & Writing Region
Harris County Department of Education

San Antonio Art Region
SAY Sí (San Antonio Youth Yes)

Travis County Art Region
St. Stephen's Episcopal School

West Texas Art Region
Wayland Baptist University Department of Art

VIRGINIA
Arlington County Art Region
Arlington Public Schools

Fairfax County Art Region
Fairfax County Public Schools

Richmond Art Region
Virginia Museum of Fine Arts

Southwest Virginia Art Region
Fine Arts Center for the New River Valley

MIDWEST

ILLINOIS
Chicago Writing Region
Chicago Area Writing Project

Mid-Central Illinois Art Region
Regional Scholastic Art Awards Council

Southern Illinois Art Region
John R. and Eleanor R. Mitchell Foundation/Cedarhurst Center for the Arts

Suburban Chicago Art Region
Downers Grove North and South High Schools

INDIANA
Central/Southern Indiana Art Region
Clowes Memorial Hall of Butler University

Central/Southern Indiana Writing Region
Clowes Memorial Hall of Butler University and
Hoosier Writing Project at IUPUI

Northwest Indiana and Lower Southwest Michigan Art Region
Regional Scholastic Art Awards Advisory Board

Northeast Indiana and Northwest Ohio Art & Writing Region
Fort Wayne Museum of Art

IOWA
Iowa Multi-State Art & Writing Region
The Belin-Blank Center for Gifted Education

KANSAS
Eastern Kansas Art Region
Wichita Center for the Arts

Western Kansas Art Region
Western Kansas Scholastic Art Awards

MICHIGAN
Macomb, St. Clair and Lapeer Art Region
Macomb Community College and College for Creative Studies

Southeastern Michigan Art Region
College for Creative Studies

West Central Michigan Art Region
Kendall College of Art and Design of Ferris State University

MINNESOTA
Minnesota Art Region
Minneapolis College of Art and Design

MISSOURI
Missouri Writing Region
Prairie Lands Writing Project at Missouri Western State University

NEBRASKA
Nebraska Art Region
Omaha Public Schools Art Department

OHIO
Cuyahoga County Art Region
Cleveland Institute of Art

Lorain County Art Region
Lorain County Regional Scholastic Arts Committee

Northeast Central Ohio Art Region
Kent State University at Stark

Northeastern Ohio Art Region
McDonough Museum of Art at Youngstown State University

**Southern Ohio, Northern Kentucky and
Southeastern Indiana Art Region**
Art Machine, Inc.

WISCONSIN
Milwaukee Writing Region
Still Waters Collective

Wisconsin Art Region
Milwaukee Art Museum

WEST

ALASKA
Alaska Art Region
MTS Gallery/Alaska Art Education Association

Alaska Writing Region
F Magazine

CALIFORNIA
California Art Region
California Arts Project

California Writing Region
California Writing Project

Los Angeles Art Region
Armory Center for the Arts

COLORADO
Colorado Art Region
Colorado Art Education Association/Rocky Mountain College of
Art+Design

Southern Colorado Writing Region
Southern Colorado Writing Project

HAWAII
Hawai'i Art Region
Hawai'i State Department of Education

NEVADA
Northern Nevada Art Region
Nevada Museum of Art

Northern Nevada Writing Region
Sierra Arts Foundation

Southern Nevada Art & Writing Region
Springs Preserve

OREGON
Central Oregon Art Region
Oregon Art Education Association

Portland Metro Art Region
Portland Metro Scholastic Art Awards

Willamette Valley Art Region
Benton County Historical Society

WASHINGTON
Snohomish County Art Region
Arts Council of Snohomish County

PERSONAL ESSAY/MEMOIR